KRONSTADT 1921

KRONSTADT
1921

PAUL AVRICH

W · W · NORTON & COMPANY

New York · London

W. W. Norton & Company, Inc., 500 Fifth Avenue, New York, N.Y. 10110
W. W. Norton & Company Ltd., 37 Great Russell Street, London WC1B 3NU

First published in the Norton Library 1974
by arrangement with Princeton University Press

Books That Live
The Norton imprint on a book means that in the publisher's
estimation it is a book not for a single season but for the years.
W. W. Norton & Company, Inc.

Library of Congress Cataloging in Publication Data
Avrich, Paul.
    Kronstadt, 1921.
    (The Norton library)
    Reprint of the ed. published by the Princeton
University Press, Princeton, N.J., in series: Studies
of the Russian Institute, Columbia University.
    1. Kronstadt, Russia—History—Revolt, 1921.
I. Title. II. Series: Columbia University. Russian
Institute. Studies.
[DK265.8.K7A88   1974]   947'.45'0841   73-22130

ISBN 0-393-00724-3

Printed in the United States of America
        7 8 9 0

For Ina, Jane, and Karen

Contents

Illustrations

Acknowledgments

I am pleased to express my gratitude to the many colleagues and friends who assisted me in the preparation of this volume. I owe a special debt of thanks to three outstanding teachers and scholars, Professors Geroid T. Robinson, Henry L. Roberts, and Michael T. Florinsky, who guided my study of Russian history at Columbia University. I am also indebted to Max Nomad and Professor Loren Graham, who read the entire manuscript and made valuable comments and criticisms. Marina Tinkoff, Xenia J. Eudin, Anna M. Bourguina, N. Zhigulev, Peter Sedgwick, Edward Weber, Alexis Struve, and Eino Nivanka were good enough to answer my inquiries and to make a number of helpful suggestions. I am grateful to Professor Philip E. Mosely for granting me access to the Archive of Russian and East European History and Culture at Columbia University, and to its curator, L. F. Magerovsky, for his assistance in finding pertinent documents. My thanks are due also to the staffs of the Columbia, Harvard, and Hoover Libraries, the New York Public Library, the Helsinki University Library, the Library of Congress, and the National Archives for their courteous help in my search for materials. Although I have drawn on numerous sources, I am especially indebted to the pioneering studies of Ida Mett and George Katkov which are listed in the bibliography. Needless to say, however, responsibility for this volume is entirely my own.

I am deeply grateful to the Russian Institute of Columbia University, with which I have been associated as a Senior Fellow, and particularly to its Director, Professor Marshall Shulman, for his warm hospitality and encouragement. I am also indebted to the John Simon Guggenheim Memorial Foundation, the American Philosophical Society, the American Council of Learned Societies, and the Social Science Research Council for supporting my research on Russian anarchism and mass revolts, of which the present study is a byproduct.

KRONSTADT 1921

NOTE: In transliterating Russian words and proper names, I have followed the Library of Congress system in the footnotes and bibliography, but have modified this slightly in the text for the sake of readability.

It should also be noted that the terms "Bolshevik" and "Communist" are used interchangeably throughout the book (the Bolsheviks officially changed their name to Communists in March 1918).

Introduction

"*This was the flash*," said Lenin of the Kronstadt rebellion, "which lit up reality better than anything else."[1] In March 1921 the sailors of the naval fortress in the Gulf of Finland, the "pride and glory" of the Russian Revolution, rose in revolt against the Bolshevik government, which they themselves had helped into power. Under the slogan of "free soviets," they established a revolutionary commune that survived for 16 days, until an army was sent across the ice to crush it. After a long and savage struggle, with heavy losses on both sides, the rebels were subdued.

The rising at once provoked a bitter controversy that has never quite abated. Why had the sailors revolted? According to the Bolsheviks, they were agents of a White Guard conspiracy hatched in the West by Russian émigrés and their Allied supporters. To their sympathizers, however, they were revolutionary martyrs fighting to restore the soviet idea against the Bolshevik dictatorship. The suppression of the revolt was, in their eyes, an act of brutality which shattered the myth that Soviet Russia was a "workers' and peasants' state." In the aftermath, a number of foreign Communists questioned their faith in a government which could deal so ruthlessly with genuine mass protest. In this respect Kronstadt was the prototype of later events which would lead disillusioned radicals to break with the movement and to search for the original purity of their ideals. The liquidation of the kulaks, the Great Purge, the Nazi-Soviet pact, Khrushchev's denunciation of Stalin—each produced an exodus of party members and supporters who were convinced that the revolution had been betrayed. "What counts decisively," wrote Louis Fischer in 1949, "is the 'Kronstadt.' Until its advent, one may waver emotionally or doubt intellectually or even

[1] V. I. Lenin, *Polnoe sobranie sochinenii*, 5th edn., 55 vols., Moscow, 1958-1965, XLIII, 138.

3

reject the cause altogether in one's mind and yet refuse to attack it. I had no 'Kronstadt' for many years."[2]

Others found their "Kronstadt" later still—in the Hungarian uprising of 1956. For in Budapest, as in Kronstadt, the rebels sought to transform an authoritarian and bureaucratic regime into a genuine socialist democracy. To the Bolsheviks, however, such heresy was a greater menace than outright opposition to the principles of socialism. Hungary—and again Czechoslovakia in 1968—was dangerous not because it was counterrevolutionary, but because, like Kronstadt, its conception of the revolution and of socialism diverged sharply from that of the Soviet leadership; yet Moscow, as in 1921, denounced the rising as a counterrevolutionary plot and proceeded to suppress it. The crushing of Budapest, noted one critic of Soviet policy, showed again that the Communists would stop at nothing to destroy those who challenged their authority.[3]

Yet such comparisons must not be pressed too far. For events separated by 35 years and occurring in different countries with entirely different participants cannot possess more than a superficial resemblance. Soviet Russia in 1921 was not the Leviathan of recent decades. It was a young and insecure state, faced with a rebellious population at home and implacable enemies abroad who longed to see the Bolsheviks ousted from power. More important still, Kronstadt was in Russian territory; what confronted the Bolsheviks was a mutiny in their own navy at its most strategic outpost, guarding the western approaches to Petrograd. Kronstadt, they feared, might ignite the Russian mainland or become the springboard for another anti-Soviet invasion. There was

[2] Richard Crossman, ed., *The God That Failed*, New York, 1950, p. 207.

[3] Emanuel Pollack, *The Kronstadt Rebellion*, New York, 1959, Introduction. Cf. Angelica Balabanoff, *Impressions of Lenin*, Ann Arbor, 1964, pp. 58-59.

mounting evidence that Russian émigrés were trying to assist the insurrection and to turn it to their own advantage. Not that the activities of the Whites can excuse any atrocities which the Bolsheviks committed against the sailors. But they do make the government's sense of urgency to crush the revolt more understandable. In a few weeks the ice in the Finnish Gulf would melt, and supplies and reinforcements could then be shipped in from the West, converting the fortress into a base for a new intervention. Apart from the propaganda involved, Lenin and Trotsky appear to have been genuinely anxious over this possibility.

Few Western historians, unfortunately, have taken proper account of these anxieties. And Soviet writers, for their part, have done considerable violence to the facts by treating the rebels as dupes or agents of a White conspiracy. The present volume tries to examine the rebellion in a truer perspective. To accomplish this, Kronstadt must be set within a broader context of political and social events, for the revolt was part of a larger crisis marking the transition from War Communism to the New Economic Policy, a crisis which Lenin regarded as the gravest he had faced since coming to power. It is necessary, moreover, to relate the rising to the long tradition of spontaneous rebellion in Kronstadt itself and in Russia as a whole. Such an approach, one hopes, will shed some interesting light on the attitudes and behavior of the insurgents.

Beyond this, there are a number of specific problems that require careful analysis. Among the more important are the social composition of the fleet, the role of national discontent, the question of White involvement, and the nature of the rebel ideology. To some of these questions, of course, no definitive answers will be possible until the relevant Soviet archives are opened for inspection, an event not likely to occur for some time. Meanwhile, this volume attempts to provide as full an account of the rebellion as the available sources permit. Use has been made of a number of pertinent documents in Western archives, and also of published Soviet materials which have often been dismissed as mere propaganda but which, when used with proper caution, are of genuine value in illuminating some of the most significant issues.

It is important, above all, to examine the conflicting motives of the insurgents and their Bolshevik adversaries. The sailors, on the one hand, were revolutionary zealots, and like zealots throughout history they longed to recapture a past era before the purity of their ideals had been defiled by the exigencies of power. The Bolsheviks, on the other hand, having emerged victorious from a bloody Civil War, were not prepared to tolerate any new challenge to their authority. Throughout the conflict each side behaved in accordance with its own particular goals and aspirations. To say this is not to deny the necessity of moral judgment. Yet Kronstadt presents a situation in which the historian can sympathize with the rebels and still concede that the Bolsheviks were justified in subduing them. To recognize this, indeed, is to grasp the full tragedy of Kronstadt.

1. The Crisis of War Communism

In the autumn of 1920 Soviet Russia began an uneasy period of transition from war to peace. For more than six years the country had known continuous upheaval, but now, after world war, revolution, and civil war, the smoke was finally lifting. On October 12 the Soviet government concluded an armistice with Poland. Three weeks later the last of the White generals, Baron Peter Wrangel, was driven into the sea, and the Civil War, though it left the country torn and bleeding, was won. In the south, Nestor Makhno, the anarchist partisan, remained at large, but in November 1920 his once formidable army was dispersed and presented no further threat to the Moscow government. Siberia, the Ukraine, and Turkestan had been regained, along with the Donets coal basin and the Baku oilfields; and in February 1921 a Bolshevik army would complete the reconquest of the Caucasus by capturing Tiflis and putting the Menshevik government of Georgia to flight. Thus, after three years of precarious existence, its fate hanging by a thread from day to day, the Soviet regime could boast effective control over the bulk of Russia's vast and far-flung territory.

The end of the Civil War signaled a new era in Soviet relations with other countries. The Bolsheviks, shelving their hopes of an imminent world upheaval, sought to obtain the "breathing spell" which had been denied them in 1918 by the outbreak of civil conflict. Among the Western powers, by the same token, expectations of the impending collapse of Lenin's government had faded. Both sides desired more normal relations, and by the end of 1920 there was no reason why this desire should not be realized; the Allied blockade having been lifted and armed intervention in European Russia brought to a halt, the most serious obstacles to diplomatic recognition and a resumption of trade had been removed. During the course of the year, moreover, formal peace treaties had been concluded with Russia's Baltic neighbors, Finland, Estonia, Latvia, and Lithuania; and in February 1921 peace and friendship pacts were signed with Persia and Afghanistan, while a similar agreement with the Turks was in the offing. Meanwhile, Soviet emissaries, notably Krasin in London and Vorovsky in Rome, were negotiating trade agreements with a number of European nations, and the prospects were bright for a successful outcome.

And yet, for all these favorable developments, the winter of 1920-1921 was an extremely critical period in Soviet history. Lenin acknowledged this when he told the Eighth Congress of Soviets, in December 1920, that a smooth transition to peaceful economic and social reconstruction would not be easy to accomplish.[1] Although the military struggle had been won and the external situation was rapidly improving, the Bolsheviks faced grave internal difficulties. Russia was exhausted and bankrupt. The scars of battle were visible in every corner of the land. During the last two years the death rate had mounted sharply, famine and pestilence claiming millions of victims beyond the millions who had fallen in combat. Not since the Time of Troubles in the seventeenth century had the country seen such suffering and devastation. Agricultural output had fallen off drastically; industry and transportation were in a shambles. Russia, in the words of a contemporary, had emerged from the Civil War in a state of economic collapse "unparalleled in the history of humanity."[2]

The time had come to bind up the nation's wounds, and for this a shift was needed in domestic policy to match the relaxation already taking place in foreign affairs. Above all, this meant the abandonment of "War Communism," a

[1] *Vos'moi vserossiiskii s"ezd sovetov rabochikh, krest'ianskikh, krasnoarmeiskikh i kazach'ikh deputatov: stenograficheskii otchet (22-29 dekabria 1920 goda)*, Moscow, 1921, p. 16.

[2] L. N. Kritsman, *Geroicheskii period velikoi russkoi revoliutsii*, 2nd edn., Moscow, 1926, p. 166.

program improvised to meet the emergency of the Civil War. As its name implies, War Communism bore the harsh stamp of regimentation and compulsion. Dictated by economic scarcity and military necessity, it was marked by an extreme centralization of government controls in every area of social life. Its cornerstone was the forcible seizure of grain from the peasantry. Armed detachments were sent into the countryside to requisition surplus produce with which to feed the cities and to provision the Red Army, a force of some five million men. Though instructed to leave the peasants enough for their personal needs, it was common for the requisitioning squads to take at pistol-point grain intended for personal consumption or set aside for the next sowing. "The essence of 'War Communism,' " Lenin himself admitted, "was that we actually took from the peasant all his surpluses and sometimes not only the surpluses but part of the grain the peasant needed for food. We took this in order to meet the requirements of the army and to sustain the workers."[3] In addition to grain and vegetables, the food detachments confiscated horses, fodder, wagons, and other items for military use, often without payment of any kind, so that the villagers had to go without such staples as sugar, salt, and kerosene, not to mention soap, boots, matches, and tobacco, or the nails and scrap metal needed for essential repairs.

There is little doubt that compulsory requisitioning (in Russian *prodrazverstka*) saved the Bolshevik regime from defeat, for without it neither the army nor the urban population, from which the government drew its main support, could have survived. Yet the inevitable price was the estrangement of the peasantry. Forced at gunpoint to hand over their surpluses and denied the compensation of badly needed consumer goods, the villagers responded in predictable fashion: the food detachments, when not met by open resistance,

[3] Lenin, *Polnoe sobranie sochinenii*, XLIII, 219.

were stymied by evasive tactics to which every ounce of peasant ingenuity was applied. In 1920, a leading authority estimated, more than a third of the total harvest was successfully hidden from the government's collection teams.[4] The peasants, moreover, began to till only enough land to meet their own direct needs, so that by the end of 1920 the amount of sown acreage in European Russia was only three-fifths of the figure for 1913, the last normal year before the onset of war and revolution.[5] A good part of this shrinkage was, of course, the result of the devastation which the Russian countryside had experienced, but the policy of *prodrazverstka* certainly contributed to the catastrophic decline of agricultural production during the Civil War period. By 1921 total output had fallen to less than half, and the quantity of livestock to about two-thirds, of prewar figures. Particularly hard hit were such basic crops as flax and sugar beets, which had dwindled to between a fifth and a tenth of their normal levels.[6]

At the same time, forcible requisitioning rekindled the age-old struggle in Russia between the rural population and the urban-based state authority. Lenin had long ago realized that, given Russia's retarded economic and social condition, a tactical alliance with the peasantry was essential if his party was to win, and afterwards to retain, power. The Bolsheviks, at the very least, had to keep the peasants neutral. It was this motive, primarily, that had led to the formation of a coalition government with the Left Socialist Revolutionaries in December 1917; and the same consideration may also have influenced the choice of M. I. Kalinin—one of the few Bolsheviks of some prominence whose peasant origins

[4] Kritsman, *Geroicheskii period velikoi russkoi revoliutsii*, pp. 135-39.

[5] A. S. Pukhov, *Kronshtadtskii miatezh 1921 g.*, Leningrad, 1931, p. 8.

[6] See Kritsman, *Geroicheskii period velikoi russkoi revoliutsii*, pp. 153-61.

were widely known—as president of the Soviet Republic. But the chief means of securing the peasants' support was to fulfill their ancient dream of a *chernyi peredel*, a general land distribution. The Bolshevik land decrees of October 26, 1917 and February 19, 1918 were in very close harmony with the populist and egalitarian urges of the rural folk. Borrowing the agrarian program of the Socialist Revolutionaries, whose doctrines were tailored to the aspirations of the peasantry, the young Soviet government abolished all private holdings and ordered the land to be apportioned on an equal basis among those who toiled on it with their own hands and without the assistance of hired labor.[7] The two decrees gave new impetus to a process which the villagers had begun on their own several months before, during the summer of 1917, and by 1920 the land had been divided into more than 20 million small holdings worked by individual family units.

Small wonder, then, that the rural population greeted these initial Bolshevik measures with exultation, tempered only by their traditional wariness of official edicts emanating from the state. To the peasants the Bolshevik Revolution meant first and foremost the satisfaction of their land hunger and the elimination of the nobility, and now they wanted only to be left in peace. Entrenching themselves on their new holdings, they guarded suspiciously against any outside intrusions. Nor were these long in coming. As the Civil War deepened and requisition teams descended into the countryside, the peasants began to regard the Bolsheviks as adversaries rather than friends and benefactors. They complained that Lenin and his party had driven away the masters and given the people the land only to take away their produce and their freedom to use the land as they saw fit. The peasants, moreover, resented the state farms which the authori-

[7] See E. H. Carr, *The Bolshevik Revolution, 1917-1923*, 3 vols., New York, 1951-1953, II, 39-46.

ties had established on some of the larger gentry estates during the Civil War period. For the villagers a true *chernyi peredel* meant the division among the people of *all* the land. It meant, too, the abolition of "wage slavery," which the state farms perpetuated. As Lenin himself put it, "the peasant thinks: if there are big farms, then I am once more a hired laborer."[8]

As a result of these policies, more than a few peasants came to believe that Bolsheviks and Communists were different people. To the former they attributed the precious gift of the land, while they bitterly accused the latter—particularly Trotsky, Zinoviev, and other Communist leaders whose "alien" origins were well known—of imposing on them a new form of bondage, this time to the state instead of the nobility. "We are Bolsheviks not Communists. We are for the Bolsheviks because they drove out the landlords, but we are not for the Communists because they are against individual holdings."[9] Thus did Lenin describe the attitude of the peasants in 1921. A year later their frame of mind, as a police report from Smolensk province shows, had changed but little: "Among the peasants there are no limits to the grumbling against the Soviet government and the Communists. In the conversation of every middle peasant and poor peasant, not to speak even of the kulak, the following is heard, 'They aren't planning freedom for us, but serfdom. The time of Godunov has already begun, when the peasants were attached to the landowners. Now we [are attached] to the Jewish bourgeoisie like Modkowski, Aronson, etc.' "[10]

Yet the bulk of the peasants, for the duration of the Civil War, continued to tolerate the Soviet regime as a lesser evil than a White restoration. However acute their antipathy for

[8] Lenin, *Polnoe sobranie sochinenii*, XXXVIII, 200.

[9] *Ibid.,* XLIV, 43. The Bolsheviks officially changed their name to Communists in March 1918.

[10] Merle Fainsod, *Smolensk under Soviet Rule*, Cambridge, Mass., 1958, p. 43.

the ruling party, still more did they fear a return of the gentry and the loss of their land. The food collection squads, it is true, often met with resistance in the villages, resistance which claimed more than a few Bolshevik lives, but the peasants shrank from armed opposition on a scale serious enough to threaten the existence of the government. However, with the defeat of Wrangel's army in the fall of 1920, the situation changed rapidly. Now that the White danger had evaporated, peasant resentment against *prodrazverstka* and the state farms flared up out of control. Waves of peasant risings swept rural Russia. The most serious outbreaks occurred in Tambov province, the middle Volga area, the Ukraine, the northern Caucasus region, and western Siberia, peripheral sectors where government control was comparatively weak and popular violence had a long pedigree.[11]

The rebellions gathered strength rapidly throughout the winter of 1920-1921. During this period, as Lenin noted, "tens and hundreds of thousands of disbanded soldiers" returned to their native villages and swelled the ranks of the guerrilla forces.[12] By early 1921 some 2,500,000 men— nearly half the total strength of the Red Army—had been demobilized in an atmosphere of violence and social unrest which menaced the very fabric of the state. It was a pattern not unfamiliar elsewhere in Europe during the years immediately after the First World War, when large-scale military demobilization aggravated existing economic tensions and sharpened popular discontent. But in Russia the situation was particularly grave. Nearly seven years of war, revolution, and civil disorder had bred a spirit of lawlessness that was difficult to eradicate. An uprooted civilian population had not yet settled down when the demobilization, as

[11] A detailed survey of the peasant risings in various parts of Soviet Russia is given in I. Ia. Trifonov, *Klassy i klassovaia bor'ba v SSSR v nachale nepa (1921-1923 gg.)*, Vol. I: *Bor'ba s vooruzhennoi kulatskoi kontrrevoliutsiei*, Leningrad, 1964.

[12] *Desiatyi s"ezd RKP(b), mart 1921 goda*, Moscow, 1963, p. 23.

Lenin remarked, set loose a horde of restless men whose sole occupation was warfare and who naturally turned their energies to banditry and rebellion. For Lenin the situation was tantamount to a revival of the Civil War, but in a different and more dangerous form—more dangerous, as he saw it, because it was being waged not by bankrupt social elements whose time in history had run out, but by the popular masses themselves. The specter of an enormous jacquerie, a new Pugachev revolt, "blind and pitiless" in Pushkin's celebrated phrase, had appeared to haunt the government—and this at a moment when the towns, the traditional centers of Bolshevik support, were in a depleted and weakened condition and themselves gripped by profound unrest.

Between November 1920 and March 1921, the number of rural outbreaks mounted sharply. In February 1921 alone, on the eve of the Kronstadt rebellion, the Cheka reported 118 separate peasant risings in various parts of the country.[13] In western Siberia the tide of rebellion engulfed nearly the entire Tiumen region and much of the neighboring provinces of Cheliabinsk, Orenburg, and Omsk. Communications along the Trans-Siberian railroad were seriously disrupted, aggravating the already severe food shortages in the large cities of European Russia. Along the middle Volga, where Stenka Razin and Pugachev had won their greatest followings, bands of armed marauders—peasants, army veterans, deserters—roamed the countryside in search of food and plunder. Only a thin line separated brigandage from social revolt. Everywhere desperate men ambushed requisitioning detachments and fought with savage determination against all who dared to interfere with them. The fiercest struggle, perhaps, occurred in the black-earth province of Tambov, a hotbed of peasant revolt since the seventeenth century. Led by A. S. Antonov, a former Socialist Revolutionary whose talents as

[13] Seth Singleton, "The Tambov Revolt (1920-1921)," *Slavic Review*, xxv (September 1966), 499.

a partisan warrior and reputation as a Robin Hood rivaled those of Nestor Makhno, the rebellion raged out of control for more than a year until the capable Red Commander, Mikhail Tukhachevsky, fresh from crushing the sailors' revolt in Kronstadt, arrived with a large force to subdue it.[14]

Apart from the high incidence of peasant insurrection during the winter of 1920-1921, one is struck by the large number of men drawn into the rebel ranks. At its height, Antonov's movement counted some 50,000 insurgents, while in a single district of western Siberia the guerrillas, according to sources not likely to exaggerate, numbered as many as 60,000.[15] Simple peasants, armed with axes, cudgels, pitchforks, and a scattering of rifles and pistols, fought pitched battles with regular army formations, their desperate courage inspiring so high a rate of defection among the government troops—many of whom shared their social background and attitudes—that special Cheka units and Communist officer cadets, whose loyalty was beyond doubt, had to be called in. Lacking up-to-date weapons and effective organization, the scattered peasant bands were in the end no match for the seasoned Red forces. The insurgents, moreover, had no coherent program, though everywhere their slogans were the same: "Down with requisitioning," "Away with food detachments," "Don't surrender your surpluses," "Down with the Communists and the Jews." Beyond this, they shared a common hatred of the cities, from which the commissars and food detachments came, and of the government which sent these intruders into their midst. The population of Tambov, noted a Bolshevik military commander in that province, regarded Soviet authority as the begetter of

---

[14] See *ibid.*, pp. 497-512; and *Antonovshchina*, Tambov, 1923.

[15] Trifonov, *Klassy i klassovaia bor'ba v SSSR*, I, 4-5; Iu. A. Poliakov, *Perekhod k nepu i sovetskoe krest'ianstvo*, Moscow, 1967, pp. 205-206. The Trotsky Archives at Harvard University contain a number of documents relating to these peasant risings of 1920-1921.

"raiding commissars and officials," a tyrannical force estranged from the lives of the people. It is hardly surprising, therefore, that one of the rebel groups in Tambov should have set as its primary goal "the overthrow of the rule of the Communists-Bolsheviks, who have brought the country to poverty, death, and disgrace."[16]

Although armed resistance and evasion of food levies were their strongest weapons, the peasants brought yet another traditional means of protest into play: humble petitions to the central government. Between November 1920 and March 1921, the authorities in Moscow were bombarded with urgent appeals from every region of the country, demanding an end to the coercive policies of War Communism. Now that the Whites had been defeated, argued the petitioners, the forcible requisitioning of grain had lost its justification. In its place the peasants called for a fixed tax on their produce and the right to dispose of surpluses as they saw fit. And, as an added incentive for production, they requested an increase in the supply of consumer goods to the countryside.[17]

These grass-roots appeals, however, found few sympathetic ears within Soviet administrative circles, where the peasant smallholder was widely regarded as an incurable petty bourgeois who, having obtained possession of the land, had ceased to support the revolution. More than anything else, the Bolsheviks feared a capitalist entrenchment in the Russian village. Ever mindful of historical parallels, they recalled the peasantry of 1848, who had served as the bulwark of reaction in Western Europe, and they shrank from any concessions which might increase the strength of the independent peasant proprietor in their own country. For more than a few Bolsheviks, moreover, the system of War Com-

---

[16] Singleton, "The Tambov Revolt," *Slavic Review*, xxv, 500; *Kak tambovskie krest'iane boriatsia za svobodu*, n.p., 1921, pp. 12-13.

[17] Poliakov, *Perekhod k nepu*, pp. 213ff.

munism, with its centralized state direction of the economy, bore the essential hallmarks of the socialist society of their dreams, and they were loath to give it up for a restoration of the free market and a solidly entrenched peasantry.

A forceful exponent of this viewpoint was Valerian Osinsky (real name Obolensky), a leader of the left-wing Democratic Centralist group within the Communist party. Osinsky set forth his position in a series of influential articles which appeared during the latter part of 1920. Rejecting any retreat to a tax in kind or a revival of free trade, he called for greater rather than less state intervention in agricultural life. The only solution to the peasant agrarian crisis, he wrote, lay in the "compulsory mass organization of production" under the direction and control of government officials.[18] To achieve this, he proposed the formation of "sowing committees" in every locality, with the primary mission of raising output by extending the area under the plough. The new committees would also regulate the use of equipment, the methods of planting, the care of livestock, and other matters affecting the efficiency of production. Osinsky further suggested that the peasants be required to pool their seed grain in a common seed bank, distribution from which would be determined by the government. His ultimate vision was a system of socialized farming in which all small holdings would be collectivized and agricultural labor performed on a common basis.

What Osinsky's recommendations implied was not merely the retention of War Communism but its reinforcement in virtually every phase of rural life. Far from pacifying the peasants, his proposals only gave them new cause for alarm, and they were not long in making their voices heard. An opportunity arose at the end of December 1920, when the Eighth Congress of Soviets assembled in Moscow. Osinsky's

[18] N. Osinskii, *Gosudarstvennoe regulirovanie krest'ianskogo khoziaistva*, Moscow, 1920, pp. 8-9.

scheme occupied a central place in the deliberations. Although the Communist majority endorsed the plan by an overwhelming margin, vocal opposition came from the Mensheviks and Socialist Revolutionaries, who were making their last appearance at a national gathering of this sort. Fyodor Dan and David Dallin for the Mensheviks, and V. K. Volsky and I. N. Steinberg for the Right and Left SR's, were unanimous in condemning the "bankrupt" policies of War Communism. They called for the immediate replacement of food requisitioning by a fixed tax in kind, with freedom of trade for surpluses in excess of the peasant's obligations to the state. Any approach founded on compulsion, argued Dan, would only hasten the decline in the sown area and further curtail the output of badly needed grain; the continued application of force would widen the gulf between town and village, driving the peasantry into the arms of the counterrevolution. In a similar vein, Volsky urged the government to encourage voluntary cooperatives and to abandon the state farms which the peasants so bitterly opposed. And Dallin, referring to Osinsky's sowing committees, warned that any new instrument of coercion would only aggravate the existing crisis.[19]

Further objections to the government's agricultural policies were voiced by the peasants themselves at a closed session of rural delegates to the congress. Lenin personally attended, and the notes which he passed on to the party Central Committee and the Council of People's Commissars are of enormous interest. Opposition to Osinsky's project, as Lenin's notes reveal, was unanimous and unsparing. With unhidden contempt, a peasant from Siberia—a region already deep in the throes of peasant rebellion—denounced the idea of sowing committees and of increased state interference in village affairs: "Osinsky does not know Siberia. I have been ploughing there for thirty-eight years, but Osinsky knows

[19] *Vos'moi vserossiiskii s"ezd sovetov*, pp. 37-43, 50-57, 122-23, 200-201.

nothing." Other delegates assailed the government's efforts to collectivize agriculture, but their worst venom was reserved for the confiscation of grain by armed detachments which, determined to fulfill their arbitrary quotas, made no distinction between the idler and the hard-working peasant. So much grain was being taken, said one delegate, that neither humans nor animals had anything to eat. A peasant from Tula protested that, owing to excessive confiscations, ten of the black-soil provinces of central Russia (including his own) had been left without seed for the next planting. If food production is to be raised, said a delegate from Perm, we must be freed from this lash of compulsory requisitioning.

One after another the speakers protested that little or no compensation was given for their produce. "If you want us to sow all the land," declared a peasant from Minsk province, "just give us salt and iron. I shall not say anything more." We need horses, wheels, harrows, other voices chimed in. Give us metal to mend our tools and sheds, or give us hard cash with real value to pay the blacksmith and the carpenter. A delegate from Kostroma province spoke the mind of the whole group when he declared: "The peasant must be given incentives, otherwise he won't work. I can saw wood under the lash, but one cannot cultivate under the lash." "How to provide incentive?" asked a peasant from Novgorod. "Simple: a fixed percent of requisitioning for grain as well as cattle."[20]

Lenin himself was by no means indifferent to the plight of the peasantry. When he learned, for example, that the peasants of a particular district had been subjected to excessive confiscations and deprived of their seed grain, he personally intervened in their behalf.[21] As early as November 1920 he had even begun to consider the possibility of "the

---

[20] Lenin, *Polnoe sobranie sochinenii*, XLII, 382-86.
[21] See his note of October 21, 1920 to the Deputy Food Commissar, N. P. Briukhanov: *ibid.*, LI, 313.

transformation of food requisitioning into a tax in kind,"[22] which is precisely what the villagers themselves were demanding. But, for the moment at least, he rejected such a step as premature. For the danger of a resumption of the Civil War, he told the Eighth Congress of Soviets, had not completely evaporated. A formal peace with Poland had yet to be concluded; and Wrangel's army, supplied by the French, remained poised in neighboring Turkey, ready to strike at the first convenient opportunity. Obviously, then, the transition to a new peacetime economic program must not be too hasty.[23] On an earlier occasion Lenin had illustrated this point with a Russian fable. Speaking before an assembly of rural representatives from Moscow province in October 1920, he admitted (to cries of agreement from the audience) that the peasantry was groaning under a heavy burden of taxation, a burden which had caused a serious rift between town and country, between worker and peasant. But if the ram and goat fall out, Lenin asked, referring to the proletariat and peasantry, must the lynx of counterrevolution be allowed to devour them both?[24]

Thus, in spite of increasing doubts, Lenin clung fast to the old policies of War Communism. In December 1920, at the Eighth Congress of Soviets, he placed his seal of approval on Osinsky's project for a public seed bank and a sowing campaign in the coming spring. The congress thereupon passed a resolution calling for a "statewide plan of compulsory sowing" under the general direction of the Commissariat of Agriculture. Sowing committees were to be established in every province, district, and township, charged with marshalling all available manpower and equipment in order to extend the area of land under cultivation.[25] But,

[22] *Ibid.*, XLII, 51.
[23] *Vos'moi vserossiiskii s"ezd sovetov*, pp. 10ff.
[24] Lenin, *Polnoe sobranie sochinenii*, XLI, 362-63.
[25] *Vos'moi vserossiiskii s"ezd sovetov*, p. 268.

for the present at least, Lenin considered any further attempt to collectivize agriculture unfeasible. He no longer believed that socialism was attainable in the near future. Russia, he told the Eighth Congress of Soviets, remained a country of small peasants, and peasants "are not socialists." To treat them as such was to build the future of Russia on shifting sand. Although the Sukharevka (Moscow's famous black market) had been shut down, its spirit lived on in the heart of every petty proprietor. "So long as we are living in a country of small peasants," said Lenin, "capitalism in Russia shall have a stronger economic base than communism." But if the transition to socialism was to be long and difficult, he added, all the more reason not to retreat before the capitalist forces in the countryside. Thus compulsion rather than concession remained the watchword of Bolshevik agricultural policy.[26]

THE situation in the towns, hitherto the main stronghold of Bolshevik support, was in many ways worse than in the countryside. Six years of turmoil had shattered the nation's industrial economy. Although published statistics vary in many details, the picture which emerges is one of near collapse.[27] By the end of 1920 total industrial output had shrunk to about a fifth of 1913 levels. The supply of fuel and raw materials had reached a particularly critical state. Although the Baku oilfields and the Donets coal basin had been recovered in the spring and autumn of 1920, damage was extensive and very difficult to repair. Many of the mines were flooded and other enterprises destroyed. The total

[26] *Ibid.*, p. 30.
[27] *Za 5 let, 1917-1922: sbornik Ts.K.R.K.P.*, Moscow, 1922, p. 408; Kritsman, *Geroicheskii period velikoi russkoi revoliutsii*, pp. 163-64. Cf. the figures in N. A. Kornatovskii, ed., *Kronshtadtskii miatezh: sbornik statei, vospominanii i dokumentov*, Leningrad, 1931, pp. 8-9; and in *Grazhdanskaia voina*, 1918-1921, 3 vols., Moscow, 1928-1930, I, 361.

production of coal in Russia at the end of 1920 was only a quarter, and of oil only a third, of prewar levels. Still worse, cast iron output had dropped to less than 3 percent of 1913 levels, and the production of copper had all but ceased. Lacking these basic materials, the major industrial centers of the country were forced to cut back production very severely. Many large factories could operate only part-time, and their work forces dwindled to fractions of what they had been four or five years earlier. Some important sectors of heavy industry ground to a complete standstill. And in consumer-goods enterprises total production fell to less than a quarter of prewar levels. The manufacture of footwear was reduced to a tenth of normal, and only one in twenty textile spindles remained in operation.

Compounding the disaster were two additional factors: the throttling effects of the recent Allied blockade and the disorganization of the country's transportation system. Imposed after the Brest-Litovsk treaty in 1918, the blockade was finally lifted in 1920, but foreign trade was not revived until the following year, and even then on a very small scale. As a result, Soviet Russia was deprived of badly needed technical equipment, machinery, and raw materials, the absence of which prevented a rapid recovery of the industrial system. At the same time, transportation facilities were seriously disrupted. In much of the country, railway lines had been torn up and bridges destroyed by retreating armies. Trotsky, who reported on the transport situation to the Eighth Congress of Soviets, noted that more than half the locomotives in Russia were in disrepair; and the production of new engines had dropped to 15 percent of the 1913 figure.[28] The supply of normal fuel being at best intermittent, railwaymen were re-

[28] *Vos'moi vserossiiskii s"ezd sovetov*, p. 160; *Za 5 let*, p. 408. All told, 3,762 railway bridges and 3,597 road bridges were destroyed, as well as some 1,200 miles of railroad and 60,000 miles of telegraph wire: Erich Wollenberg, *The Red Army*, London, 1938, p. 110.

duced to running the trains on wood, and this increased the number of breakdowns. Nearly everywhere communications were severely impaired, and in some districts total paralysis had set in.

The breakdown of the railroads held back the delivery of food to the hungry cities. Provisions became so scarce that workmen and other townspeople were put on starvation rations. The small quantities of food on hand were distributed according to a preferential system which, originally designed to favor workers in arms industries, was retained even after the Civil War had ended. Thus, at the beginning of 1921, the workers of Petrograd's metal-smelting shops and blast furnaces (*goriachie tsekhi*) received a daily ration of 800 grams of black bread, while shock workers (*udarniki*) received 600 grams, and lesser categories only 400 or even 200 grams.[29] But even this meager allotment was doled out on an irregular basis. The diet of transport workers was said to average between 700 and 1,000 calories a day,[30] a figure far below the minimum necessary to sustain a full day's labor.

The food crisis in the towns was greatly complicated by the disintegration of the regular market during the Civil War period. Under the system of War Communism, all private trade was abolished, and the normal exchange of goods between town and country virtually ceased to exist. In its place, a black market quickly sprang into being. Swarms of "bagmen" tramped from village to village, buying bread and vegetables which they would sell or barter to the famished inhabitants of the cities. By the end of 1920 illicit trade had grown to such proportions that it largely supplanted the official channels of distribution. At the same time, inflation mounted to dizzying heights. During 1920 alone the price of bread increased more than tenfold.[31] The Soviet government,

[29] Lazarevich, "Kronshtadtskoe vosstanie," *Bor'ba*, 1921, Nos. 1-2, pp. 3-5.

[30] Pukhov, *Kronshtadtskii miatezh*, p. 23.

[31] A. Slepkov, *Kronshtadtskii miatezh*, Moscow, 1928, p. 13.

in order to meet its own expenses, set its printing presses to work at a furious pace, and as a result of this action a gold ruble worth 7 paper rubles and 85 kopecks in 1917 brought at least 10,000 paper rubles three years later.[32] By the end of 1920 the real wages of factory workers in Petrograd had, according to official estimates, fallen to 8.6 percent of their prewar levels.[33] As the value of money drained away, an increasing proportion of wages was paid to the workers in kind. The food ration (*payok*) came to form the nucleus of the workman's wage, in addition to which he received shoes and clothing from the government and sometimes a fraction of his output, which was normally bartered for food.

Still, the factory hands seldom had enough to nourish themselves and their families, and they joined the droves of city folk who were abandoning their homes and flocking to the countryside in search of food. Between October 1917 and August 1920 (when a new census was taken), the population of Petrograd fell from almost 2.5 million to about three-quarters of a million, a drop of nearly two-thirds. During the same period Moscow lost nearly half its inhabitants, while the total urban population of Russia declined by about a third. A good proportion of these migrants were industrial workers who drifted back to their native villages and reverted to their former peasant existence. In August 1920 Petrograd, for example, was left with only a third of the nearly 300,000 factory hands of which it could boast three years before, and the overall decrease of workingmen throughout Russia exceeded 50 percent.[34] Part of this dramatic decline was attributable, of course, to the high death rate at the front, and part to the large number who returned to their

[32] Pukhov, *Kronshtadtskii miatezh*, p. 11.

[33] *Ibid.*, p. 23; Lazarevich, "Kronshtadtskoe vosstanie," *Bor'ba*, 1921, Nos. 1-2, pp. 3-5.

[34] The above statistics are derived from *Krasnaia Gazeta*, February 9, 1921; Kritsman, *Geroicheskii period velikoi russkoi revoliutsii*, p. 52; and Pukhov, *Kronshtadtskii miatezh*, p. 19.

villages to share in the division of land; the dislocation of industry and the lack of fuel and clothing also contributed to the exodus. But the majority went to seek food, especially during 1919 and 1920, when supplies in the cities rapidly approached starvation levels.

Even among those who chose to remain behind, many workers reestablished old ties with their village, making periodic trips for food or returning during illness or to assist with the harvest. Ironically, this took place at a moment when, according to the ideological canons of the Bolshevik party, the country should have been acquiring an increasingly urban and industrial character. But instead, owing to the effects of the land partition and of the Civil War, Russia in large measure reverted to the primitive agrarian society from which it had only recently begun to emerge. For the Soviet government, ruling as it did in the name of the industrial proletariat, the situation was fraught with dangerous implications. Not only did the shift of people from the city to the village dilute the social basis of Bolshevik authority, but the renewed contact between peasants and workers served to heighten existing popular tensions. The grievances of the peasants caused very strong reactions among the urban visitors, who were able to see with their own eyes the impact of War Communism in the countryside. And disaffection quickly spread from the peasants and workers to their plebeian cousins in the army and navy. The result was a mounting wave of rural disturbances, industrial agitation, and military unrest, which was to reach an explosive climax at Kronstadt in March 1921.

Meanwhile, the condition of the cities and towns continued to deteriorate. By the beginning of 1921 the very elements of city life were falling apart. Because of the fuel crisis, workshops, dwellings, and offices went without heat through the unusually severe winter months. Warm clothing and footgear were nowhere to be bought, and one heard of people freezing to death in unheated apartments. Typhus and cholera swept the cities, taking an alarming toll. But food remained the worst problem: in spite of the sharp decline in urban population, there was still not enough to go around. Laborers were sapped of their physical energy and fell victim to every form of demoralization. By the end of 1920 average productivity had sunk to a third of the 1913 rate.[35] Driven by cold and hunger, men abandoned their machines for days on end to gather wood and forage for food in the surrounding countryside. Traveling on foot or in overcrowded railway cars, they brought their personal possessions, and materials which they had filched from the factories, to exchange for whatever food they could get. The government did all it could to stop this illegal trade. Armed roadblock detachments (*zagraditel'nye otriady*) were deployed to guard the approaches to the cities and to confiscate the precious sacks of food which the "speculators" were carrying back to their families. The brutality of the roadblock detachments was a byword throughout the country, and complaints about their arbitrary methods flooded the commissariats in Moscow.[36]

Another major grievance of the working class was the growing regimentation of labor under the system of War Communism. The driving force behind this development was Trotsky, the Commissar of War. Encouraged by his success in whipping the hastily improvised Red Army into shape, Trotsky sought to apply similar methods of military discipline to the crumbling industrial economy. In January 1920 the Council of People's Commissars, largely at Trotsky's instigation, decreed a general labor obligation for all able-bodied adults and, at the same time, authorized the assign-

[35] S. N. Prokopovitch, *The Economic Condition of Soviet Russia*, London, 1924, pp. 20-25. See also K. Leites, *Recent Economic Developments in Russia*, London, 1922, pp. 131ff.

[36] See Alexander Berkman, *The Kronstadt Rebellion*, Berlin, 1922, p. 10.

ment of idle military personnel to civilian work. As the Civil War drew to a close, whole detachments of Red Army soldiers, instead of being discharged, were kept on as "labor armies" and set to work to relieve the growing fuel and transport crises and to rescue basic industry from collapse. Thousands of veterans were employed in cutting timber, mining coal, and repairing railway lines, while thousands more were assigned to heavy tasks in the large urban factories. Meanwhile, an attempt was made to reinforce labor discipline among the civilian working force in order to curtail pilfering and absenteeism and to raise individual productivity. The results of these policies, however, were disappointing. As might be expected, the tightening of discipline and the presence of troops in the factories were strongly resented by the regular workmen, provoking a shrill outcry in workshop and union meetings against the "militarization of labor." And the soldiers, for their part, were anxious to go home now that the war was over. To many Russians it seemed that the "militarization of labor" had lost its justification at the very moment when the government was seeking to extend it. Menshevik leaders compared the new regimentation to Egyptian slavery, when the Pharaohs used forced labor to build the pyramids. Compulsion, they insisted, would achieve no more success in industry than in agriculture.[37] To the alarm of government observers, such arguments were winning a sympathetic response among the industrial rank and file, whose disillusionment with the Bolsheviks and their program of War Communism was approaching the point of open demonstrations against the regime.

The "militarization of labor" was part of a wider effort to impose central control over the nation's faltering economy.

[37] See James Bunyan, *The Origin of Forced Labor in the Soviet State, 1917-1921: Documents and Materials*, Baltimore, 1967, pp. 89ff., 135-36.

During 1917 and 1918 the industrial workers had put into practice the syndicalist slogan of "workers' control" over production.[38] What this meant was that local factory and shop committees supervised the hiring and firing of labor, participated in fixing wages, hours, and working conditions, and in general kept watch over the activities of the administration. In some enterprises unpopular directors, engineers, and foremen were ejected, and the workers' committees took upon themselves the tasks of management, usually with disastrous results. By the summer of 1918 effective administration had all but vanished from Russian industry, and the country was moving towards the brink of economic collapse. The Bolsheviks, who had encouraged workers' control in 1917 as a means of undermining the Provisional Government, were now compelled to act lest they themselves should be engulfed by the same elemental tide which had swept away their predecessors. Thus, beginning in June 1918, the larger factories were nationalized, and workers' control was gradually abandoned in favor of one-man management and strict labor discipline. By November 1920 four out of five large enterprises were back under individual direction, and nationalization had been extended to most small factories and shops.[39] Wherever possible, "bourgeois specialists" were returned to their duties in order to provide badly needed technical advice and supervision. Before the year was out the ratio of white-collar employees to manual laborers was nearly double that of 1917.[40] A new bureaucracy had begun to flourish. It was a mixed lot, veteran administrative personnel rubbing shoulders with untrained neophytes; yet however disparate their

[38] See Paul Avrich, "The Bolshevik Revolution and Workers' Control in Russian Industry," *Slavic Review*, XXII (March 1963), 47-63.

[39] Kritsman, *Geroicheskii period velikoi russkoi revoliutsii*, p. 206.

[40] *Ibid.*, pp. 197-98. On February 2, 1921, Lenin complained that "the population of Moscow is being swollen by employees" and said that something must be done about it: Lenin, *Polnoe sobranie sochinenii*, LII, 65.

values and outlook, they shared vested interests of their own that set them apart from the workers at the bench.

For the rank-and-file workmen, the restoration of the class enemy to a dominant place in the factory meant a betrayal of the ideals of the revolution. As they saw it, their dream of a proletarian democracy, momentarily realized in 1917, had been snatched away and replaced by the coercive and bureaucratic methods of capitalism. The Bolsheviks had imposed "iron discipline" in the factories, established armed squads to enforce the will of management, and contemplated using such odious efficiency methods as the "Taylor system." That this should be done by a government which they had trusted and which professed to rule in their name was a bitter pill for the workers to swallow. Small wonder that, during the winter of 1920-1921, when economic and social dislocation reached a critical point, murmurings of discontent could no longer be silenced, not even by threats of expulsion with the loss of rations. At workshop meetings, where speakers angrily denounced the militarization and bureaucratization of industry, critical references to the comforts and privileges of Bolshevik officials drew indignant shouts of agreement from the listeners. The Communists, it was said, always got the best jobs and seemed to suffer less from hunger and cold than everyone else. Anti-Semitism and anti-intellectualism began to rear their heads, often simultaneously; the charge was made that the Bolsheviks were an alien breed of Jewish intellectuals who had betrayed the Russian people and contaminated the purity of the revolution.

This growing mood of bitterness and disillusionment coincided with a period of acute controversy within the Communist party itself, where opposition to the policies of War Communism was not lacking. The controversy, which continued from December 1920 to March 1921, reaching a climax at the Tenth Party Congress while the Kronstadt rebellion was in progress, centered on the role of the trade unions in Soviety society.[41] During the prolonged and turbulent dispute, three conflicting positions emerged. Trotsky, guided by the military conception of manpower which he had formed as Commissar of War, favored the complete subordination of the unions to the state, which alone would enjoy the authority to appoint and dismiss union officials. The staunchest opponents of this plan were members of the Workers' Opposition, a group composed largely of workers and former workers (notably Alexander Shliapnikov and Yuri Lutovinov) who had retained their proletarian allegiance and sympathies. What the Workers' Opposition found particularly disturbing was the apparent drift of the Soviet regime towards a new bureaucratic state dominated by a privileged nonproletarian minority. Shliapnikov, Lutovinov, Alexandra Kollontai, and their sympathizers decried the militarization of the labor force and the inauguration of one-man management in the factories. They demanded not only full independence of the trade unions from state and party control, but the transfer of industrial administration to the unions and their local factory committees, which were to be organized into an all-Russian Congress of Producers. The party, they insisted, must not allow the creative initiative of the workers to become "crippled by the bureaucratic machine which is saturated with the spirit of routine of the bourgeois capitalist system of production and control."[42]

Lenin and his supporters (who formed a large majority of the party's membership) sought to heal the breach between Trotsky's appeal for the subjugation of the trade unions and the syndicalist program of the Workers' Opposition. As they

[41] For good discussions of the trade union controversy, see Robert V. Daniels, *The Conscience of the Revolution*, Cambridge, Mass., 1960, pp. 119-36; and Isaac Deutscher, *Soviet Trade Unions*, London, 1950, pp. 42-52.

[42] Alexandra Kollontai, *The Workers' Opposition in Russia*, Chicago, 1921, pp. 22-23. Cf. the theses of the Workers' Opposition group in *Pravda*, January 25, 1921.

saw it, the unions must neither be absorbed into the state apparatus nor granted control over industry; rather, they should be allowed to retain a real measure of autonomy, with the right to choose their own leaders and engage in free discussion of labor problems, while the government continued to hold the reins of the economy in its own hands. Lenin hoped that his compromise proposals would succeed in bringing the other groups together. He was deeply disturbed by the dispute, which threatened, at so critical a moment in Soviet history, to shatter the party's fragile unity. "We must have the courage to look the bitter truth in the face," he said in January 1921, at the height of the controversy. "The party is sick. The party is shaking with fever." Unless it can cure its illness "quickly and radically," he warned, there will occur "an inevitable split" that might prove fatal to the revolution.[43]

THE debates within the Communist party reflected the rising tensions within Russian society as a whole as the winter months advanced. For the past three years the people had waged a desperate struggle to preserve the fruits of the revolution and to achieve a freer and more comfortable life. Once the enemy had been defeated, they believed, the government would promptly release them from the rigors of wartime discipline, and before long the system of War Communism would become a fading memory of a troubled era which had passed into history. But nothing of the sort took place. When the Civil War was won, the policies of War Communism were neither abandoned nor even relaxed. Months after Wrangel's defeat, the government showed little sign of restoring elementary liberties, either economic or political. The overriding thrust of Bolshevik policy, rather, remained in the direction of compulsion and rigid control. As a result, a feeling of bitter disappointment rapidly set in.

[43] Lenin, *Polnoe sobranie sochinenii*, XLII, 234.

It was this feeling which lay at the heart of the unfolding crisis. Even those who conceded that War Communism had served a necessary purpose, that during the life-and-death struggle against the Whites it had saved the army from defeat and the towns from starvation, were convinced that compulsion had outlived its usefulness. In their eyes, War Communism had been nothing more than a temporary expedient to meet an emergency situation; as a peacetime program it was an abysmal failure and a burden which the people would no longer tolerate.

Yet the Bolsheviks were not willing to scrap it any more than they were willing to halt the smothering of political opposition. By way of justification, party spokesmen insisted that the wartime emergency had not yet passed, that the country remained isolated and beset by powerful enemies on every side, ready to pounce at the first sign of internal weakness. But each repressive measure, even when dictated by economic or political urgency, further undermined the government's democratic and egalitarian pretensions. Critical voices argued that it was the Bolsheviks themselves who were betraying the ideals of the revolution. For Alexander Berkman, a leading anarchist who had supported the Soviet regime during the Civil War, the slogans of 1917 had been forsworn, the people's most cherished hopes trampled underfoot. Injustice prevailed on every hand, he wrote in 1921, and alleged exigency had been made the cloak of treachery, deceit, and oppression; the Bolsheviks, while ruling in the name of the workers and peasants, were destroying the initiative and self-reliance on which the revolution depended for its growth, indeed for its very survival.[44]

Berkman's sentiments were widely shared by other parties of the Left, which, like the anarchists, had been rudely

[44] Alexander Berkman, *The Bolshevik Myth* (*Diary 1920-1922*), New York, 1925, p. 319; Berkman, *The "Anti-Climax,"* Berlin, 1925, p. 12.

shunted aside after the Bolshevik seizure of power. In a speech to the Eighth Congress of Soviets, the Menshevik leader Fyodor Dan went so far as to charge that, with the stifling of popular initiative, the whole system of soviets had ceased to function except as a mere facade for a one-party dictatorship. Free speech and assembly, said Dan, had been brutally suppressed, citizens imprisoned or banished without trial, and political executions carried out on a mass scale. Decrying these terrorist practices, he demanded the immediate restoration of political and civil liberties and called for new elections to the soviets in every locality. Dan's appeal was echoed in a speech by the prominent Left SR I. N. Steinberg. Himself a former Commissar of Justice in the Soviet government, Steinberg called for the revival of "soviet democracy" with broad autonomy and self-direction on the local level.[45]

Here, in effect, was the old Leninist demand for "all power to the soviets," now being turned against the Bolsheviks by their left-wing critics. Within the very ranks of the Communist party the Democratic Centralists advocated more power to the local soviets as a cure for the excessive centralization of political authority during the Civil War. Nor were such appeals confined to a handful of radical intellectuals. During the winter months popular anger developed on a wide front, embracing sailors and soldiers as well as peasants and workers, who yearned for the anarchic freedom of 1917 while craving at the same time a restoration of social stability and an end to bloodshed and economic privation. Out of these somewhat contradictory aspirations there arose one of the most serious internal crises that the Bolsheviks had faced since their assumption of power. By March 1921 the Soviet regime was in danger of being swept away by a swelling wave of peasant insurrections, labor disturbances, and

[45] *Vos'moi vserossiiskii s"ezd sovetov*, pp. 55-57, 122-23.

military ferment which reached their culmination in the Kronstadt uprising.

Above all, it was hunger and deprivation that had set the stage for the crisis, and it is easy to criticize the Bolsheviks for their failure to provide relief by abandoning the system of War Communism. Yet, no less than the governments of the West, they needed time to assess the new situation that confronted them. The transition from war to peace, as Lenin told the Eighth Congress of Soviets, was no simple matter. No one was sure which course of action was best; there was no strategic blueprint, no precedent to follow. From the moment the Bolsheviks took power, their policies had been groping, experimental, uncertain; and now, more than three years later, improvisation continued to mark their discussions and actions. Some of the party's leaders, including Lenin himself, had in fact begun to contemplate a moderation of War Communism as early as November 1920, but at that time it had been far from evident—as it was to become only two or three months later—that an immediate reorientation was necessary to avert a major social upheaval.

Yet the fact remains that a relaxation in domestic affairs was too long in coming. Still in the grip of a wartime psychology, and unwilling to give up a program which suited their ideological preconceptions, the Bolsheviks clung to the policies of War Communism and did not let go until February 1921, when Lenin took the first steps towards setting a New Economic Policy in motion. By then, however, it was too late to avoid the tragedy of Kronstadt.

2. Petrograd and Kronstadt

In February 1921 an open breach occurred between the Bolshevik regime and its principal mainstay of support, the working class. Since the onset of winter, an unusually severe one even by Muscovite standards, cold and hunger, combined with the undiminished rigors of War Communism, had produced a highly charged atmosphere in the large towns. This was particularly true of Moscow and Petrograd, where only a single spark was needed to set off an explosion. It was provided on January 22, when the government announced that the already meager bread ration for the cities would immediately be cut by one-third.[1] Severe though it was, the reduction apparently was unavoidable. Heavy snows and shortages of fuel had held up food trains from Siberia and the northern Caucasus, where surpluses had been gathered to feed the hungry towns of the center and north. During the first ten days of February, the disruption of railway links became so complete that not a single carload of grain reached the empty warehouses of Moscow.[2] But the fact that the cut in rations had been dictated by urgent and unforeseeable circumstances did little to diminish its impact on the starving urban population. An outburst of some sort seemed inevitable.

The first serious trouble erupted in Moscow during the middle of February. It began with a rash of spontaneous factory meetings, at which angry workmen called for the immediate scrapping of War Communism in favor of a system of "free labor." So assertive was this demand that the government sent emissaries to the factories to try to justify its policies. This, however, was no easy task. Facing extremely hostile audiences, the official spokesmen were seldom allowed to finish their remarks before being driven from the

[1] *Pravda*, January 22, 1921.
[2] Poliakov, *Perekhod k nepu*, p. 233.

platform to a chorus of jeers and catcalls. According to one report, Lenin himself, appearing before a noisy gathering of Moscow metal workers, asked his listeners, who had accused the Bolsheviks of ruining the country, if they would prefer to see a return of the Whites. His question drew a bitter retort: "Let come who may—whites, blacks, or devils themselves—just you clear out."[3]

Unrest in the capital escalated swiftly, as factory meetings were succeeded by strikes and demonstrations. Workers took to the streets with banners and placards demanding "free trade," higher rations, and the abolition of grain requisitions. Nor did they stop at economic demands. Some of the demonstrators appealed for the restoration of political rights and civil liberties, and here and there a placard even called for the revival of the Constituent Assembly, while others bore the uglier legend "Down with the Communists and Jews."[4] At first, the authorities tried to end the demonstrations with promises of relief, but these were unavailing and regular troops and officer cadets (*kursanty*) had to be called in to restore order.

No sooner had the Moscow disturbances begun to subside than a far more serious wave of strikes swept the former capital of Petrograd. An air of tragedy hung over the city, "a ghost of its former self," in the description of a contemporary, "its ranks thinned by revolution and counter-revolution, its immediate future uncertain."[5] Situated in the northwestern corner of Russia, remote from the main centers

[3] *New York Times*, March 6, 1921.

[4] "Sobytiia v Petrograde," Maklakov Archives, Series A, Packet 5, No. 13; "Pis'mo iz Petrograda ot poloviny fevralia 1921 goda," Miller Archives, File 5M, No. 5; *Novyi Mir*, March 1, 1921; H. B. Quarton, Viborg, to Secretary of State, March 3, 1921, National Archives, 861.00/8245. According to Quarton, these demonstrations were not reported in the Soviet press to prevent their spread to other cities.

[5] Angelica Balabanoff, *My Life as a Rebel*, New York, 1938, p. 261.

of food and fuel supply, Petrograd suffered even more than Moscow from hunger and cold. Available stores of food had shrunk to only a fifth of what they had been before the First World War.[6] Townsmen went for miles on foot into the neighboring forests, without warm clothing or decent shoes, to chop wood to heat their homes. In early February more than 60 of the largest Petrograd factories were forced to close their gates for lack of fuel.[7] Meanwhile, food supplies had all but vanished. According to a Menshevik witness, Fyodor Dan, starving workers and soldiers begged in the streets for a crust of bread.[8] Angry citizens protested against the unequal system of rations which favored some categories of the population over others. Tensions were aggravated by reports that party members had received new shoes and clothing. Rumors of this kind, always rife in times of stress and hardship, were widely believed and figured prominently in the turmoil preceding the revolt at Kronstadt.

As in Moscow, street demonstrations were heralded by a rash of protest meetings in Petrograd's numerous but depleted factories and shops. Economic grievances led the list, above all the question of food. Speaker after speaker called for an end to grain requisitioning, the removal of roadblocks, the abolition of privileged rations, and permission to barter personal possessions for food. On February 23 a clamorous meeting took place at the Trubochny factory, still one of Petrograd's largest metal producers, although its working force had dwindled to a fraction of what it had been three or four years earlier. Before the gathering dispersed, a resolution was passed demanding an increase in food rations and the immediate distribution of all shoes and winter clothing on hand. The men returned the next morning but soon laid

[6] Pukhov, *Kronshtadtskii miatezh*, p. 19.

[7] *Pravda*, February 12, 1921.

[8] F. I. Dan, *Dva goda skitanii* (*1919-1921*), Berlin, 1922, pp. 104-105.

down their tools and walked out of the factory. Making their way to Vasili Island on the northern side of the Neva, they tried to organize a mass demonstration to dramatize their grievances. A delegation was sent to the barracks of the Finland Regiment but failed to draw the soldiers into the demonstration. Nevertheless, additional workers from nearby factories and students from the Mining Institute began to arrive, and before long a crowd of 2,000 had collected to shout their disapproval of the government. According to one account, the Bolshevik chairman of the Petrograd Council of Trade Unions, N. M. Antselovich, rushed to the scene and urged the workers to return to their jobs but was dragged from his car and beaten.[9] Before the situation could get completely out of hand, Zinoviev, party chairman in Petrograd and chairman of the Soviet, dispatched a company of armed military cadets with orders to break up the demonstration. After some buffeting and shouting, and a few shots fired into the air, the strikers were dispersed without bloodshed.[10]

The demonstration on Vasili Island was only a foretaste of what was to come. The following day, February 25, the Trubochny workers again took to the streets, fanning out through the surrounding factory districts and calling their fellow workmen off the job. Their efforts were immediately successful. Walkouts took place at the Laferme tobacco factory, the Skorokhod shoe factory, and the Baltic and Patronny metal plants; then, fanned by rumors that some of the Vasili Island demonstrators had been killed or wounded the previous day by the military cadets, the strike spread to other large enterprises, including the Admiralty shipyards and the Galernaya drydocks. In several places crowds

9 "Sobytiia v Petrograde," Maklakov Archives, Series A, Packet 5, No. 13; *Novaia Russkaia Zhizn'*, March 8, 1921.

10 *Pravda o Kronshtadte*, Prague, 1921, p. 6; Pukhov, *Kronshtadskii miatezh*, pp. 29-30; Kornatovskii, ed., *Kronshtadtskii miatezh*, p. 130; Berkman, *The Bolshevik Myth*, pp. 291-92.

gathered to hear impromptu attacks on the policies of the government, and once again the *kursanty* were summoned to disperse them.

Alerted by the strikes in Moscow, the Petrograd authorities, under Zinoviev's supervision, had been keeping a watchful eye for signs of trouble in their own bailiwick. When it came, they acted swiftly to restore order. On February 24, the very day of the Vasili Island demonstration, the Petrograd Committee of the Communist party met and organized a three-man Defense Committee, consisting of M. N. Lashevich, a member of the Revolutionary War Council of the Soviet Republic, D. N. Avrov, commander of the Petrograd Military District, and N. M. Antselovich of the Trade Union Council. Vested with emergency powers, the Petrograd Defense Committee ordered every district of the city to set up its own "revolutionary troika" to prevent the disturbances from spreading. Modeled after the Defense Committee itself, the *revtroiki* were composed of the district party organizer, the local military commander, and either the chairman of the district soviet or the commissar of the local military school. That same day the Executive Committee of the Petrograd Soviet, chaired by Zinoviev, proclaimed martial law throughout the city. An 11 P.M. curfew was imposed, and gatherings in the streets were forbidden at any time.[11]

While the Trubochny strikers made the rounds of the factories, exhorting the workmen to join them in a mass protest against the authorities, Zinoviev and his colleagues sought ways to avert a bloodbath. On February 25 the Petrograd Soviet, the Trade Union Council, and the party committee addressed a joint appeal "To the Workers of Red

---

[11] *Petrogradskaia Pravda*, February 25 and 26, 1921; *Izvestiia Petrogradskogo Soveta*, February 26, 1921. Antselovich appears to have served on the Petrograd Defense Committee only during the first few days of its existence. Thereafter all orders and decrees of the committee were signed by Zinoviev, Lashevich, and Avrov.

Petrograd," urging them to stay on the job. The appeal admitted that the workers were suffering many hardships but explained that this was the cost of defending the revolution against its enemies. Even now, it said, the White Guards, aided by the Mensheviks and Socialist Revolutionaries, were seeking to exploit the food crisis for their own malevolent purposes. Had the workers of "Red Peter" already forgotten the Yudeniches and Kolchaks, the Denikins and Wrangels? What could a White restoration give the people? Only "the landlord's whip and the tsarist crown." And what would result from quitting the factories? Even greater hunger and cold. The workers had indeed made enormous sacrifices, but all the more reason not to abandon the revolution at the very moment when victory had been achieved.[12]

With this appeal the Petrograd Bolsheviks launched a major propaganda campaign to stem the unrest within the city. From every official quarter the strikers were warned not to play into the hands of the counterrevolution. Hunger, exhaustion, and cold, ran the government's argument, were the inevitable consequences of the "Seven Years' War" through which the country had just passed. Did it make any sense to forfeit such a costly victory to the "White Guard swine" and their supporters? The sole beneficiaries of the strikes and demonstrations, declared the Petrograd Soviet, were the Polish landlords in Riga and the English capitalists in London, who might be tempted to demand greater concessions at the negotiating table. In the same vein, a proclamation by the *kursanty* of Petrograd denounced the Trubochny workers for actions which could please only "the English, French, and other landlords, the White Guard agents who are scattered everywhere, and their servants, the lackeys of capitalism—the SR's and Mensheviks."[13] The Petrograd

[12] *Krasnaia Gazeta*, February 25, 1921.

[13] *Izvestiia Petrogradskogo Soveta*, February 25, 1921; *Petrogradskaia Pravda*, February 26, 1921.

Defense Committee warned that British, French, and Polish spies had been smuggled into the city to take advantage of the confusion. Meanwhile, the daily press printed a spate of resolutions from various Petrograd factories and trade unions condemning the "provocateurs" and "idlers" responsible for the disturbances.[14] The favorite epithet for the alleged troublemakers was *shkurniki* or "self-seekers"—literally, persons concerned only for their own skins. And instead of the usual words for "strike" (*stachka* or *zabastovka*), the term *volynka* was employed, a colloquialism embracing not only regular walkouts but sitdown strikers and slowdowns as well. According to Fyodor Dan, the authorities preferred this pejorative rather than admit that genuine strikes could be launched against a "workers' government."[15]

On February 26, as the disturbances mounted, the Petrograd Soviet held a special session to consider further action. An ominous note was sounded when N. N. Kuzmin, a commissar of the Baltic Fleet who was to acquire a certain notoriety in the weeks ahead, called attention to the rising temper of the sailors and warned that an explosion might occur if the strikes were allowed to continue. Pursuing this line, Lashevich, a member of the Petrograd Defense Committee, declared that stern measures were the only way to deal with the strikers. He demanded in particular that the Trubochny workers, the chief instigators of the movement, be locked out of their factory and thus automatically deprived of their rations. The Soviet concurred and immediately issued the necessary orders. The Laferme factory, a second hotbed of proletarian discontent, was also shut down, and workers from other enterprises were directed to return to their machines or suffer the same punishment.[16]

[14] See, for example, Kornatovskii, ed., *Kronshtadtskii miatezh*, pp. 138, 144.

[15] Dan, *Dva goda skitanii*, p. 105.

[16] *Pravda o Kronshtadte*, p. 6; Berkman, *The Kronstadt Rebellion*, p. 7.

This thinly veiled attempt to starve the strikers into submission merely added to the existing tensions. During the remaining days of February the movement continued to spread, forcing factory after factory to suspend operations. On the 28th the contagion reached the giant Putilov metal works with its 6,000 workers, a formidable body though only a sixth of what it had been during the First World War.

By now the fourth anniversary of the February Revolution was approaching, and the disquiet in Petrograd, as Dan noted, recalled the mood of the city in 1917, just before the collapse of the autocracy.[17] Another factor provoking official concern was a change in the character of the workers' demands. Initially, the resolutions passed at factory meetings dealt overwhelmingly with familiar economic issues: regular distribution of rations, issuance of shoes and warm clothing, removal of roadblocks, permission to make foraging trips into the countryside and to trade freely with the villagers, elimination of privileged rations for special categories of workingmen, and so on. On the last two days of February these economic demands acquired a more urgent tone; one leaflet, for example, cited cases of workers who had been found frozen or starved to death in their homes.[18] But even more alarming, from the standpoint of the authorities, was the fact that political grievances had begun to occupy a prominent place in the strike movement. Among other things, the workers wanted the special squads of armed Bolsheviks, who carried out a purely police function, withdrawn from the factories, as well as the disbandment of the labor armies, some of which had recently been posted to the larger Petrograd enterprises. On a more fundamental level, pleas for the restoration of political and civil rights, which at first had been sporadic, became insistent and widespread.

At such a moment, it is hardly surprising that the political

17 Dan, *Dva goda skitanii*, p. 107.
18 Berkman, *The Bolshevik Myth*, p. 292.

opposition should be stirred into action. The Menshevik and SR organizations in Petrograd, though decimated by arrests and hounded by the police, managed to distribute a number of proclamations among the working-class population. On the 27th, for example, the following manifesto appeared in the streets of the city:

A fundamental change is necessary in the policies of the government. First of all, the workers and peasants need freedom. They do not want to live by the decrees of the Bolsheviks. They want to control their own destinies. Comrades, support the revolutionary order. In an organized and a determined manner demand:

Liberation of all arrested socialists and nonparty workingmen; abolition of martial law; freedom of speech, press, and assembly for all who labor; free elections of factory committees, trade unions, and soviets.

Call meetings, pass resolutions, send delegates to the authorities, bring about the realization of your demands.[19]

Although the manifesto was unsigned, it bore earmarks of the agitation which, by their own admission, Dan and his fellow Menshevik leaders were actively conducting at the end of February. Aided by sympathetic printers, among whom the Mensheviks had always enjoyed a large following, the Petrograd organization was able to issue many leaflets and proclamations calling for freely elected soviets and labor unions, the restoration of civil liberties, an end to the terror, and the liberation of socialists and other left-wing political prisoners from Communist jails. In the economic sphere, the Mensheviks appealed to the government to end grain requisitioning and the compulsory establishment of state farms, and to restore freedom of trade between town and country, with regulations to prevent speculation.

These were demands which the Mensheviks had been

[19] Kornatovskii, ed., *Kronshtadtskii miatezh*, p. 26.

making since the early stages of the Civil War, and which Fyodor Dan and David Dallin had so vigorously advanced at the Eighth Congress of Soviets in December 1920. What the Mensheviks wanted, in essence, was the fulfillment of the existing constitution, so that all socialist parties might have a place in the Soviet system and the working people could enjoy the freedoms arbitrarily denied them by the Bolshevik dictatorship. In keeping with their role as a legal opposition, a role which they had performed since 1917, the Mensheviks shrank from any appeal for the overthrow of the government by force of arms. Rather, as the above manifesto indicates, they called on the workers of Petrograd to hold meetings, pass resolutions, and petition the authorities—in short, to apply "in an organized and a determined manner" every legal pressure for political and economic reform. Nonetheless, their criticisms aroused the concern and indignation of the government, for they amounted to nothing less than the accusation that the Bolsheviks had betrayed the fundamental principles of the revolution. Besides, who could guarantee that the workers, once stirred into action, would stop at legal methods of protest and not erupt into an open rebellion?

Unlike the Mensheviks, the Socialist Revolutionaries had long pinned their hopes on a mass uprising to oust Lenin's regime from power. In its place they aimed to restore the popularly elected Constituent Assembly, in which their party had won a majority of the seats but which the Bolsheviks had dispersed in January 1918. In 1921 these twin objectives—the overthrow of Bolshevik power and the revival of the Constituent Assembly—remained at the heart of their program, and the following proclamation, pasted on the walls of Petrograd on February 28, over the signature of the "Socialist Workers of the Neva District," was probably of SR origin:

We know who is afraid of the Constituent Assembly. It is they who will no longer be able to rob the people, but will have to answer before the people's representatives for their deceit, their robberies, and all their crimes.

Down with the hated Communists! Down with the Soviet government! Long live the Popular Constituent Assembly![20]

This leaflet (and others like it) was much more militant and uncompromising than anything the Mensheviks were capable of turning out. Actually, in tone and content it was closer to the propaganda of such underground organizations as the Union for the Resurrection of Russia, an alliance of liberals and right-wing socialists who shared an overriding desire to bring an end to Bolshevik rule.

The flood of anti-Communist propaganda let loose during the February strikes raises the question of leadership of the movement. Was it the Mensheviks and Socialist Revolutionaries, as the government charged, who had brought the workers into the streets? There can be no question that both groups did their best to encourage the strikes once they had broken out. This was particularly true of the Mensheviks, who by 1921 had regained much of the working-class support that they had lost during the 1917 Revolution. At the time of the Petrograd disturbances, Menshevik influence in the Trubochny factory and other troublesome enterprises was considerable.[21] Menshevik agitators received a sympathetic hearing at workers' meetings, and their leaflets and manifestos passed through many eager hands. Yet, for all this activity, which undoubtedly played a role in fanning the disturbances, there is no evidence that the Mensheviks or any other group had planned and organized them in advance. The workingmen of Petrograd, as we have seen, had ample

[20] *Ibid.* The text of this leaflet and that of the Mensheviks quoted above are also to be found in *Pravda o Kronshtadte*, pp. 6-7; Berkman, *The Kronstadt Rebellion*, pp. 7-8; and Slepkov, *Kronshtadtskii miatezh*, p. 18.

[21] See P. I. Boldin, "Men'sheviki v Kronshtadtskom miatezhe," *Krasnaia Letopis'*, 1931, No. 3, pp. 13-14.

causes of their own for erupting into open protest against the government. In the sense that they were unplanned— though hardly unmotivated—the February strikes were a spontaneous expression of popular discontent.

After a week of turmoil, the Petrograd authorities finally succeeded in bringing the situation under control. No mean feat, this was achieved through a combination of force and concessions which Zinoviev and his associates applied with determined efficiency. Complicating their task was the fact that a good part of the regular garrison, having themselves been caught up in the general ferment, could not be relied upon to carry out the government's orders. Units considered untrustworthy were disarmed and confined to their barracks. It was even rumored that the issue of boots was prohibited so as to prevent the soldiers from leaving their quarters and mingling with the crowds, as they had done with such fateful results four years earlier.[22] In place of the regular troops, the authorities relied on the *kursanty*, the Communist officer cadets, who were called in by the hundreds from neighboring military academies to patrol the city. In addition, all party members in the area were mobilized in case they too should be needed to restore order.

Overnight Petrograd became an armed camp. In every quarter pedestrians were stopped and their documents checked. Theaters and restaurants were closed and the curfew strictly enforced. From time to time an isolated shot rang out in the streets. As tensions rose, there occurred, particularly among the industrial workers, a flareup of anti-Semitic feeling, which the Petrograd Soviet attributed to the Jew-baiting literature circulated by White agitators.[23] To a certain extent, perhaps, this charge was justified, although anti-Semitism was a traditional response of Russian peasants and workers during times of unusual hardship. In any case, the Jewish inhabitants of Petrograd were apprehensive, and some

[22] Dan, *Dva goda skitanii*, p. 107.
[23] *Izvestiia Petrogradskogo Soveta*, March 1, 1921.

of them left the city, fearing a pogrom if the government should collapse and the mobs be allowed free rein in the streets.[24]

Beyond concentrating heavy military force within the city, the Bolsheviks tried to break the protest movement by locking more strikers out of their factories. This entailed—as in the case of Trubochny and Laferme—denying the workers their rations. At the same time, widespread arrests were carried out by the Petrograd Cheka. Speakers who criticized the regime at factory meetings and street demonstrations were taken into custody. During the last days of February, by Dan's reckoning, some 500 recalcitrant workmen and union officials ended up behind bars.[25] Students, intellectuals, and other nonworkers who were also caught in the dragnet probably numbered in the thousands, many of them belonging to opposition parties and groups. The Menshevik organization in Petrograd was particularly hard hit by Cheka raids. Virtually every active leader who had thus far escaped arrest was carted off to prison. Kazukov and Kamensky were arrested towards the end of February, after organizing a workers' demonstration. A few, including Rozhkov and Dan, remained at large a day or two longer, feverishly turning out and distributing their proclamations and leaflets, until they too were rounded up by the police. All told, during the first three months of 1921, it has been estimated that some 5,000 Mensheviks were arrested in Russia, including the party's entire Central Committee.[26] At the same time, the few prominent SR's and anarchists who still found themselves at liberty were also rounded up. According to Victor Serge, in his

[24] *Novaia Russkaia Zhizn'*, March 8, 1921; Quarton to Secretary of State, March 5, 1921, National Archives, 861.00/8253. On the resurgence of anti-Semitism, see also Pukhov, *Kronshtadtskii miatezh*, p. 32; and Emma Goldman, *Living My Life*, New York, 1931, pp. 875-76.

[25] Dan, *Dva goda skitanii*, p. 108.

[26] Leonard Schapiro, *The Origin of the Communist Autocracy*, Cambridge, Mass., 1956, p. 205.

Memoirs of a Revolutionary, the Cheka wanted to shoot its Menshevik prisoners as the principal instigators of the strikes, but Maxim Gorky intervened and saved them.[27]

Meanwhile, the Bolsheviks stepped up their propaganda drive in a last effort to persuade the strikers to return to work without bloodshed. To supplement the press, party members—particularly those who enjoyed popular esteem—were recruited for agitation in the streets, factories, and barracks. Their reception, by and large, was not very cordial, although Mikhail Kalinin, president of the All-Russian Congress of Soviets, seems to have been more successful than most of his colleagues (possibly because of his own plebeian origins) in gaining a hearing in the workshops and military installations around the city. As their central theme, the agitators blamed the strikes and demonstrations on counterrevolutionary plots hatched by the White Guards and their Menshevik and SR allies. This formula, as Emma Goldman noted, had grown stale from three years of repetition,[28] yet it still had some effect, especially since the Mensheviks and SR's made no attempt to conceal their active role in the disturbances.

But it was not by force and propaganda alone that order was restored in Petrograd. Of equal importance was a series of concessions of sufficient magnitude to take the edge off the opposition movement. As an immediate step, extra rations were distributed to the soldiers and factory workers, amounting to a tin of preserved meat and a pound and a quarter of bread per day, which, the American consul in Viborg reported, "made quite a hole in Petrograd's dwindling food supply."[29] At the same time, emergency supplies

[27] Victor Serge, *Memoirs of a Revolutionary, 1901-1941*, London, 1963, p. 130. Gorky himself left the country soon afterwards.

[28] Goldman, *Living My Life*, p. 875.

[29] Quarton to Secretary of State, March 4, 1921, National Archives, 861.00/8241.

were rushed in from other locations to be used when existing stores were exhausted.

Beyond this, Zinoviev, on February 27, announced a number of additional concessions to the workers' most pressing demands. Henceforward they would be permitted to leave the city in order to forage for food. To facilitate this, Zinoviev even promised to schedule extra passenger trains into the surrounding countryside. Moreover, the roadblock detachments around Petrograd were instructed not to confiscate food from ordinary workingmen but to confine themselves to guarding against genuine speculation. Zinoviev also announced that the government had purchased some 18 million poods of coal from abroad, which would arrive shortly and help ease the fuel shortage in Petrograd and other cities. But most important, he revealed for the first time that plans were afoot to abandon the forcible seizure of grain from the peasants in favor of a tax in kind.[30] In other words, the system of War Communism was at long last to be replaced by a new economic policy, a policy which would at least partially restore freedom of trade between town and country. On March 1, as if to confirm this intention, the Petrograd Soviet announced the withdrawal of all roadblocks from the whole of Petrograd province. That same day, moreover, the Red Army soldiers who had been assigned to labor duties in Petrograd—some two or three thousand in all—were demobilized and allowed to return to their native villages. According to the official explanation, curtailments of production had made their further presence unnecessary.[31]

As a result, after several days of tense excitement, the Petrograd disturbances rapidly petered out. By March 2 or 3

[30] *Krasnaia Gazeta*, February 27, 1921. The decision to buy the coal (18.5 million poods—a pood is 36 pounds) had already been made by the Council of Labor and Defense on February 1: see Lenin, *Polnoe sobranie sochinenii*, LII, 63.

[31] *Izvestiia Petrogradskogo Soveta*, March 1, 1921; *Krasnaia Gazeta*, March 1, 1921.

nearly every striking factory was back in operation. The concessions had done their work, for more than anything else it was cold and hunger which had stimulated popular disaffection. Yet there is no denying that the application of military force and the widespread arrests, not to speak of the tireless propaganda waged by the authorities, had been indispensable in restoring order. Particularly impressive in this regard was the discipline shown by the local party organization. Setting aside their internal disputes, the Petrograd Bolsheviks swiftly closed ranks and proceeded to carry out the unpleasant task of repression with efficiency and dispatch. This applies as much to Zinoviev, the local party chieftain, as to any of his subordinates. For all his reputation as a craven, liable to panic when danger threatened, Zinoviev appears to have acted with remarkable presence of mind to quell the disorders in his midst.

Then, too, the collapse of the movement would not have come so soon but for the utter demoralization of Petrograd's inhabitants. The workers were simply too exhausted to keep up any sustained political activity. Hunger and cold had reduced many to a state of listlessness bordering on total apathy. What is more, they lacked effective leadership and a coherent program of action. In the past these had been supplied by the radical intelligentsia. But in 1921, as Emma Goldman noted, Petrograd's intellectuals were themselves in no condition to lend the workers any meaningful support, let alone active guidance. Once the torchbearers of revolutionary protest, they now felt too weary and terrorized, too paralyzed by the futility of individual effort, to raise their voices in opposition. With most of their comrades in prison or exile, and some already executed, few of the survivors were willing to risk the same fate, especially when the odds against them were so overwhelming and when the slightest protest might deprive their families of their rations.[32] For

[32] Goldman, *Living My Life*, p. 885.

many intellectuals and workers, moreover, the Bolsheviks, with all their faults, were still the most effective barrier to a White resurgence and the downfall of the revolution.

For these reasons, the strikes in Petrograd were fated to lead a brief existence. Indeed, they ended almost as suddenly as they had begun, never having reached the point of armed revolt against the regime. Nevertheless, their consequences were enormous. By arousing the sailors of neighboring Kronstadt, who were closely attuned to insurrectionary developments in the old capital, they set the scene for what was in many ways the most serious rebellion in Soviet history.

KRONSTADT is a fortified city and naval base on Kotlin Island, situated in the Gulf of Finland about 20 miles west of Petrograd. Constructed by Peter the Great at the beginning of the eighteenth century, the original fortress was designed to protect the new Russian capital on the Neva—Peter's celebrated "window on the West"—from the open sea. The island itself, however, has possessed strategic importance since the ninth century, when the mouth of the Neva formed the starting point of the famous water route "from the Varangians to the Greeks." Today, a visitor to Peterhof, Peter's majestic palace on the mainland southeast of Kotlin, can stand at the water's edge and see the vague outline of the island off in the distance, guarding the sea approaches to the former capital. A narrow piece of land, some eight miles long by about a mile and a half wide at its greatest breadth, its irregular contours form a rough elongated triangle. Inaccessible to outsiders, its coasts are well defended by chains of forts and batteries on rocks projecting far out into the sea to the north and south.

The eastern end of the island, which faces Petrograd, is occupied by the city of Kronstadt. A thick ancient wall encircles the town, the main point of entry being the Petrograd Gate on the east. On the southern side lie the harbors and

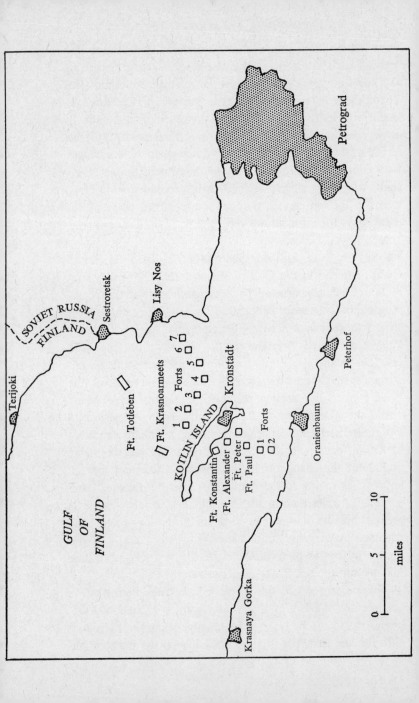

drydocks for vessels of the Baltic Fleet. The Gulf of Finland is frozen for more than four months of the year, from late November until the end of March or the beginning of April. Before the First World War, during the summer months, pleasure steamers plied regularly between Petersburg and Kronstadt. In winter the standard route was by train to Oranienbaum, a town and military base on the mainland five miles due south of Kotlin Island, and from there by sleigh over a snow road atop the thick ice of the gulf. By all accounts, Kronstadt, in the early part of the twentieth century, was a very picturesque place. Its numerous canals, tree-lined streets, and stately public buildings resembled those of the nearby imperial capital. Among its principal landmarks were the striking Cathedral of St. Andrew, with its golden dome and ochre-colored walls, the old Arsenal and Admiralty buildings, and the School of Naval Engineering (renamed the House of Education in 1917). Dominating the center of the city was the immense Anchor Square, with its huge Seamen's Cathedral (Morskoi Sobor), built at the end of the nineteenth century. The square acquired its name in the middle of the eighteenth century, when large warehouses were erected there to store ships' anchors.[33] Capable of holding more than 25,000 people, it was subsequently used for training recruits and for military reviews. During 1905 and 1917 Anchor Square became Kronstadt's revolutionary forum, the daily meeting-place for throngs of enthusiastic sailors, soldiers, and workingmen who practiced a kind of rough-and-ready direct democracy which recalled the Cossack popular assemblies of an earlier age.

In 1921 Kronstadt served as the main base of the Baltic

[33] *Kronshtadt: kratkii putevoditel'*, Leningrad, 1963, p. 77. Other descriptions of Kronstadt are to be found in the *Entsiklopedicheskii slovar'*, St. Petersburg, 1895, xviA, 823-24; *Encyclopedia Britannica*, 11th edn., xv, 927-28; and Voline, *La Révolution inconnue (1917-1921)*, Paris, 1947, pp. 408-10. For Kronstadt's early history see A. V. Shelov, *Istoricheskii ocherk kreposti Kronshtadt*, Kronstadt, 1904.

Fleet. Its total population numbered some 50,000, about half of whom were civilians and half military. The latter in turn were divided between the crews of the fleet (who formed the majority) and the soldiers of the garrison, mostly artillery-men who manned the main bastion and the outlying forts and gun emplacements. Many of the civilians were associated with the fortress and naval station, either as military de-pendents or as workmen employed at the dockyards, ware-houses, and other shore establishments. The rest were mainly factory hands, artisans, fishermen, small tradesmen, and employees of cooperatives and government institutions within the city proper.[34]

The name of Kotlin—kettle or cauldron—was a fitting one for the island on which Kronstadt was situated, as its prin-cipal inhabitants, the Baltic sailors, were perpetually seething with discontent. A restless and independent breed who loathed all privilege and authority, they seemed forever on the verge of exploding into open violence against their officers or against the central government, which they regarded as an alien and a coercive force. Temperamentally, they bore a close resemblance to those audacious freebooters of a former age, the Cossacks and *strel'tsy* (musketeers) of the seventeenth and eighteenth centuries, whose garrisons were hotbeds of *buntarstvo*, or spontaneous rebellion. Like their tempestuous forebears, the sailors were *vol'nitsy*, or untamed spirits, who instinctively resisted external discipline and lusted for freedom and adventure. When inflamed by rumor or drink, they were as prone as their predecessors to run riot and to vent their fury on the wealthy and powerful.

Kronstadt had a history of volatile radicalism reaching back to the first great upheaval in twentieth-century Russia, the Revolution of 1905. Illegal literature first appeared at the naval base in 1901, and soon after this the sailors began

[34] Pukhov, *Kronshtadtskii miatezh*, p. 49.

to form circles to discuss political and social questions and to air their grievances—above all, low wages, bad food, and the rigorous discipline to which they were continually subjected. The wave of strikes, jacqueries, and terrorism that swept the country between 1902 and 1905 found a sympathetic chord among them and heightened their social and political awareness. Insubordination towards officers and other breaches of discipline became everyday occurrences. By 1905, after the outbreak of war and revolution, whatever semblance of morale still remained suffered a devastating blow at the Straits of Tsushima, where a large part of the fleet was wiped out by the Japanese. A further stimulus to revolutionary activity, if any was needed, was provided by the dramatic *Potemkin* mutiny of June 1905 in the Black Sea Fleet.

The first serious trouble at Kronstadt began in October 1905, at the height of the revolution. It traced a pattern which was to become increasingly familiar in the years ahead. First came a mass meeting in Anchor Square. Thousands of disgruntled sailors and soldiers gathered to air their discontents. Mingled with the familiar appeals for better food and clothing, higher pay and shorter tours of duty, and a relaxation of military discipline were cries for the immediate overthrow of the autocracy and the inauguration of a democratic republic with full civil liberties for all. In the succeeding days tempers rose with appalling swiftness. On October 25 a commotion occurred in the seamen's mess after someone complained about the food. Shouts of "Kill the commandant" rose above the din of stamping feet and hammering mess trays.[35] The next day Kronstadt rose in open rebellion. Completely spontaneous in origin, the revolt quickly degenerated into an orgy of plunder and destruction akin to the *strel'tsy* mutinies during the reign of Peter the Great.

[35] F. Kogan, *Kronshtadt v 1905-1906 gg.*, Moscow, 1926, pp. 7-13.

Crowds of sailors and soldiers rampaged through the city streets, smashing shop windows and setting buildings aflame. Barricades went up and several houses were occupied as shelters against the expected arrival of punitive forces from Petersburg. The rioting lasted for two days, leaving 17 dead and 82 injured before government troops could restore order. Nearly 3,000 mutineers were arrested. Many of them were condemned to years of prison or exile, though no death sentences were meted out.[36]

On July 19, 1906, in the afterglow of the 1905 Revolution, a second and more serious explosion occurred in Kronstadt, sparked by a mutiny at its sister port of Sveaborg. Like its predecessor of October, the new outbreak was a spontaneous and disorganized affair which raged out of control for two days before government reinforcements were able to crush it. The rebel demands, while essentially the same as before, took on a note of bitter disillusionment after the failures of the preceding months. Hatred of authority and discipline remained the motive force behind the sailors' fury. "You have drunk our blood long enough!" shouted one bluejacket to an officer in the midst of the tumult, a cry which epitomized the feelings of the insurgents.[37] Both sides fought with unprecedented ferocity, the rebels driven by frustration and outrage, the authorities by the confidence of a swift victory now that the revolutionary tide in Russia had begun to ebb. An atmosphere of stern repressiveness having set in, this time

---

[36] V. Voronevskii and N. Khenrikson, *Kronshtadtskaia krepost'—kliuch k Leningradu*, Leningrad, 1926, pp. 10-16; Iu. Korablev, *Revoliutsionnye vosstaniia na Baltike v 1905-1906 gg.*, Leningrad, 1956, pp. 24-30; L. A. Lentsner, *Kronshtadt v 1905-1906 gg., vospominaniia*, Moscow, 1956, pp. 156-65. For further material on the Kronstadt revolts of 1905 and 1906, see the documents collected in *Voennye vosstaniia v Baltike v 1905-06 gg.*, Moscow, 1933; and *Voennye moriaki v period pervoi russkoi revoliutsii, 1905-1907 gg.*, Moscow, 1955.

[37] "Kronshtadtskoe vosstanie 1906 g.," *Krasnyi Arkhiv*, 1936, No. 4, p. 103.

36 ringleaders were executed and hundreds were imprisoned or banished to Siberia.[38]

It is important to dwell on these early cases of spontaneous rebellion in Kronstadt because, as we shall see presently, in many ways they foreshadowed the stormy events of March 1921. This was especially true of the 1917 upheaval, when once again Kronstadt was a center of unbridled revolutionary activity. Under the influence of the extreme Left, which throughout the year held ideological sway over Kotlin Island's tempestuous population, Kronstadt set itself up as a revolutionary commune on the model of the Paris Commune of 1871, an event enshrined in the history and legend of social rebellion. In May 1917 the maverick Kronstadt Soviet, led by Bolsheviks, anarchists, left-wing SR's and unaffiliated radicals of an anarcho-populist bent, refused to bow to the authority of the Provisional Government and proclaimed itself "the sole power in the city."[39] Thereafter the Soviet exercised overall political authority, supported by the general meetings in Anchor Square, which were held nearly every day. Anchor Square, in the description of Efim Yarchuk, an outspoken anarchist in the Kronstadt Soviet, became a "free university" where revolutionary orators of every stripe held forth to vast crowds of eager sailors, soldiers, and workingmen. A local Bolshevik leader, Ivan Flerovsky, proudly dubbed the square "Kronstadt's *veche*," a reference to the rowdy popular assemblies which flourished in the towns of Russia during the middle ages.[40]

[38] Korablev, *Revoliutsionnye vosstaniia na Baltike*, pp. 89-103; Lentsner, *Kronshtadt v 1905-1906 gg.*, pp. 101-24. According to Lentsner, 70 mutineers received the death sentence (perhaps some were reprieved).

[39] R. P. Browder and A. F. Kerensky, eds., *The Russian Provisional Government, 1917*, 3 vols., Stanford, 1961, III, 1296-99.

[40] E. Iarchuk, *Kronshtadt v russkoi revoliutsii*, New York, 1923, p. 54; I. P. Flerovskii, *Bol'shevistskii Kronshtadt v 1917 godu (po lichnym vospominaniiam)*, Leningrad, 1957, p. 17.

Together, the Soviet and the forum in Anchor Square satisfied the political needs of Kronstadt's inhabitants. There seems to have been no widespread desire for a national parliament or for any other central ruling body. For the most part, the social and economic life of the city was administered by the citizens themselves, through the medium of local committees of every sort—house committees, ship committees, food committees, factory and shop committees—which throve in the prevailing libertarian atmosphere. A popular militia was organized to defend the island from any outside encroachments upon its sovereignty. Kronstadt's residents displayed a real talent for spontaneous self-organization. Apart from their various committees, men and women working in the same shop or living in the same neighborhood formed tiny agricultural communes, each with about 50 members, which undertook to cultivate whatever arable land could be found on the empty stretches of the island. During the Civil War, says Yarchuk, these collective vegetable gardens helped save the city from starvation.[41]

Cherishing their local autonomy, the Kronstadt population warmly endorsed the appeal for "All power to the soviets" put forward in 1917 by Lenin and his party. They interpreted the slogan in a literal sense, to mean that each locality would run its own affairs, with little or no interference from any central authority. This, says Yarchuk, they understood to be the true essence of "socialism."[42] They regarded their own revolutionary commune as a model of decentralized self-rule and confidently expected the rest of the country to follow suit. "For all their revolutionary virtues," noted Ivan Flerovsky, "the Kronstadt sailors had one serious weakness: they naïvely believed that the force of their own enthusiasm would suffice to establish the power of the soviets through-

[41] Iarchuk, *Kronshtadt v russkoi revoliutsii*, pp. 22-23.
[42] *Ibid.*, pp. 37, 50.

out all of Russia."[43] Such hopes, however, were not to be realized, and in the ensuing years of Bolshevik dictatorship the libertarian commune of 1917 took on the aspect of a lost revolutionary utopia. The revolt of 1921 was at bottom an effort by the Kronstadters to recapture this golden age of spontaneity, and "All power to the local soviets" was their slogan.

Throughout the 1917 Revolution, the Baltic Fleet remained in a state of turbulence, punctuated by violent outbursts against every form of political and military authority. As in 1905, the sailors vented their greatest fury on their officers, whom they saw as living symbols of outworn privilege and arbitrary power. The Kronstadters were particularly eager to rid themselves of the severe discipline and the atmosphere of penal servitude which had earned Kotlin Island the reputation of a "sailors' Sakhalin."[44] Thus, when the February Revolution erupted, they seized the opportunity to remove the shackles of regimentation and to settle accounts with their unpopular superiors. On February 28 an angry mob of bluejackets dragged the base commander, Admiral R. N. Viren, from his quarters and carried him to Anchor Square, where he was summarily executed. This act signaled an orgy of bloodletting in which more than 40 Kronstadt navy and army officers were killed. Some 200 others were arrested and put behind bars. During the February turmoil a wave of violence swept through the whole complex of Baltic Fleet bases. A total of 76 naval officers, not to mention those of the army garrisons, were done to death by their men. Besides Viren, these included his counterpart at Sveaborg, Admiral Butakov, and Admiral Nepenin, commander in chief of the

---

[43] I. P. Flerovskii, "Iiul'skii politicheskii urok," *Proletarskaia Revoliutsiia*, 1926, No. 7, pp. 58-59.

[44] F. F. Raskol'nikov, *Kronshtadt i Piter v 1917 godu*, Moscow, 1925, pp. 29-32.

entire Baltic Fleet, whose headquarters was then at Helsingfors (Helsinki).[45]

This thirst for personal vengeance was only one aspect of
the revolutionary extremism which the February upheaval
let loose in Kronstadt. A spirit of libertarian abandon seized
hold of the place. Of course, the Bolsheviks, anarchists, SR
Maximalists, and other ultra-radical groups did what they
could to encourage it, and before long they came to exercise
a strong influence among the seamen and the rest of the Kronstadt population. The principal target of these groups was not
the military officers but the Provisional Government itself.
And in the ensuing months they could count on the sailors to
support any revolutionary manifestation directed against the
new regime. The Kronstadters figured prominently in the
Petrograd street demonstrations of April 1917, and also of
June, when they came to the aid of a group of anarchists who
had barricaded themselves against an anticipated government attack. Again, during the stormy July Days, they rushed
to Petrograd at the first news of trouble and played a central
part in the abortive insurrection, for which Trotsky christened
them "the pride and glory of the revolution." (In a well-
known incident, a group of sailors seized Victor Chernov,
the SR Minister of Agriculture, and it was only Trotsky's
fast talking that saved him from being lynched.)[46]

At the end of August, during General Kornilov's march on
the capital, the sailors rallied to the defense of the revolution.
The crew of the battleship *Petropavlovsk*, who had been in
the vanguard of the July uprising, called again for the immediate transfer of power to the soviets and demanded

[45] *Baltiiskie moriaki v podgotovke i provedenii Velikoi Oktiabr'skoi
sotsialisticheskoi revoliutsii*, Moscow, 1957, pp. 19-22; V. V. Petrash,
Moriaki Baltiiskogo flota v bor'be za pobedu Oktiabria, Leningrad,
1966, p. 52.

[46] N. N. Sukhanov, *The Russian Revolution, 1917*, New York,
1955, pp. 444-46. On the June and July events in Petrograd, see Alexander Rabinowitch, *Prelude to Revolution*, Bloomington, Ind., 1968.

Kornilov's arrest and execution. Four officers who protested were themselves seized and put to death.[47] In the weeks that followed, the sailors, true to their reputation of revolutionary intransigence, continued to press for the overthrow of the Provisional Government. On October 25 their moment arrived when Lenin launched his successful bid for power. Taking to their boats, the sailors hurried to the capital to lend their strength to the insurgents, joining the Petrograd Red Guards in storming the Winter Palace, while the Petrograd cruiser *Aurora* fired blank rounds to demoralize the defenders. For their role in October the men of Kronstadt earned the accolade "the pride and glory of the revolution," with which Trotsky had honored them during the July Days.

Even after Kerensky's fall Kronstadt's revolutionary militancy remained undiminished. Victory, in fact, only whetted the sailors' appetite for revenge against the social elements which they had driven from power. Their propensity for violent outbursts had particularly tragic results on the night of January 6-7, 1918, when a band of Kronstadt hotheads invaded a Petrograd hospital where two former Kadet ministers of the Provisional Government, Shingarev and Kokoshkin, were being held in custody, and murdered them in their beds. On Lenin's instructions, I. N. Steinberg, the Commissar of Justice, began an inquiry, but Lenin reconsidered and decided to drop it rather than risk a confrontation with the sailors.[48] Indeed, it was precisely because of their ruthlessness that Lenin wanted the sailors on his side. He placed no small value on their role as a kind of praetorian guard, ready at a moment's notice to take up arms for the cause of the soviets. In fact, on the night before the murders, he had sent a detachment of Kronstadters, led by a fierce young anarchist

[47] Browder and Kerensky, *The Russian Provisional Government*, III, 1581-82.

[48] I. N. Steinberg, *Als ich Volkskommissar war*, Munich 1929, pp. 138-63.

named Anatoli Zhelezniakov, to disperse the Constituent Assembly, in which the Bolsheviks had failed to gain a majority.[49] The sailors, of course, had their own reasons for opposing the assembly. As we have seen, they had little use for any central political institutions, particularly if dominated by parties too conservative for their taste. In their eyes, direct democracy through the local soviets was the political wave of the future; a national parliament, by contrast, could only be a step backward, a retreat towards the kind of "bourgeois" society represented by the Provisional Government, which they had been at such pains to liquidate.

Throughout the Civil War of 1918-1920, the sailors of Kronstadt, and of the Baltic Fleet as a whole, remained the torchbearers of revolutionary militancy. More than 40,000 bluejackets threw themselves into the struggle against the Whites.[50] Noted for their courage and ferocity in combat, they manned river flotillas and armored trains and replenished the ranks of the Red Army on every front. At the critical battle of Sviiazhsk—"the Valmy of the Russian Revolution"—they provided Trotsky with his most ardent shock troops, helping to turn back a large enemy force which threatened to penetrate into the heartland of Bolshevik territory.

At the same time, however, serious friction was developing between the sailors and the government. The first discordant notes had sounded when Lenin, immediately after the October coup, announced a cabinet composed exclusively of Bolsheviks. Wary of strong concentrations of authority, the Kronstadt Soviet began to press for a coalition government in which all socialist groups would enjoy representation—an early foretaste of the Kronstadt program of March 1921. Ominous murmurings arose among the sailors, cautioning against the possibility of a new dictatorial regime. If the

---

[49] See Paul Avrich, *The Russian Anarchists*, Princeton, 1967, p. 156.
[50] P. G. Sofinov, *Istoricheskii povorot (perekhod k novoi ekonomicheskoi politike)*, Moscow, 1964, p. 45.

new Council of People's Commissars should dare betray the democratic ideals of the revolution, it was said, then the guns which took the Winter Palace could just as easily be turned against the Smolny Institute, headquarters of the new administration.[51] Lenin apparently overlooked these hostile sentiments when he threatened, in November 1917, to "go to the sailors" after several of his colleagues demanded that other socialists be admitted into the government.[52]

By early 1918 complaints against the arbitrary and bureaucratic character of Communist rule were no longer isolated occurrences. In March the situation was aggravated when the fleet's own elected central committee (*Tsentrobalt*) was dissolved and its functions transferred to a council of commissars appointed by the party. For a growing number of sailors the revolution had been betrayed, a belief which the Brest-Litovsk treaty of the same month did much to strengthen. Many sided with the Left Communists, anarchists, and Left SR's, who opposed the treaty as a surrender to German imperialism and a retreat from the goal of world revolution. In April the crews of several Baltic vessels passed a strongly worded resolution accusing the government of planning to liquidate the fleet in compliance with German demands. The resolution went so far as to call for a general uprising to dislodge the Bolsheviks and install a new regime that would adhere more faithfully to the principles of the revolution. Nothing came of this, but a number of sailors joined the Left SR revolt in Moscow in July 1918, raided the headquarters of the Cheka, and briefly arrested a high-ranking official, M. I. Latsis.[53]

Further trouble occurred in October, when a mass meeting at the Petrograd naval base adopted a resolution in favor of

---

[51] Voline, *La Révolution inconnue*, p. 200.

[52] See Schapiro, *The Origin of the Communist Autocracy*, p. 74.

[53] L. D. Trotskii, *Kak vooruzhalas' revoliutsiia*, 3 vols. in 5, Moscow, 1923-1925, I, 140, 278.

tearing up the Brest-Litovsk agreement and resisting the German forces which had occupied the Ukraine, an area from which many of the sailors were recruited.[54] At the same time, the sailors went on record against the Bolshevik monopoly of political power. Condemning the suppression of the anarchists and opposition socialists, they called for free elections to the soviets in order to achieve a broader representation of the various left-wing parties. Finally, they denounced the compulsory seizure of grain, which the government had recently inaugurated, branding the food detachments as "thieves" and "plunderers of the peasants."[55]

The mutiny of October 1918 never got off the ground; troops were called in and the sailors quickly brought to order. But their demands strikingly anticipated the Kronstadt program of 1921, down to the slogans of "free soviets" and "Away with the commissarocracy." The two events, indeed, form part of a long historical pattern. A glance at the behavior of the Baltic Fleet from 1905 to 1921 reveals many elements of continuity, attesting to what Pavel Dybenko, a Bolshevik military leader who himself had been a Kronstadt seaman, called the "eternally rebellious spirit" of the sailors.[56] Over the years, one finds the same loathing of privilege and authority, the same hatred of regimentation, the same dream of local autonomy and self-administration. One finds, moreover, a powerful antagonism towards the central government and its appointed officials, an antagonism that was deeply rooted in the anarchist and populist traditions of the lower classes, dating from the rise of a powerful bureaucratic state during the seventeenth and eighteenth centuries. Isolated from the mainland, Kronstadt, even more than its sister

[54] G. S. Pukhov, *Kak vooruzhalsia Petrograd*, Moscow, 1933, p. 36.

[55] I. Flerovskii, "Miatezh mobilizovannykh matrosov v Peterburge 14 oktiabria 1918 g.," *Proletarskaia Revoliutsiia*, 1926, No. 8, pp. 218-37.

[56] P. E. Dybenko, *Iz nedr tsarskogo flota k velikomu Oktiabriu*, Moscow, 1928, p. 69.

bases on the Baltic, became a stronghold of primitive anarchic rebellion. The Kronstadt sailors, renowned for their revolutionary fervor and independent spirit, had little tolerance
for arbitrariness or compulsion from any source. Spontaneity
and decentralization were their watchwords. They yearned
for a free social order anchored in the local soviets, a direct
popular democracy patterned after the Cossack *krug* and
medieval *veche*. They were forever prone to sudden par-
oxysms of violence against the holders of authority, the
officers, the bureaucrats, the men of property or privilege. In
March 1921 all of these urges were to find their final and
most formidable expression.

Meanwhile, as the Civil War expanded, the grievances of
the sailors accumulated. Discontent, as in the past, centered
on the question of military discipline. The Revolution of
1917 had left the army and navy in a state of total disorganization. The traditional hierarchy of command had fallen
apart, leaving a vacuum of authority which was filled by in-
numerable committees of soldiers and sailors who elected
their own leaders and passed upon orders received from
above. The resulting chaos closely paralleled the situation in
industry, where local factory committees were establishing
"workers' control" in enterprise after enterprise. In the first
months after the October Revolution, Bolshevik policy tended
to foster this spontaneous process of decentralization. By
government decree, traditional military ranks and titles were
abolished, and a "socialist" fighting force was proclaimed
into existence, "built up from below on the principle of
election of officers and mutual comradely discipline and
respect."[57] In practice, this led to the final collapse of central authority and of the normal chain of command, and
encouraged the age-old tendency of Russian service men to
run amok and indulge in marauding and plunder.

The outbreak of Civil War in 1918, however, brought

[57] Wollenberg, *The Red Army*, p. 41.

about a quick reversal in Bolshevik military policy. The regime's very survival demanded an end to the chaotic decentralization of authority and the restoration of discipline in the ranks. As Commissar of War, Trotsky was the chief opponent of the "partisan spirit" (*partizanshchina*) which had infected the armed services. Following traditional military procedures, he soon whipped a new and effective fighting force into shape. The old ranks were not restored, but thousands of former imperial officers were returned to service as "military specialists" (*voenspetsy*) under the watchful supervision of political commissars. In this way, badly needed command experience and technical knowledge were provided until a new corps of Red Commanders could be trained. Within the Red Army the committee system was eliminated, obedience of orders strictly enforced, and the holiday from discipline brought to a swift and sudden conclusion.[58]

It was not long before the government began to extend these measures to the navy. But here stiffer opposition was encountered. As Dybenko noted, Bolshevik efforts to liquidate the ship committees and to impose the authority of centrally appointed commissars aroused a storm of protest in the Baltic Fleet.[59] For the sailors, whose aversion to external authority was proverbial, any attempt to restore discipline meant a betrayal of the freedoms for which they had struggled in 1917. Not only were they reminded of the harsh regimentation of tsarist times, but they felt that military efficiency would be better served by allowing free rein to their own initiative. They were determined not to have the fruits of victory denied them by the very party which they had helped lift into power. As a result, there was continuous friction between the rank and file and their Bolshevik commissars and commanders, and skirmishes occasionally broke out with the Cheka units

[58] See John Erickson, *The Soviet High Command*, London, 1962, pp. 25-52.

[59] Dybenko, *Iz nedr tsarskogo flota*, p. 199.

which fought alongside the regular troops at the height of the Civil War.

When the Civil War ended, the situation, instead of improving, took a turn for the worse. Overnight the stringent policies of the government lost their raison d'être. Just as the peasants saw no further need for the confiscation of their produce and the suppression of the free market, and just as the workers chafed at the subjugation of their trade unions and at the restoration of factory discipline, one-man management, and "bourgeois" technical specialists, so the sailors and soldiers demanded the return to democratic principles in military life. In the turbulent Baltic Fleet opposition to the reinforcement of discipline, the abolition of ship committees, and the appointment of commissars and "military specialists" to command positions quickly assumed threatening dimensions. Furthermore, several new factors came to bear which nurtured the mutinous spirit among the ships' crews as well as the troops of the Baltic garrisons. In the first place, since the White danger had been removed, the men were able to obtain leave for the first time in many months, and, returning to their native villages, were confronted at first hand with the policy of grain requisitions and the violent methods by which it was carried out. Some were themselves stopped by roadblock detachments and searched for illegal food. In the towns they saw the full extent of human misery which the war had brought about. Everywhere they were exposed to a restless and discontented population. They listened to the complaints of their fathers and brothers, which in so many ways resembled their own grievances against the authorities. "For years," remarked Stepan Petrichenko, a leading figure in the Kronstadt rising, "the happenings at home while we were at the front or at sea were concealed by the Bolshevik censorship. When we returned home our parents asked us why we fought for the oppressors. That set us thinking."[60] It is easy

[60] *New York Times*, March 31, 1921.

to imagine the extent to which accounts of men like Petrichenko fanned the unrest of their comrades when they returned to their posts. So drastic, in fact, was the effect on morale that the government took steps to curtail furloughs in the fleet. In December 1920 this touched off angry protests aboard the *Sevastopol*, one of the two dreadnoughts in Kronstadt harbor which were to play a central role in the events of the coming February and March. During the winter of 1920-1921 the rate of desertions among the Baltic sailors mounted steadily. By early 1921 the fleet was falling apart as an organized military force.[61]

Another danger which loomed large during this period was the impact of the food and fuel crises on the fleet. The sailors suffered only slightly less than the general civilian population from hunger and cold. With the onset of winter, the lack of heat in the barracks and aboard ship made life difficult to bear. Nor was there any stock of boots or warm uniforms on hand to mitigate the effects of the unusually severe cold that gripped the Baltic area between November and April. Worse still was the decline in both the quantity and the quality of the food rations which the men were issued.[62] A traditional complaint within the Russian navy, bad food had more than once given rise to disturbances in the past. And now, towards the end of 1920, an epidemic of scurvy broke out in the Baltic Fleet. In December, according to émigré sources in Helsingfors, the sailors of Kronstadt sent a delegation to Moscow to appeal for an improvement in rations, but when they arrived they were locked up by the authorities. Interceding for his men, F. F. Raskolnikov, the commander of the fleet, warned that unless the delegates were released at once Kronstadt might turn its guns on Petrograd. His prophetic words, however, went unheeded.[63]

[61] Pukhov, *Kronshtadtskii miatezh*, pp. 44-54.

[62] *Ibid.*, p. 42; Pukhov, "Kronshtadt i Baltiiskii flot pered miatezhem 1921 goda," *Krasnaia Letopis'*, 1930, No. 6, pp. 150-53.

[63] *Obshchee Delo*, January 2, 1921.

Even those sailors who belonged to the Communist party were not immune from the rising temper of opposition within the fleet. Sharing the independent spirit of their comrades, they had never been readily amenable to party or military discipline. By the end of 1920 a "fleet opposition" had taken shape, the counterpart of the "military opposition" in the Red Army and the "workers' opposition" in the factories, each of which stood for local initiative and party democracy and against regimentation and rigid central control. The "fleet opposition" advocated a Soviet navy organized on "socialist" lines, as distinguished from what they regarded as the outmoded hierarchical and authoritarian concepts of the past. Defending the elective ship committees, they scorned the introduction of "military specialists" as well as the "dictatorial behavior" (*diktatorstvo*) of certain Bolshevik officials in the political administration of the fleet.[64]

Even more alarming, a growing number of Bolshevik sailors, for whom the "fleet opposition" was an inadequate outlet for their disaffection, took the bolder step of tearing up their party cards. In January 1921 alone some 5,000 Baltic seamen quit the Communist party. Between August 1920 and March 1921, the Kronstadt party organization lost half of its 4,000 members.[65] Bolshevik officials blamed the exodus on unreliable elements which had inundated the party's ranks during the Civil War when qualifications for membership had been relaxed or lifted entirely, as in the "party week" recruitment drive of August 1919. It was largely these newcomers, according to party sources, who made up the recent wave of defectors. As a precautionary measure, moreover, hundreds more who did not leave of their own accord were purged from the rolls, and some of these were

[64] Lazarevich, "Kronshtadtskoe vosstanie," *Bor'ba*, 1921, Nos. 1-2, p. 3.

[65] Ida Mett, *La Commune de Cronstadt: Crépuscule sanglant des Soviets*, Paris, 1949, p. 26; Kornatovskii, ed., *Kronshtadtskii miatezh*, pp. 13-15.

transferred to the Black Sea and Caspian fleets or to posts in the Far East.[66]

The authority of the party was further undermined by a struggle for political control in the fleet, which pitted Trotsky, the War Commissar, against Zinoviev, the party chief in Petrograd. Zinoviev had resented Trotsky ever since October 1917, when the latter replaced him as Lenin's closest associate. During the final months of 1920, according to Fyodor Raskolnikov, the fleet's commander, and E. I. Batis, the head of its political directorate (*Pubalt*)—both of whom were loyal to Trotsky—Zinoviev tried to discredit his rival by casting him in the role of a "dictator" while projecting himself as a champion of party democracy and local initiative. In November 1920, at Zinoviev's urging, the Petrograd party committee demanded that the political administration of the Baltic Fleet be transferred from *Pubalt* into its own hands, a demand which Trotsky's supporters stubbornly resisted.[67]

As a result of this dispute, the commissars and other party administrators lost much of their hold over the rank and file. This was already evident in early December, when a large group of sailors walked out of a general meeting at the Petrograd naval base in protest against the manner of choosing delegates to the Eighth Congress of Soviets (the election, it appears, had been dominated by party officials from the local political department of the fleet). As winter set in tempers continued to rise until a stormy climax was reached at the Second Conference of Baltic Fleet Communists, held in Petrograd on February 15. The "fleet opposition," having emerged as a potent force, won an overwhelming majority in favor of its resolution calling for the immediate decentralization of political control. This was to be

[66] *Sotsialisticheskii Vestnik*, March 18, 1921, p. 1.

[67] Pukhov, "Kronshtadt i Baltiiskii flot," *Krasnaia Letopis'*, 1930, No. 6, pp. 174-94. Cf. Schapiro, *The Origin of the Communist Autocracy*, p. 299.

accomplished by transferring the seat of authority from *Pubalt* and its political departments to the local party committees, along the lines proposed by Zinoviev and his associates the previous November. The resolution criticized *Pubalt* for its lack of contact with the masses and its aloofness from the party activists on the grass-roots level. *Pubalt*, in the words of the resolution, had become a "bureaucratic organ without widespread authority" among the rank and file; to restore local initiative, the whole political structure of the fleet had to be refashioned "on the lines of democratism." Some of the delegates also called for the outright abolition of the political departments of the fleet, a demand shortly to be echoed by the Kronstadt rebels. And one party official warned that unless reforms were inaugurated, "in two or three months we shall have a rising."[68]

BY THE middle of February 1921, therefore, tensions in the Baltic Fleet had clearly reached the bursting point. Before the month was out the strike wave broke in Petrograd. Almost immediately, news of the disturbances reached Kronstadt, where a tradition of revolutionary solidarity with the working class of "Red Peter" had existed since 1905 and 1917. Mingled with the initial reports was an assortment of bogus rumors which quickly roused the passions of the sailors. It was said, for example, that government troops had fired on the Vasili Island demonstrators and that strike leaders were being shot in the cellars of the Cheka.[69] In the prevailing atmosphere of unrest such stories spread like wildfire, filling the local commissars with alarm and leading Kuzmin to warn the Petrograd Soviet that an explosion would occur unless the strikes were crushed swiftly. But Kuzmin's warning came too late. That very day, February 26, the

---

[68] Pukhov, *Kronshtadtskii miatezh*, pp. 50-52; G. P. Maximoff, *The Guillotine at Work*, Chicago, 1940, p. 169.

[69] Dan, *Dva goda skitanii*, p. 108; Goldman, *Living My Life*, p. 876.

crews of the *Petropavlovsk* and *Sevastopol* held an emergency meeting and decided to send a delegation to Petrograd to find out what was happening. Both battleships, now frozen side by side in the ice of Kronstadt harbor, had long been hotbeds of rebellious sentiment and activity. During the July Days of 1917, as we have seen, the *Petropavlovsk* had set an example of militant opposition to the Provisional Government; and the following month four of its officers had been shot on dubious charges of supporting General Kornilov. It is without exaggeration, therefore, that Pavel Dybenko, himself a former member of the crew, speaks in his memoirs of "the eternally stormy *Petropavlovsk*."[70] The *Sevastopol* too had had a history of intemperate behavior, its crew only recently having rioted over the curtailment of furloughs in the fleet.

When the Kronstadt delegation arrived in Petrograd, it found the factories surrounded by troops and military cadets. In the shops still in operation, armed Communist squads kept a watchful eye on the workmen, who remained silent when the sailors approached. "One might have thought," noted Petrichenko, a leading figure in the impending revolt, "that these were not factories but the forced labor prisons of tsarist times."[71] On February 28 the emissaries, filled with indignation at the scenes they had witnessed, returned to Kronstadt and presented their findings at an historic meeting on board the *Petropavlovsk*.

Their report, of course, expressed full sympathy for the strikers' demands, and called for greater self-determination in the factories as in the fleet. The meeting then voted for a long resolution which was destined to become the political charter of the Kronstadt rebellion:

[70] Dybenko, *Iz nedr tsarskogo flota*, p. 159.

[71] S. M. Petrichenko, *Pravda o Kronshtadtskikh sobytiiakh*, n.p., 1921, p. 6; Petrichenko, "O prichinakh Kronshtadtskogo vosstaniia," *Znamia Bor'by*, Nos. 14-15, December 1925-January 1926, pp. 6-7.

Having heard the report of the representatives sent by the general meeting of ships' crews to Petrograd to investigate the situation there, we resolve:

1. In view of the fact that the present soviets do not express the will of the workers and peasants, immediately to hold new elections by secret ballot, with freedom to carry on agitation beforehand for all workers and peasants;

2. To give freedom of speech and press to workers and peasants, to anarchists and left socialist parties;

3. To secure freedom of assembly for trade unions and peasant organizations;

4. To call a nonparty conference of the workers, Red Army soldiers, and sailors of Petrograd, Kronstadt, and Petrograd province, no later than March 10, 1921;

5. To liberate all political prisoners of socialist parties, as well as all workers, peasants, soldiers, and sailors imprisoned in connection with the labor and peasant movements;

6. To elect a commission to review the cases of those being held in prisons and concentration camps;

7. To abolish all political departments because no party should be given special privileges in the propagation of its ideas or receive the financial support of the state for such purposes. Instead, there should be established cultural and educational commissions, locally elected and financed by the state;

8. To remove immediately all roadblock detachments;

9. To equalize the rations of all working people, with the exception of those employed in trades detrimental to health;

10. To abolish the Communist fighting detachments in all branches of the army, as well as the Communist guards kept on duty in factories and mills. Should such guards or detachments be found necessary, they are to be ap-

pointed in the army from the ranks and in the factories and mills at the discretion of the workers;

11. To give the peasants full freedom of action in regard to the land, and also the right to keep cattle, on condition that the peasants manage with their own means, that is, without employing hired labor;

12. To request all branches of the army, as well as our comrades the military cadets (*kursanty*), to endorse our resolution;

13. To demand that the press give all our resolutions wide publicity;

14. To appoint an itinerant bureau of control;

15. To permit free handicrafts production by one's own labor.

> PETRICHENKO, Chairman of the Squadron Meeting
> PEREPELKIN, Secretary[72]

The *Petropavlovsk* resolution echoed the discontents not only of the Baltic Fleet but of the mass of Russians in towns and villages throughout the country. Themselves of plebeian stock, the sailors wanted relief for their peasant and worker kinfolk. Indeed, of the resolution's 15 points, only one—the abolition of the political departments in the fleet—applied specifically to their own situation. The remainder of the document was a broadside aimed at the policies of War Communism, the justification for which, in the eyes of the sailors and of the population at large, had long since vanished. The fact that some of the resolution's sponsors, including Petrichenko, had recently gone home on leave and witnessed the plight of the villagers with their own eyes doubtless influenced their demands on the peasantry's behalf. This was especially true of Point 11, which would have allowed the peasants to make free use of their land so long as they did not employ hired

---

[72] *Pravda o Kronshtadte*, pp. 46-47; Berkman, *The Kronstadt Rebellion*, pp. 9-11.

help. What this implied was nothing less than the abolition of food requisitions, and possibly the liquidation of the state farms as well. By the same token, the sailors' inspection tour of Petrograd's factories may account for their inclusion of the workingmen's chief demands—the abolition of road-blocks, of privileged rations, and of armed factory squads—in their program.

But it was not these economic demands which so alarmed the Bolshevik authorities when word of the *Petropavlovsk* meeting reached them. Some of the demands, indeed, such as the removal of the roadblock detachments (Point 8), were about to be granted by Zinoviev and his subordinates in Petrograd. Moreover, at that very moment the government was in the midst of drafting a new economic policy that would go considerably further than the sailors' program in satisfy-ing popular wishes. It was the political demands, rather, aimed as they were at the very heart of the Bolshevik dictator-ship, which prompted the authorities to call for immediate suppression of the Kronstadt movement. True, the sailors did not appeal for the overthrow of the Soviet government; nor did they advocate a restoration of the Constituent As-sembly or of political rights for the gentry and middle classes. They despised the moderate and conservative ele-ments of Russian society as much as ever and had no thought of granting them a new lease on life. But the resolution's opening declaration—that "the present soviets do not express the will of the workers and peasants"—represented a clear challenge to the Bolshevik monopoly of political power. The call for new elections to the soviets, linked as it was to a demand for free expression for all workers, peasants, and left-wing political groups, was something that Lenin and his followers were not prepared to tolerate. In effect, the *Petropavlovsk* resolution was an appeal to the Soviet gov-ernment to live up to its own constitution, a bold statement of those very rights and freedoms which Lenin himself had professed in 1917. In spirit, it was a throwback to October, evoking the old Leninist watchword of "All power to the soviets." But the Bolsheviks saw it in a different light: by rejecting their claims to sole guardianship of the revolution, to exclusive representation of the workers and peasants, it was nothing but a manifesto of counterrevolution and had to be dealt with accordingly.

With the adoption of the *Petropavlovsk* resolution the pace of events quickened. The following day, March 1, a mass meeting of sailors, soldiers, and workingmen was held in Anchor Square. Some 15,000 attended, more than a quarter of Kronstadt's combined military and civilian population. Several eyewitness accounts have come down to us, both from Communist and non-Communist sources,[73] and together they provide a vivid and detailed picture of what took place. At the speakers' platform stood two high-ranking Bolshevik officials, M. I. Kalinin and N. N. Kuzmin, who had been sent from Petrograd to save the situation. According to some reports, Zinoviev had accompanied his colleagues as far as Oranienbaum but decided not to proceed any further for fear of rough handling by the sailors.[74] Kalinin, president of the Soviet Republic, was a former factory worker born of a peasant family in Tver province, and ordinary Russians, it seems, felt a certain affection for him. During the previous week he had been one of the few Bolshevik speakers in Petrograd to gain a sympathetic hearing from the strikers.

[73] V. Kuznetsov, *Iz vospominanii politrabotnika*, Moscow, 1930, pp. 67-68; *Revoliutsionnaia Rossiia*, 1921, No. 7, p. 20; G. A. Cheremshanskii, "Kronshtadtskoe vosstanie, 28 fevralia-18 marta 1921," manuscript, Columbia Russian Archive. See also Pukhov, *Kronshtadtskii miatezh*, p. 61; and Kornatovskii, ed., *Kronshtadtskii miatezh*, pp. 71-72.

[74] "Prichiny, povody, techenie i otsenka Kronshtadtskikh sobytii," manuscript, Hoover Library; Quarton to Secretary of State, April 23, 1921, National Archives, 861.00/8619; *Novaia Russkaia Zhizn'*, March 6, 1921.

Perhaps, then, it was thought that his popularity might now be helpful in bringing the sailors to their senses.

When Kalinin arrived, he was met by music, banners, and a military guard of honor, a hopeful sign that serious trouble might still be averted. Moreover, the Anchor Square meeting opened in a friendly spirit, with the Bolshevik chairman of' the Kronstadt Soviet, P. D. Vasiliev, himself presiding. But tempers began to flare when the report of the delegates sent to investigate the Petrograd disturbances was read. When the *Petropavlovsk* resolution was put before the assembly, excitement reached a high pitch. Kalinin rose and began to speak against it but was repeatedly interrupted by hecklers: "Stow it, Kalinych, you manage to keep warm enough." "Look at all the jobs you've got. I'll bet they bring you plenty." "We know ourselves what we need. As for you, old man, go back to your woman." Kalinin struggled to make himself heard, but his words were drowned out by whistles and catcalls.

Kuzmin, a ranking commissar attached to the Revolutionary War Council of the fleet, was given the same treatment. In an effort to win the crowd's attention, he reminded them of their heroic role in the Revolution and Civil War. Suddenly a voice broke in: "Have you forgotten how you had every tenth man shot on the Northern Front? Away with him!" The meaning of this is unclear, but perhaps during the Civil War Kuzmin had served as a commissar at the Northern Front (the Archangel and Murmansk area) and had been involved in the shooting of Bolshevik troops after some mutiny or other breach of discipline. (Such incidents were not uncommon. A notorious case occurred when a group of Petrograd recruits seized a steamer on the Volga and fled towards Nizhni Novgorod; on Trotsky's orders, an improvised gunboat intercepted the deserters, and a field tribunal condemned the commander, the commissar, and every tenth man in the ranks to death.)[75] Whatever the explanation, Kuzmin delivered a menacing reply: "The working people have always shot traitors to the cause, and they will continue to shoot them in the future. In my place you would have shot every fifth man, not every tenth." "Enough of that," someone shouted. "You can't threaten us. Kick him out!" For several minutes the jeers and heckling forced Kuzmin to remain silent. Then, in a final attempt to speak, he denounced the *Petropavlovsk* resolution as a counterrevolutionary document, shouting that indiscipline and treason would be smashed by the iron hand of the proletariat—whereupon he was driven from the platform to a loud chorus of booing.[76]

Once Kalinin and Kuzmin had stepped down, the rostrum became the property of the sailors and soldiers. One after another they lashed out at the authorities for the lack of food and fuel, the confiscation of grain, the roadblocks, and above all for the fact that there was still no relief in sight months after the Civil War had ended. While ordinary citizens suffered, they declared, the commissars were warm and well-fed. Among the principal orators was Petrichenko, a senior clerk from the *Petropavlovsk* and a leader of the revolt from its very inception. Echoing a traditional folk myth, formerly aimed at the boyars and officials of old Muscovy, he accused the Bolsheviks of "hiding the truth from the people." Popular legends of this type, as we shall see in a moment, were deeply embedded in the psychology of the rebellion and occupied a central place in its rather primitive ideology. Petrichenko urged the crowd to endorse the *Petropavlovsk* resolution (which bears his signature) and to demand free elections to the soviets throughout the country.

The resolution was then put to a vote and approved by an overwhelming majority, over the protests of Kalinin, Kuz-

[75] See Erickson, *The Soviet High Command*, p. 39.
[76] Berkman, *The Bolshevik Myth*, p. 294; Serge, *Memoirs of a Revolutionary*, p. 127.

min, and Vasiliev. Next, it was decided to summon a special conference to arrange for new elections to the Kronstadt Soviet, whose term, it appears, was in any case due to expire that very day. Finally, the meeting voted to send a 30-man delegation to Petrograd to acquaint the people with its demands and to request that they send nonparty representatives to Kronstadt in order to observe the situation at first hand. The delegates, duly dispatched, were arrested on arrival and never heard of again.[77]

When the gathering dispersed, Kalinin and Kuzmin went to local party headquarters to consider their next move. Kalinin, says Emma Goldman, the well-known anarchist who was following events from the Astoria Hotel in Petrograd, then departed from Kronstadt in a spirit of continued friendship.[78] In view of what had just taken place, this seems hard to believe. According to Soviet sources, Kalinin was detained for a time at the Petrograd Gate before being allowed to leave the island; and we have it from the insurgents themselves, interviewed afterwards in Finland, that many of the sailors wanted to throw him in jail but were dissuaded by arguments that this would violate the principle of freedom enunciated in their own resolution.[79] In any event the point is not crucial. What seems reasonably clear is that, with the passage of the sailors' resolution at Anchor Square, events turned sharply in the direction of outright mutiny.

For this development Victor Serge places the blame squarely on the shoulders of Kalinin and Kuzmin, whose brutal attitude and bungling speeches, he says, could not but provoke the sailors into a fury. Far from calming the angry Kronstadters, writes Serge in his memoirs, the two officials

---

[77] *Pravda o Kronshtadte*, p. 10.

[78] Goldman, *Living My Life*, p. 877.

[79] Pukhov, *Kronshtadtskii miatezh*, p. 62; "Interv'iu s chlenami Vremennogo Revoliutsionnogo Komiteta (s matrosami 'Petropavlovska' Iakovenko, Karpenko i Arkhipovym)," manuscript, Hoover Library.

treated them as rogues and traitors and threatened them with merciless reprisals unless they came to their senses.[80] This, certainly, is an exaggeration, for the unfolding rebellion had far deeper causes than mere provocative speeches. The sailors, moreover, seemed predisposed to bait the Communists, scarcely allowing them to utter a sentence before interrupting with shouts and catcalls. On the other hand, it cannot be denied that Kalinin and Kuzmin might have shown greater discretion before such an excitable audience. There can be little doubt that their tactless words reinforced the sailors' hostile feelings towards Bolshevik officialdom.

Meanwhile, the authorities were greatly alarmed by the failure of the Kronstadt Communists to oppose the decisions of the Anchor Square meeting. Though present in substantial numbers, the party rank and file seem to have been swept along by the rebellious tide, and when Kalinin and Kuzmin raised their voices in protest not one of their fellow Bolsheviks (other than Vasiliev) came forward to support them. Indeed, the majority evidently voted for the *Petropavlovsk* resolution, while the rest abstained. It was this feature, as Leonard Schapiro notes, which distinguished the Kronstadt rising from all previous outbursts against the Soviet government.[81]

The next day, March 2, the incipient revolt advanced a further step when a conference (summoned by the meeting in Anchor Square) was held to arrange for the reelection of the Kronstadt Soviet. Some 300 delegates attended, two from each ship, military unit, factory, trade union, and the like, hastily elected the same morning or the night before. The Communists, it appears, were not permitted to dominate these electoral meetings and to choose their own delegates

---

[80] Serge, *Memoirs of a Revolutionary*, p. 127.

[81] Schapiro, *The Origin of the Communist Autocracy*, p. 303. Cf. George Katkov, "The Kronstadt Rising," *St. Antony's Papers*, No. 6, London, 1959, p. 28.

as in the past. When addressing their comrades, they were heckled and interrupted in the same way Kalinin and Kuzmin had been the day before. In the main garrison, for instance, the Bolshevik commissar barely had time to object to the irregular proceedings before being cut off by the "military specialist" in charge of artillery, a former tsarist general named Kozlovsky, who will figure very largely in our story. "Your time is past," Kozlovsky declared. "Now I shall do what has to be done." It is likely that scenes such as this were repeated in other units that morning. Nonetheless, although most of the elected delegates were nonparty, the Communists managed to win a very substantial minority, amounting perhaps to as much as a third of the total number.[82]

The conference assembled in the large auditorium of the House of Education, the former School of Marine Engineering and one of the most prominent buildings in the city. Armed sailors from the battleship *Petropavlovsk* were posted outside and in the halls to prevent any interference with the meeting. Their presence may also have been designed to intimidate any would-be defenders of the existing order. Not unexpectedly, it was their shipmate Petrichenko who chaired the conference. From the very outset, as we have seen, he had assumed a leading role in the Kronstadt movement, a role which he retained until the bitter end more than two weeks later. Born of a peasant family in the Ukraine, Stepan Maksimovich Petrichenko was well endowed with the qualities of a rebel leader. He was an intense young sailor of about thirty, handsome and solidly built, with a strong, magnetic character that won him a devoted following. Despite his Ukrainian accent, he spoke effectively in a simple and direct language which reflected his peasant upbringing.

---

[82] Pukhov, *Kronshtadtskii miatezh*, p. 63. For details of the March 2 conference, see *Pravda o Kronshtadte*, pp. 115-17; and *Revoliutsionnaia Rossiia*, 1921, No. 7, pp. 21-22.

He was an experienced seaman, having joined the navy in 1912, nearly a decade before the tragic events in which he now became embroiled. Before that, he had worked as a plumber in his native district. From all accounts, he was possessed of a keen intellect which belied the mere two years of formal schooling he had received as a child. His energy and resourcefulness, moreover, are widely affirmed by those with whom he came into contact.[83]

With Petrichenko in the chair, the conference opened by electing a five-man presidium. The delegates then listened to a few speeches before turning to their principal business of organizing new elections to the Soviet. The first to mount the rostrum were the Communist officials Kuzmin and Vasiliev, who had opposed the *Petropavlovsk* resolution the day before in Anchor Square. Now, to the consternation of their listeners, they pursued the same critical tack. Kuzmin's speech in particular aroused the indignation of the delegates. Reminding them that a formal peace with Poland had not yet been concluded, he warned that any division in governmental authority—any *dvoevlastie*, or dual power—might at this point tempt Marshal Pilsudski to revive hostilities. The eyes of the West, he said, were fixed on Soviet Russia, watching for signs of internal weakness. As for the disturbances in Petrograd, Kuzmin went on, Kronstadt was grossly misinformed both as to their gravity and extent. There had indeed been a momentary flareup, but it had passed very quickly, and now the city was quiet. At one point, Kuzmin, alluding to the unrest within the Baltic Fleet, defended the conduct of commissars like himself, whom the sailors, at their recent meetings, had held up as objects of scorn. This could hardly have pleased his listeners. But what incensed them more

[83] See *Volia Rossii*, March 15, 1921; *Revoliutsionnaia Rossiia*, 1921, No. 8, pp. 6-7; *New York Times*, March 31, 1921; and the interview with Petrichenko by Edmond Stratton, March 19, 1921, National Archives, 861.00/8470.

than anything else were Kuzmin's concluding remarks, which carried the same implicit threat as his speech of the previous day. "You have me at your mercy," he told them. "You can even shoot me if it suits your fancy. But should you dare to raise your hand against the government, the Bolsheviks will fight with their last ounce of strength."[84]

The defiant tone of Kuzmin's address left his audience completely alienated. Given the explosive atmosphere in the hall, a more tactful approach was surely in order. Yet his remarks were by no means lacking in point. Since it was a fact that no treaty had yet been signed with Poland (an armistice had been in effect since October and peace talks were being conducted at Riga), the threat of renewed Polish intervention, backed once more by French officers, was not to be lightly dismissed. Petrograd remained in a particularly exposed position, and Soviet officials genuinely feared that any evidence of internal difficulties might strengthen the Polish position at the bargaining table or even lead to an outright resumption of the war. It was true, moreover, that the Petrograd strikes were on the wane, having reached a peak on the last day of February. But the rumors of shootings and full-scale rioting had already aroused the sailors, and on March 2, at a time when the disturbances had all but ceased, they were drafting the erroneous announcement (for publication the following day) that the city was in the throes of a "general insurrection."[85] This misapprehension, by emboldening the Kronstadters with visions of a mass upheaval on the mainland, plunged them into serious acts which more than a few would later have cause to regret.

When Kuzmin stepped down, Vasiliev, chairman of the defunct Soviet, addressed the assembly in a similar vein. By the time he had finished, the general attitude of the meeting had become plainly anti-Bolshevik, notwithstanding the large number of Communists among the delegates. The hostility

---

[84] *Pravda o Kronshtadte*, p. 116.   [85] *Ibid.*, p. 47.

of the sailors, as Alexander Berkman noted, was not directed against the party as such, but against its bureaucrats and commissars, whose arrogance, as they saw it, was exemplified by the speeches of Kuzmin and Vasiliev. Kuzmin's speech, said Berkman, was "a firebrand thrown into gunpowder."[86] So infuriated were the delegates that the hapless officials, together with the commissar of the Kronstadt Battleship Squadron (a Bolshevik named Korshunov, whose jurisdiction included the *Petropavlovsk* and *Sevastopol*), were placed under arrest and removed from the hall. This was a flagrant act of insubordination, far more serious than the brief detention of Kalinin the day before. It marked a giant step down the road towards open mutiny. On the other hand, the delegates rejected a motion to arrest the other Communists present and to deprive them of their arms. Although a vocal minority expressed strong anti-Communist feelings, most of their comrades were determined to adhere to the principles of the *Petropavlovsk* resolution, the charter of their budding movement, which guaranteed a voice for all left-wing political groups, Bolsheviks included.

Serious as it was, the arrest of the three officials did not represent an irreversible step. This, however, was not long in coming. After the guards ushered their prisoners from the auditorium, Petrichenko recalled the meeting to order. The *Petropavlovsk* resolution, in what by now seemed a firmly established ritual, was read aloud and once again enthusiastically approved. The conference then turned to the main item on its agenda, the election of a new Soviet. But suddenly they were interrupted by a voice from the floor. It belonged to a seaman from the *Sevastopol*, who shouted that 15 truckloads of Communists armed with rifles and machine guns were on their way to break up the meeting. The news had the effect of a bombshell, throwing the delegates into

[86] Berkman, *The Kronstadt Rebellion*, pp. 12-13.

alarm and confusion, and only after a period of great commotion was sufficient calm restored for the meeting to resume. Someone proposed sending a new delegation to Petrograd to seek an alliance with the strikers, but this was rejected for fear of more arrests. Then, unsettled by the prospect of a Bolshevik attack, the conference took a fateful step. It decided to establish a Provisional Revolutionary Committee, charged with administering the city and garrison pending the formation of a new Soviet. For lack of time to hold proper elections, the conference's five-men presidium was designated as the Provisional Revolutionary Committee, with Petrichenko as its chairman. By this action the Kronstadt movement placed itself outside the pale of mere protest. The rebellion had begun.[87]

Once again, therefore, rumor had played a critical role in shaping the course of events in Kronstadt. The speeches of Kuzmin and Vasiliev, by arousing the indignation of the delegates, had set the stage for the impetuous acts which followed. But it was the bogus report that Communists were preparing to attack the meeting that actually precipitated the formation of the Provisional Revolutionary Committee, the step by which the sailors crossed the Rubicon of insurrection. Who was responsible for launching the rumor? According to Petrichenko, it was the work of the Communists themselves, with the object of breaking up the conference.[88] Although certainly possible, there is no evidence that this was the case. It is just as likely that the sailor who shouted the news wanted to stir things up *against* the Communists. And it is worth noting that Petrichenko himself took up the rumor and announced that a detachment of 2,000 Commu-

---

[87] *Pravda o Kronshtadte*, p. 46. Cf. Robert V. Daniels, "The Kronstadt Revolt of 1921: A Study in the Dynamics of Revolution," *American Slavic and East European Review* x (December 1951), 244; and John G. Wright, *The Truth About Kronstadt*, New York, 1938.

[88] *Revoliutsionnaia Rossiia*, 1921, No. 8, p. 8.

nists were indeed on their way to disperse the meeting. Once again pandemonium broke loose, and the delegates left the hall in great excitement.[89]

What may have inspired the rumor was the fact that a group of Communist trainees, headed by a member of the Kronstadt Cheka, were observed leaving the Higher Party School while the conference at the House of Education was in progress. Far from intending to attack the meeting, however, they were actually fleeing Kronstadt for Krasnaya Gorka, a fort located on the mainland to the southwest. Another incident, on the previous day, may also have contributed to the insurgents' fears. Following the Anchor Square meeting, a number of Bolshevik loyalists did in fact consider taking military action to head off the rebellion. Novikov, the commissar of the Kronstadt fortress, even obtained light artillery and machine guns from the arsenal. But when it became apparent that they lacked sufficient support for such an undertaking, Novikov's group decided to quit the island. Novikov himself was intercepted at Fort Totleben, near the Karelian coast, but managed to escape on horseback across the ice.[90]

The insurgents, at all events, did not remain idle. The newly created Provisional Revolutionary Committee took up headquarters on board the flagship *Petropavlovsk*, where two days before all the ferment had originated. Acting with great dispatch, the committee sent armed detachments to occupy the arsenals, telephone exchange, food depots, water-pumping station, power plants, Cheka headquarters, and other strategic points. By midnight the city had been secured without any resistance. Moreover, all the warships, forts, and batteries recognized the authority of the Revolutionary Committee. Earlier in the day copies of the *Petropavlovsk* resolution had been taken by courier to the mainland and distributed in

[89] *Pravda o Kronshtadte*, p. 117.   [90] *Ibid.*, pp. 12, 48.

Oranienbaum, Petrograd, and other towns in the vicinity. That evening the Naval Air Squadron at Oranienbaum recognized the Revolutionary Committee and sent representatives across the ice to Kronstadt. The revolt had begun to spread.

The following day, March 3, the Provisional Revolutionary Committee began to publish a daily newspaper, the *Izvestiia Vremennogo Revoliutsionnogo Komiteta Matrosov, Krasnoarmeitsev i Rabochikh gor. Kronshtadta* [News of the Provisional Revolutionary Committee of Sailors, Soldiers, and Workers of the City of Kronstadt], which was to appear without interruption until the 16th, the day before the decisive assault against the rebels. In the first issue, Petrichenko, as chairman of the committee, appealed to the population of Kronstadt for their support: "Comrades and citizens, the Provisional Committee is determined that not a single drop of blood be spilled. . . . The task of the Provisional Revolutionary Committee is to organize in the city and fortress, through friendly and cooperative effort, the conditions for fair and proper elections to the new Soviet. AND SO, COMRADES, FOR ORDER, FOR CALM, FOR FIRMNESS, FOR THE NEW AND UPRIGHT SOCIALIST CONSTRUCTION THAT WILL PROMOTE THE WELL-BEING OF ALL THE TOILING PEOPLE."[91] That same day the Revolutionary Committee banned all exit from the city without special permission. All military leaves were canceled. Further, an 11 P.M. curfew was imposed and local *revtroiki* established,[92] as though in imitation of Zinoviev's *ad hoc* Petrograd Defense Committee. Kronstadt had passed the point of no return. With three Bolshevik leaders in jail, and with the rebels in full control of the city, a trial of strength with the government seemed inevitable.

[91] *Ibid.*, p. 46.
[92] *Ibid.*, p. 49; Pukhov, *Kronshtadtskii miatezh*, p. 69.

3. Kronstadt and the Russian Emigration

From the outset, the Soviet authorities recognized the danger of the turbulence in Kronstadt. Given the acute discontent among the Russian people, the revolt of the sailors might spark a mass conflagration throughout the country. The possibility of outside intervention gave added cause for concern, and Kronstadt's strategic position at the gateway to the Neva placed Petrograd under serious jeopardy. Mindful of historical parallels, the Bolsheviks might well recall that four years earlier mutinous outbreaks in the armed forces, in conjunction with strikes and demonstrations in the former capital, had brought about the downfall of the autocracy. Now their own regime faced a similar danger. If "Red Kronstadt" and "Red Peter" could turn against the government, what might be expected from the rest of the country?

Small wonder, therefore, that every effort was made to discredit the rebels. This was no easy task, for Kronstadt had long had a reputation for revolutionary fidelity. In 1917 Trotsky himself had called the Kronstadt sailors "the pride and glory" of the Russian Revolution. Yet now he was at pains to show that these were not the same loyal revolutionaries of four years ago but new elements of a completely different stamp. Thousands of Kronstadt stalwarts had perished in the Civil War, argued Trotsky, and many of the survivors had since been scattered around the country. Thus the best men were gone, and the ranks of the fleet had been filled with raw peasant recruits from the Ukraine and the western borderlands who were largely indifferent to the revolutionary struggle and sometimes, owing to class and national differences, openly hostile to the Soviet regime. It was further charged that many of the recruits came from regions where Makhno, Grigoriev, and other anti-Communist guerrillas had attracted a large following, and had brought with them an "anarcho-bandit frame of mind"—indeed, in some cases had even fought in these partisan bands or in the White armies of Denikin and Wrangel.[1]

As portrayed by the Bolsheviks, then, the Kronstadt seaman of 1921 was "of a different social and psychological makeup" from his predecessor of the Revolution and Civil War: at worst, a corrupt and demoralized roughneck, undisciplined, foul-mouthed, and given to card playing and drink; at best, "a peasant lad in a sailor suit," a simple country bumpkin sporting bell-bottom trousers and a heavily pomaded pompadour to attract female admirers.[2] To these green recruits from the countryside, said the Bolsheviks, the older "salts" pinned an assortment of abusive epithets: *Kleshniki*, a term derived from the broad-bottomed pants they favored; *Zhorzhiki*, or dandified hayseeds; and, worst of all, *Ivanmory* (sea-yokels), a derisive parody of *Voenmory* (sea-warriors), the proud title borne by veterans of the Civil War.[3]

How accurate were such characterizations? There can be little doubt that during the Civil War years a large turnover had indeed taken place within the Baltic Fleet, and that many of the old-timers had been replaced by conscripts from the rural districts who brought with them the deeply felt discontents of the Russian peasantry. By 1921, according to official figures, more than three-quarters of the sailors were of peasant origin, a substantially higher proportion than in 1917, when industrial workers from the Petrograd area made up a

[1] Trotskii, *Kak vooruzhalas' revoliutsiia*, III, part 1, 203-204; Pukhov, *Kronshtadtskii miatezh*, pp. 40-41; Kornatovskii, ed., *Kronshtadtskii miatezh*, pp. 12-13; M. L. Lur'e, "Kronshtadtskii miatezh 1921 goda v sovetskoi i beloi literature i pechati," *Krasnaia Letopis'*, 1931, No. 2, p. 226.

[2] Slepkov, *Kronshtadtskii miatezh*, p. 20; Pukhov, *Kronshtadtskii miatezh*, p. 42; Leon Trotsky, "Hue and Cry Over Kronstadt," *The New International*, April 1938, p. 104.

[3] Kornatovskii, ed., *Kronshtadtskii miatezh*, p. 21; M. Kuz'min, *Kronshtadtskii miatezh*, Leningrad, 1931, p. 17. Cf. Katkov, "The Kronstadt Rising," *St. Antony's Papers*, No. 6, p. 21.

sizable part of the fleet.[4] Petrichenko himself later acknowledged that many of his comrades-in-arms were peasants from the south aroused by the plight of the villagers back home. Yet this does not necessarily mean that the behavioral patterns of the fleet had undergone any fundamental change. On the contrary, alongside the technical ratings, who were drawn largely from the working class, there had always been a large and unruly peasant element among the sailors, an element lacking in discipline and prone to run amok at the least provocation. Indeed, in 1905 and 1917 it was these very youths from the countryside who had given Kronstadt its reputation as a hotbed of revolutionary extremism. And throughout the Civil War the Kronstadters had remained an independent and headstrong lot, difficult to control and far from constant in their support of the government. It was for this reason that so many of them—especially the chronic troublemakers and malcontents—had found themselves transferred to new posts remote from the centers of Bolshevik power. Of those who remained, many hankered for the freedoms they had won in 1917 before the new regime began to establish its one-party dictatorship throughout the country.

Actually, there was little to distinguish the old-timers from the recent recruits in their midst. Both groups were largely of peasant background; both—the one while on furlough, the other before reporting for active duty—had seen for themselves the misery in their native districts; and both longed to cast off the coercive authority of the central government. Not unexpectedly, when the rebellion finally erupted, it was the older seamen, veterans of many years of service (dating in some cases from before the First World War) who took the lead. Petrichenko had joined the fleet as early as 1912, and had been a crew member of the *Petro-*

[4] See the figures in Pukhov, *Kronshtadtskii miatezh*, p. 43; Petrash, *Moriaki Baltiiskogo flota*, pp. 20-21; and A. V. Bogdanov, *Moriaki-baltiitsy v 1917 g.*, Moscow, 1955, p. 15.

pavlovsk since 1918. His deputy chairman of the Provisional Revolutionary Committee, an old "salt" named Yakovenko, had fought on the barricades in 1917. Given their maturity and experience, not to speak of their keen disillusionment as former participants in the revolution, it was only natural that these seasoned bluejackets should be thrust into the forefront of the uprising. This was particularly true of the higher ranking seamen and qualified technicians (Petrichenko, for example, was a senior clerk on a battleship), who had been carefully chosen from the most alert and literate recruits and were accustomed to acting on their own initiative. The proximity of Petrograd, moreover, with its intense intellectual and political life, had contributed towards sharpening their political awareness, and a good many had engaged in revolutionary activity during 1917 and after.[5]

The Kronstadters had long been regarded as the torchbearers of revolutionary militancy, a reputation which remained largely untarnished throughout the Civil War, despite their volatility and lack of discipline. As late as the autumn of 1920, Emma Goldman recalled, the sailors were still held up by the Communists themselves as a glowing example of valor and unflinching courage; on November 7, the third anniversary of the Bolshevik seizure of power, they were in the front ranks of the celebrations, and their reenactment of the storming of the Winter Palace in Petrograd was wildly acclaimed by the crowd.[6] No one at that time spoke of any "class degeneration" at Kronstadt. The allegation that politically retarded *muzhiks* had diluted the revolutionary character of the fleet, it would seem, was largely a device to explain away dissident movements among the sailors, and had been used as such as early as October 1918, following the

[5] Cf. D. Fedotoff White, *The Growth of the Red Army*, Princeton, 1944, p. 155; and Voline, *La Révolution inconnue*, pp. 411-12.

[6] Emma Goldman, *Trotsky Protests Too Much*, Glasgow, 1938, p. 7.

abortive mutiny at the Petrograd naval station, when the social composition of the fleet could not yet have undergone any sweeping transformation.

The charge that the Kronstadters were mostly non-Russians—conscripts from the Ukraine, Latvia, Estonia, and Finland, who bore strong national antagonisms against the Soviet regime—also warrants a closer look. Some three or four hundred names appear in the journal of the rebel movement, as signers of articles, proclamations, letters, poems, and the like. So far as one can judge from these surnames alone—admittedly an uncertain procedure—Great Russians are in the overwhelming majority. There is no unusual proportion of Ukrainian, Germanic, Baltic, or other names. Yet the picture is somewhat different when one looks at the membership of the Provisional Revolutionary Committee, the general staff of the insurrection:[7]

1. PETRICHENKO, senior clerk, battleship *Petropavlovsk*
2. YAKOVENKO, telephone operator, Kronstadt district
3. OSOSOV, machinist, battleship *Sevastopol*
4. ARKHIPOV, senior machinist
5. PEREPELKIN, electrician, battleship *Sevastopol*
6. PATRUSHEV, senior electrician, battleship *Petropavlovsk*
7. KUPOLOV, senior medical assistant
8. VERSHININ, seaman, battleship *Sevastopol*
9. TUKIN, worker, electro-mechanical factory
10. ROMANENKO, watchman of drydocks
11. ORESHIN, principal of the Third Workers' School
12. VALK, sawmill worker
13. PAVLOV, worker, mine factory
14. BAIKOV, transport chief of fortress construction department
15. KILGAST, deep-sea navigator

[7] *Pravda o Kronshtadte*, pp. 131, 158. For another list, with interesting comments about the members, see "Kak nachalos' vosstanie v Kronshtadte," Miller Archives, File 5M, No. 5.

Of the 15 committee members, three (Petrichenko, Yako-venko, and Romanenko) bore patently Ukrainian names and two others (Valk and Kilgast) Germanic names. Petrichenko, Yakovenko, and Kilgast, moreover, occupied key places on the committee, as its chairman, deputy chairman, and secretary, respectively. According to Soviet sources, Petrichenko's nationalist feelings were so strong that his shipmates nicknamed him "Petliura," after the well-known Ukrainian leader.[8] And we have it from Petrichenko himself that "three-quarters" of the Kronstadt garrison were natives of the Ukraine, some of whom had served with the anti-Bolshevik forces in the south before entering the Soviet navy.[9]

What all this indicates is that national feelings probably played some role in sparking the rebellion. But precisely how great a role must, for want of further evidence, remain uncertain. Much clearer are the humble social origins of the committee members. Sailors—normally of peasant and working-class background—formed a preponderant majority: apparently there were nine of them, mostly qualified ratings from the *Petropavlovsk* and *Sevastopol*, the powder kegs of the rising. In addition, there were four workmen and two white-collar employees (a school principal and a transportation official). Thus the leadership of the movement was undeniably plebeian, unlike that of the Whites, and this was clearly embarrassing to the authorities, who spared no effort to prove that the ringleaders actually sprang from antiproletarian social groups. Vershinin, a seaman from the *Sevastopol* who fell into Bolshevik hands at an early stage of the revolt, was said to be a "speculator" and dandified peasant, or *Zhorzhik.* Worse still, Pavlov was identified as a former detective, Baikov as a property holder in Kronstadt, and Tukin

---

[8] *Krasnaia Gazeta*, March 11, 1921.

[9] Petrichenko et al. to General Wrangel, May 31, 1921, Giers Archives, File 88; U.S. Chargé d'Affaires in Helsingfors to Secretary of State, April 22, 1921, National Archives, 861.00/8628.

as an ex-gendarme who had once owned no less than six houses and three shops in Petrograd. Another committee member, Kilgast, had reportedly been convicted of embezzling government funds in the Kronstadt transportation department but had been released in a general amnesty on the third anniversary of the Bolshevik Revolution.[10]

Efforts to discredit the Provisional Revolutionary Committee continued long after the rebellion had been suppressed. Apart from defaming the character of its members, Soviet writers sought to associate them with the political opposition. Petrichenko was repeatedly identified as a Left SR, Valk and Romanenko as Mensheviks, and Oreshin as a Populist Socialist. Another figure, Lamanov, who was said to be the chief ideologist of the movement and editor of its daily newspaper, was an SR Maximalist.[11] Unfortunately, no reliable information has come to light to confirm or deny these affiliations. Of Petrichenko, however, we know from contemporary Soviet records that he was a "former Communist," having enrolled during the "party week" recruitment drive of August 1919, when regular qualifications for admission were suspended, and that he left during the next re-registration period.[12]

Petrichenko's brief association with the Communists was not untypical—Kilgast, the secretary of the Revolutionary Committee, being another case in point. Thousands of Baltic sailors followed the same course. By March 1921 party membership in Kronstadt was only half of what it had been just six months before. Some of the apostates seized the first

[10] *Petrogradskaia Pravda*, March 11, 1921; Kornatovskii, ed., *Kronshtadtskii miatezh*, p. 34; Pukhov, *Kronshtadtskii miatezh*, p. 77.

[11] Slepkov, *Kronshtadtskii miatezh*, p. 33; Kornatovskii, ed., *Kronshtadtskii miatezh*, p. 156n; I. Vardin, *Revoliutsiia i men'shevizm*, Moscow, 1925, p. 140. More will be said about Lamanov and the Maximalists in Chapter 5.

[12] *Krasnaia Gazeta*, March 11, 1921. Cf. the archival document in Kornatovskii, ed., *Kronshtadtskii miatezh*, p. 228.

opportunity to go home on leave. Petrichenko returned to his native village in April 1920 and apparently remained until September or October, having had ample time to see the Bolshevik food detachments in action and to build up considerable hostility against the government. The authorities, he later told an American journalist, had arrested him more than once on suspicion of counterrevolutionary activity. He had even tried to join the Whites, only to be turned away as a former Bolshevik. Yet he insisted that the Kronstadt Revolutionary Committee had no ties with any political group. "Our revolt," he said, "was an elemental movement to get rid of Bolshevik oppression; once that is done, the will of the people will manifest itself."[13]

THE chief object of Bolshevik propaganda was to show that the revolt was not a spontaneous outbreak of mass protest but a new counterrevolutionary conspiracy, following the pattern established during the Civil War. According to the Soviet press, the sailors, influenced by Mensheviks and SR's in their ranks, had shamelessly cast their lot with the "White Guards," led by a former tsarist general named Kozlovsky. "Behind the backs of the SR's and Mensheviks," declared *Pravda*, "the ex-tsarist generals have already bared their fangs."[14] This, in turn, was said to be part of a carefully laid plot hatched in Paris by Russian émigrés in league with French counterintelligence. Furthermore, a network of Red Cross organizations—the International Red Cross, the American Red Cross, and the Russian Red Cross in Finland—was accused of acting as a front for the plotters. On March 2 the Council of Labor and Defense issued an order, over the signatures of Lenin and Trotsky, outlawing General Kozlovsky and his confederates and denouncing the *Petropavlovsk*

[13] *New York Times*, March 31, 1921; Quarton to Secretary of State, April 9, 1921, National Archives, 861.00/8740.
[14] *Pravda*, March 5, 1921.

resolution as a "Black Hundred-SR" document. Martial law was extended from the city of Petrograd to the whole province, and Zinoviev's Defense Committee received emergency powers to deal with the insurrection.[15]

As proof that the rising had been concocted by anti-Soviet groups in Paris, Bolshevik spokesmen pointed to a rash of French newspaper reports of a revolt in Kronstadt that appeared two weeks before the actual event. These reports, said Trotsky in a statement to the British and American press, clearly betrayed the nefarious schemes already brewing among the Russian émigrés and their Entente supporters. The choice of Kronstadt as their target, said Trotsky, was dictated by its proximity to Petrograd and its easy accessibility from the west, and also by the recent influx of unreliable elements into the Baltic Fleet.[16] Trotsky's allegations were repeated by Lenin in a speech to the Tenth Congress of the Communist party on March 8. In back of the revolt, Lenin declared, "looms the familiar figure of the White Guard general." "It is perfectly clear," he said, citing stories from *Le Matin* and *L'Echo de Paris*, "that this is the work of SR's and émigré White Guards."[17]

Since the Paris news reports played a central role in the Bolshevik case for a White conspiracy, it is well to look into their content and origins. What, precisely, did they say? The announcement in *Le Matin*, appearing on February 13 under the headline "Moscow Takes Measures Against Kronstadt Rebels," stated that a rising had broken out at the Kronstadt naval base, and that the Bolshevik authorities had initiated steps to prevent it from spreading to Petrograd. On February 14 *Matin* carried a second article attributing the revolt to the arrest of a sailors' delegation which had gone to Moscow to ask for better rations. The situation in Kron-

---

[15] *Ibid.*, March 3, 1921.

[16] Trotskii, *Kak vooruzhalas' revoliutsiia*, III, part 1, 203-204.

[17] *Desiatyi s"ezd RKP(b)*, p. 33.

stadt, said *Matin*, had meanwhile deteriorated, and the rebels had "trained their guns on Petrograd." That same day the story appeared in *L'Echo de Paris* with the added news that the sailors had arrested the chief commissar of the fleet and launched several warships (presumably aided by an ice-breaker) against Petrograd. The insurgents, according to a second item of February 15, were counting on the support of the Petrograd garrison, and the authorities were carrying out mass arrests in the Petrograd area. Between February 13 and 15 similar reports appeared in other Western journals. An account in the *New York Times* went so far as to claim that the sailors had taken full control in Petrograd and were defying the troops sent by Trotsky to dislodge them.[18]

Nothing of the sort, of course, took place at Kronstadt or at any other Baltic base during February 1921. False rumors of this type—stimulated by wishful thinking and by the general ferment inside Russia—were by no means rare at the time. Yet, in the case of Kronstadt, they do foreshadow (even to the arrest of a leading fleet commissar) what was actually to happen two weeks later. Some historians suggest that they had been sparked by the stormy Second Conference of Baltic Fleet Communists, when the sailors raised the cry for greater democracy in the fleet's political administration.[19] But this conjecture may be safely ruled out since the bogus reports antedated the conference (held on February 15) by several days. Indeed, similar stories had appeared even earlier in the Russian émigré press, providing the basis for the Western accounts. On February 12 *Volia Rossii* (Russian Freedom), an SR journal in Prague, reported the outbreak of "a major uprising in the Russian Baltic Fleet." And two days before, the Paris *Obshchee Delo* (The Common Cause),

---

[18] *New York Times*, March 14, 1921.

[19] See Mett, *La Commune de Cronstadt*, p. 80; and Katkov, "The Kronstadt Rising," *St. Antony's Papers*, No. 6, p. 55.

edited by the veteran populist Vladimir Burtsev, had announced the same news under the headline of "Rising of Sailors in Kronstadt." This was probably the earliest such report, and it contained virtually all the elements which were to turn up in succeeding accounts and which anticipate so strikingly the real thing a fortnight later: that the Kronstadt sailors had risen against the government, occupied the port, and arrested the chief commissar of the fleet; that they were planning to launch military operations against Petrograd; and that the Petrograd authorities had proclaimed a state of siege in the city and were carrying out wide-scale arrests.[20] The rumors appear to have come from a single source: a correspondent for the "Russunion" news agency stationed in Helsingfors, a notorious center of anti-Soviet propaganda. What touched them off, however, remains unclear. Beyond the general unrest within the fleet, the reported detention in Moscow of a delegation from Kronstadt may have been partly to blame. The Baltic commandant Raskolnikov, so the story goes, warned that the sailors might open fire on Petrograd unless their comrades were released, but the government refused and even threatened Kronstadt with reprisals.[21]

The Kronstadt Revolutionary Committee rejected the charges of conspiracy as sheer calumny, unsupported by a single shred of truth but revealing only the baseness and deception to which the authorities had sunk. In a declaration to the workers and peasants of Russia, the committee issued an indignant reply: "Our enemies are trying to deceive you. They say that the Kronstadt rebellion was organized by Mensheviks, SR's, Entente spies, and tsarist generals. The leading role they assign to Paris. Nonsense! If our rebellion was made in Paris, then the moon was made in Berlin."[22] To the charge that White officers were leading the movement

---

[20] *Obshchee Delo*, February 10, 1921.
[21] *Ibid.*, January 2, 1921.
[22] *Pravda o Kronshtadte*, p. 120.

the committee's response was equally firm: "In Kronstadt, total power is in the hands only of the revolutionary sailors, Red Army soldiers, and workers, and not of the White Guards headed by some General Kozlovsky, as the slanderous Moscow radio proclaims." "We have only one general here," declared the rebels sardonically, "commissar of the Baltic Fleet Kuzmin. And he has been arrested."[23] In order to demonstrate the popular character of the revolt, the Revolutionary Committee published a full list of its members. As we already know, no officers of any rank appear among the names, let alone a general, but only ordinary sailors and workingmen. "These are our generals: our Brusilovs, Kamenevs, etc.," declared the Kronstadt *Izvestiia*, alluding to the abundance of former tsarist officers within the Bolsheviks' own camp.[24]

Nevertheless, a General Kozlovsky did exist; and he was in Kronstadt in March 1921. What role, if any, did he play in the uprising? Alexander Nikolaevich Kozlovsky was an army career officer with a long and distinguished record of military service. Born in 1861 in the town of Krasnoe Selo near Petrograd, he was graduated from Cavalry Cadet School, Artillery Officers' School, and the Imperial Military Academy, and during the First World War rose to the rank of Major General in the artillery branch. Following the Bolshevik Revolution, he became one of the many ex-imperial officers who were pressed into service as "military specialists" (*voenspetsy*), and in 1921 he was chief of artillery at the Kronstadt fortress. When trouble erupted at the beginning of March, the Bolsheviks at once denounced him as the evil genius of the movement. Kozlovsky was outlawed, and his wife and children were seized in Petrograd as hostages. Three other former officers serving under his command (Burkser, Kostromitinov, and Shirmanovsky) were linked with him as fellow conspirators. Kozlovsky himself maintained that he

[23] *Ibid.*, pp. 57, 65.   [24] *Ibid.*, pp. 131, 158.

was singled out by the authorities because he happened to be the only ex-tsarist general in Kronstadt at the time, the sole convenient actor to fill the fictitious role of the White Guard commander plotting to crush the revolution.[25]

This may indeed be true. Yet, from the available evidence, it is clear that Kozlovsky and his colleagues did in fact play a part in the events of March 1921. When the commander of the fortress fled to the mainland in the early hours of the revolt, Kozlovsky declined to succeed him, but he nevertheless remained at his regular post as director of artillery. The Provisional Revolutionary Committee appointed another artillery specialist as fortress commander, former Lieutenant Colonel E. N. Solovianov, with whom Kozlovsky worked in close cooperation. Most of their fellow *voenspetsy* —in particular those of the artillery branch—apparently followed suit and placed themselves at the disposal of the insurgents, furnishing them with technical advice and assistance. These ex-officers had little use for the Bolshevik regime. Typifying their attitude was a remark quoted earlier and purportedly made by Kozlovsky on March 2 to the Bolshevik commissar of the fortress: "Your time is past. Now I shall do what has to be done."

From the very outset, the specialists threw themselves into the task of planning military operations on behalf of the insurrection. On March 2, as Kozlovsky himself admitted, he and his colleagues advised the Revolutionary Committee to take the offensive at once in order to gain the initiative against the Bolsheviks.[26] The officers worked out a plan for an immediate landing at Oranienbaum (on the mainland some five miles to the south) in order to seize its military equipment and make contact with sympathetic army units, then to move against Petrograd before the government had

[25] A. S. Pukhov, "Kronshtadt vo vlasti vragov revoliutsii," *Krasnaia Letopis'*, 1931, No. 1, p. 23; *Pravda o Kronshtadte*, p. 14.

[26] *Sotsialisticheskii Vestnik*, April 5, 1921, pp. 5-6.

The City of Kronstadt

The Battleship *Sevastopol*

A Kronstadt Refugee in Finland

Lieutenant Colonel E. N. Solovianov

Kronstadt Refugees Arriving at Terijoki

Kronstadt Refugees at Work in Finland

Lenin (right-front) with party delegates fresh from Kronstadt victory.
Behind Lenin is Voroshilov (in dark coat).

time to muster any effective opposition. The officers also proposed a surprise raid on the Oranienbaum flour mills to obtain badly needed food supplies. In still another plan, since no icebreakers were available to do the job (Kronstadt's large icebreaker, the *Ermak*, had gone to Petrograd for fuel), the artillery specialists urged the sailors to use the guns of the fortress and surrounding batteries to free the *Petropavlovsk* and *Sevastopol*, which were frozen in the ice and partially blocking each other's line of fire, and also to create a moat around the island so as to render it inaccessible to an infantry invasion.[27]

For all their activity, however, the officers remained in a purely advisory capacity throughout the rebellion. They had no share, so far as one can tell, in initiating or directing the revolt, or in framing its political program, which was altogether alien to their way of thinking. No officers took part in drawing up the *Petropavlovsk* resolution, none addressed the mass meeting in Anchor Square, none attended the March 2 conference in the House of Education, none served on the Provisional Revolutionary Committee. Their role, rather, was confined to providing technical advice, just as it had been under the Bolsheviks. Some of the rebels later told Fyodor Dan when they were in the same Petrograd jail that Kozlovsky merely carried on his duties as before and enjoyed no other authority in their movement.[28] Given the sailors' independent spirit and traditional hatred of officers, it is unlikely in any case that Kozlovsky and his colleagues could have won real influence among them. The Provisional Revolutionary Committee, which remained firmly in the saddle throughout the revolt, showed its distrust of the specialists by repeatedly rejecting their counsel, however sound and appropriate it might be. Despite the urging

---

[27] Pukhov, *Kronshtadtskii miatezh*, pp. 83-85; Quarton to Secretary of State, April 23, 1921, National Archives, 861.00/8619.

[28] Dan, *Dva goda skitanii*, p. 154.

of the officers, the sailors did not blast the ice around the island or even try to free the icebound battleships. Nor did they attempt to seize a bridgehead on the mainland and exploit the early confusion in the Bolshevik camp. Instead, they limited their offensive efforts to sending a small detachment over the ice to Oranienbaum on the night of March 2-3, after receiving news that the Naval Air Squadron there had voted to join the revolt, but the expedition was greeted by a hail of machine-gun fire and forced to withdraw.[29]

WHEN all this is said, however, the most important question remains to be answered: Was there any truth to the Bolshevik charges that the revolt had been masterminded by Russian émigrés in Paris? Certainly, the expatriates indulged in wishful thinking about an anti-Soviet uprising. Much was said and written on the subject, particularly by a group known as the National Center (or National Union), a loose-knit coalition of Kadets, Octobrists, and other moderates, with headquarters in Paris and branches in a number of other European capitals. Take, for example, an article by the prominent Kadet leader F. I. Rodichev, which appeared in *Obshchee Delo*—the principal organ of the National Center—ten days before the rebellion erupted. "To take Petrograd," wrote Rodichev, "would not be difficult. The difficulty would be to feed the city and organize it. Once this is prepared, then the hour to act will not be far off. Petrograd is closest of all to the borders open from the west. It is this point in Soviet Russia which is easiest to reach for the work of regeneration. . . . It is time to begin."[30]

At the time, however, open threats of this sort did not raise undue concern among the Bolshevik leaders. Far more alarm-

---

[29] Petrichenko, *Pravda o Kronshtadtskikh sobytiiakh*, pp. 8-9.

[30] F. Rodishchev [*sic*], "V poiskakh spaseniia," *Obshchee Delo*, February 20, 1921.

ing were the unknown conspiracies which they suspected the exiles of hatching in secret. Nor were their suspicions entirely groundless. Hitherto undisclosed evidence reveals that plans for just such an uprising had been drawn up within the National Center several weeks before the outbreak in Kronstadt. Before describing this evidence, however, a brief account of the National Center's past activities is in order.

The National Center originally came into being in 1918, at the beginning of the Civil War, as a self-proclaimed "underground organization formed in Russia for the struggle against the Bolsheviks."[31] Founded in Moscow by A. V. Kartashev, P. B. Struve, and other erstwhile leaders of the Kadet party, its chief object was to overturn Lenin's government and establish a constitutional regime in its place. The Center concentrated the bulk of its resources in Moscow and along the Baltic coast; there were branches in Petrograd and at the fortresses of Krasnaya Gorka and Kronstadt. In 1919 it was involved in the attempt by General Yudenich, aided by British equipment and naval support, to take Petrograd. Kartashev, a former professor of church history at Petrograd Theological Academy and Minister of Religious Affairs in the Provisional Government of 1917, sat on Yudenich's five-man Political Council; and among the Center's agents at Kronstadt, according to Soviet sources,[32] was Professor D. D. Grimm, the former rector of Petrograd University, who was to figure prominently in the events of 1921.

Throughout the Yudenich offensive, Kronstadt remained loyal to the Bolsheviks, withstanding British air and torpedo attacks in which several of its warships were sunk or disabled. Krasnaya Gorka, by contrast, went over to the Whites and opened fire on Kronstadt when it refused to follow suit.

[31] "Obrazovanie severo-zapadnogo Pravitel'stva," *Arkhiv russkoi revoliutsii*, I, 1922, p. 295. Cf. A. S. Lukomskii, *Vospominaniia*, 2 vols., Berlin, 1922, II, 116.

[32] A. S. Pukhov, *Baltiiskii flot na zashchite Petrograda (1919 g.)*, Moscow, 1958, pp. 65-66.

There is evidence that the National Center was involved, possibly with the connivance of British intelligence;[33] but the mutiny was crushed when, following a devastating bombardment by the *Petropavlovsk*, a detachment of Kronstadt sailors and Red soldiers captured the fort by storm.

In the wake of Yudenich's defeat, many of the Center's adherents were arrested by the Cheka and condemned to execution or long terms in prison. But a number of its leaders, among them Professor Kartashev, were able to flee the country, and, taking up new headquarters in Paris, they immediately started rebuilding their organization. By the end of 1920 the National Center could boast of affiliates in London, Berlin, Helsingfors (where its chief agent was Professor Grimm), and other centers of the White emigration. Besides Kartashev, Struve, and Rodichev, its leadership included such eminent Kadets and Octobrists as V. D. Nabokov and A. I. Guchkov, as well as several right-wing populists, notably V. L. Burtsev, the editor of *Obshchee Delo*. Some of the most distinguished liberals, however, such as Pavel Miliukov and M. M. Vinaver, refused to join, having abandoned hope that Russia could be liberated by an armed invasion, even with Allied assistance.[34]

By late 1920 the National Center had made a sufficient recovery to prepare for a European-wide Congress of National Union. The congress eventually met in Paris in June 1921 and elected a Russian National Committee, with Professor Kartashev as chairman, whose goal was "the liberation

[33] *Ibid.*, pp. 68-74; *Izvestiia VTsIK*, June 18, 1921. See also Louis Fischer, *The Soviets in World Affairs*, 2 vols., Princeton, 1951, I, 206. Paul Dukes, a British agent in Russia during this period whom the Soviets accused of complicity in the affair, denies any personal involvement and any British connection with the National Center. See his *Red Dusk and the Morrow*, New York, 1922, p. 223; and *The Story of "ST 25,"* London, 1938, p. 314.

[34] P. N. Miliukov, *Russia Today and Tomorrow*, New York, 1922, pp. 125-26.

of Russia from Communist slavery."[35] This, of course, had been the objective of the National Center ever since its formation in 1918, but one by one the White commanders— Yudenich, Kolchak, Denikin, Wrangel—had gone down in defeat. General Wrangel, however, succeeded in evacuating a large part of his Russian Army, as it was called, with their weapons intact. Some 70 or 80 thousand men were interned at Constantinople, Gallipoli, and Lemnos, and thousands more in Serbia and Bulgaria, retaining their military ranks and discipline. A protégé of France, which in August 1920 had recognized his regime as the *de facto* government of South Russia (the only country to accord him this honor), Wrangel placed his forces under French protection. The armada in which he had made his escape, including a dreadnought, several destroyers, and dozens of other ships from the Black Sea Fleet with some 5,000 crew members, was interned at the Tunisian port of Bizerte. In November 1920 Paris withdrew its recognition of Wrangel's defunct government, but continued to feed his troops on "humane grounds," meanwhile urging him to disband.[36] But their efforts came to nothing. "General Wrangel," noted the British envoy in Constantinople in March 1921, at the time of the Kronstadt rebellion, "may be expected vigorously to oppose any suggestions to disband his formations, as he contends that it is particularly desirable that his army, which is the only anti-Bolshevik force outside Russia, should be ready to benefit by the present events in that country."[37]

To return to the activities of the National Center, in the archives of that organization is an unsigned handwritten manuscript labeled "Top Secret" and bearing the title "Mem-

[35] *Obshchee Delo*, June 6, 1921.

[36] P. N. Wrangel, *The Memoirs of General Wrangel*, London, 1930, pp. 338-39.

[37] Sir H. Rumbold to Lord Curzon, March 17, 1921, Great Britain, *Documents on British Foreign Policy, 1919-1939*, First Series, XII, 838.

orandum on the Question of Organizing an Uprising in Kronstadt."[38] The Memorandum is dated "1921" and puts forward a detailed contingency plan for an anticipated revolt in Kronstadt. From internal evidence, it is clear that the plan was drawn up in January or early February 1921 by an agent of the Center located either in Viborg or Helsingfors. He predicts that a rising of the sailors would erupt during "the coming spring." There are "numerous and unmistakable signs" of discontent with the Bolsheviks, he writes, and if a "small group of individuals, by quick and decisive action, should seize power in Kronstadt," the rest of the fleet and garrison would eagerly follow them. "Among the sailors," he adds, "such a group has already been formed, ready and able to take the most energetic actions." And if outside support can be secured, he concludes, "one may count entirely on the success of the rising."

The author is obviously well acquainted with the situation in Kronstadt. There is a long and well-informed analysis of the base's fortifications, in which the danger of artillery bombardment from Krasnaya Gorka is carefully assessed but discounted as a serious threat to the rebellion. The document, moreover, stresses the need to prepare food supplies for the rebels well in advance of the insurrection. On this point its author is most emphatic. With French assistance, he writes, stores of food must be placed on transport vessels in the Baltic, which will await orders to proceed to Kronstadt. As a military task force, he continues, the Russian Army of General Wrangel must be mobilized, supported by a French naval squadron and units of the Black Sea Fleet at Bizerte. (An underlying assumption of the Memorandum is that the revolt would not occur until after the springtime thaw, when the ice had melted and Kronstadt was immune from an in-

[38] "Dokladnaia zapiska po voprosu ob organizatsii vosstaniia v Kronshtadte," manuscript, Columbia Russian Archive. For the full text of the Memorandum in English translation, see Appendix A.

vasion from the mainland, and when the necessary food supplies had been prepared and Wrangel's forces made ready for action.)

On the arrival of the Russian Army, the Memorandum continues, all authority in Kronstadt would pass immediately into the hands of its commanding officer. The fortress would then serve as "an invulnerable base" for a landing on the mainland "to overthrow Soviet authority in Russia." The success of the operation, however, would hinge on the willingness of the French to provide money, food, and naval support. Otherwise a revolt would take place all the same and would be doomed to failure. If the French government should agree, the Memorandum concludes, then it would be desirable for it to appoint "an individual with whom the representatives of the organizers of the rebellion can enter into more detailed agreements on this subject and to whom they may communicate the details of the plan of the uprising and further actions, as well as more exact information concerning the funds required for the organization and further financing of the uprising."

Although the author's identity is not known, what evidence there is points to Professor G. F. Tseidler, a Russian expatriate in Viborg. Tseidler had been director of the Russian Red Cross in Petrograd until the Bolshevik Revolution, when he emigrated to Finland and became head of the Russian Red Cross branch in that country. He was closely associated with David Grimm, his former colleague at Petrograd University, who now served in Helsingfors as chief agent of the National Center (with which Tseidler was also connected) and as General Wrangel's official representative in Finland. As a Red Cross official, Tseidler was particularly concerned with the question of food supply in Kronstadt and Petrograd, a subject which occupies a central place in the Secret Memorandum. In October 1920, for instance, he sent a report to the Paris headquarters of the American Red Cross on the food crisis in Petrograd.[39] More significant is a telegram he addressed to the National Center in Paris some months later: "The situation requires an immediate decision on the questions relating to my memorandum on necessary food supply. Real activity can erupt at any time."[40] The date on the telegram is "28/ /1921." Unfortunately, no month is given, but February would seem very likely, the 28th being the date when the Petrograd strikes reached their climax and the *Petropavlovsk* resolution was adopted in Kronstadt. At the bottom of the telegram is the handwritten notation "Right!" followed by the signature of G. L. Vladimirov, a former tsarist general who acted as a military expert for the National Center. The "memorandum on necessary food supply" to which Tseidler refers may well be the Secret Memorandum described above. Further evidence of Tseidler's authorship is the fact that, on April 5, 1921, shortly after the Bolsheviks reoccupied Kronstadt, he published a leaflet in Viborg lamenting the failure of the émigrés to provision the insurgents and offering a new plan for supplying Petrograd in case of a fresh outburst there.[41] During the March rising itself, as we shall see, Tseidler was second to none in his efforts to supply the rebels in time to avert a disaster.

Apart from the Secret Memorandum, there are other indications that the National Center had been watching Kronstadt during the early weeks of 1921. It is worth noting, for example, that the fictitious newspaper reports of a rising among the sailors in February originated with the Russunion

[39] *New York Tribune*, October 7, 1921.

[40] Columbia Russian Archive.

[41] G. Tseidler, *O snabzhenii Peterburga*, Viborg, 1921. One piece of evidence, however, points to the possibility of a different author with the initials "L. G." During the rebellion an article signed by "L. G." appeared in a Helsingfors journal published by associates of Kartashev and Grimm, and its contents bear a certain similarity to the Secret Memorandum. See L. G., "Boesposobnost' Kronshtadta," *Novaia Russkaia Zhizn'*, March 15 and 17, 1921.

agency, an organization of émigré journalists closely tied to the National Center. Vladimir Burtsev, a leading figure in the Center and editor of its organ *Obshchee Delo*, the journal in which the stories first appeared, was at the same time one of the heads of Russunion, and the offices of *Obshchee Delo* served as the agency's Paris headquarters.[42] Perhaps the rumors merely reflected the earnest wishes of the expatriates that such a rebellion would soon erupt. This, however, was not the opinion of the London *Daily Herald*, a left-wing Labour journal, well-informed if at times uncritical in its pro-Bolshevik sympathies. The stories in *Matin* and other newspapers, wrote the *Herald's* diplomatic correspondent, revealed what was "confidently expected to happen" in Kronstadt, for they betrayed the existence of a counterrevolutionary plot hatched by White exiles with Allied encouragement.[43] However dubious this assertion, it is entirely possible, in the light of the Secret Memorandum, that the National Center at least informed the French of its plans in the Baltic and asked for help in carrying them out.[44]

In any case, there is no question that plans were afoot within the National Center to support an anticipated rising at Kronstadt. And to judge from the Secret Memorandum, the Center's Baltic agents had no intention of confining themselves to a mere auxiliary role; their object, rather, was to enter into active collaboration with the rebels at the earliest possible moment, after having secured the cooperation of the French High Command "in the preparation

[42] It may also be noted that the Russian National Committee, chaired by Professor Kartashev, held its meetings there during the summer of 1921. See the announcement in *Obshchee Delo*, June 23, 1921.

[43] *Daily Herald*, March 7, 1921.

[44] According to the *Daily Herald's* Riga correspondent, White plans for a rising in Kronstadt had been communicated to both the French and the British sometime in January 1921 by the well-known SR Boris Savinkov: *ibid.*, March 18, 1921.

and direction of the uprising." Ultimately, it is clear, the Center intended to exploit the revolt for its own purposes.

But were prior links in fact established with the sailors who carried out the rebellion? In the Secret Memorandum, written during the first weeks of 1921, the author speaks of "the presence of a closely knit group of energetic organizers for the rising," and says that his information "emanated from Kronstadt," presumably from sources friendly to the Center. That an organized group of would-be insurgents had already sprung into being is by no means impossible or even unlikely, for disaffection among the sailors had been growing for several months. Nor is it unlikely that a rebel organization, if it did exist, would have included future members of the Provisional Revolutionary Committee. Petrichenko's dominant role from the earliest hours of the rising—his signature on the *Petropavlovsk* resolution, his speech in Anchor Square, his chairmanship of the March 2 conference and of the Revolutionary Committee which sprang from it—encourages speculation about his activities before the outbreak. Then, too, there is the assertion by another committee member that "we" rescinded the arrest of Kalinin on March 1—a day before the committee had even been formed.[45]

It is conceivable, then, that Petrichenko and his confederates were the "closely knit group" on whom the Secret Memorandum pinned its hopes, and even that they had been approached by agents of the National Center in January or February of 1921. There is undeniable evidence—which will be examined later—that the Revolutionary Committee entered into an agreement with the Center *after* the rebellion was suppressed and some of its members found sanctuary

[45] "Interv'iu s chlenami Vremennogo Revoliutsionnogo Komiteta," manuscript, Hoover Library. Cf. the mysterious reference to a letter from Kronstadt, dated February 21, 1921, in which a "participant of the uprising" declares that he and his comrades will fight to the end to overthrow the Bolsheviks: Baron Rozen to M. N. Giers, March 12, 1921, Miller Archives, File 5M, No. 5.

in Finland, and one cannot rule out the possibility that this was the continuation of a longstanding relationship. Yet a careful search has yielded no evidence to support such a belief. Nothing has come to light to show that the Secret Memorandum was ever put into practice or that any links had existed between the émigrés and the sailors before the revolt. On the contrary, the rising bore the earmarks of spontaneity, and the fact that a group of determined leaders quickly rose to the forefront does not provide evidence to the contrary. For every uprising, even the most elemental, has its "agitators" and "ringleaders" who rouse the discontented to action, who organize and direct them. In the case of Kronstadt, there was little in the behavior of the rebels to suggest any careful advance preparation. Had there been a prearranged plan, surely the sailors would have waited a few weeks longer for the ice to melt, thereby eliminating the danger of an infantry assault and simultaneously freeing the two battleships for action and opening up a supply route from the west. The rebels, moreover, allowed Kalinin to return to Petrograd, though he would have made a valuable hostage. Further, they made no attempt to take the offensive, sending only a token force across the ice to Oranienbaum. Significant, too, is the large number of Communists who took part in the movement. In the early stages at least, the Kronstadters apparently saw themselves not as revolutionary conspirators but as a pressure group for social and political reform. This, as George Katkov points out, was also what the Petrograd authorities believed, otherwise they would not have sent Kalinin and Kuzmin to Kronstadt on March 1, nor would Vasiliev, the Bolshevik chairman of the Kronstadt Soviet, have presided at the mass meeting in Anchor Square at which the *Petropavlovsk* resolution was put to a vote.[46]

[46] Katkov, "The Kronstadt Rising," *St. Antony's Papers*, No. 6, p. 27. Cf. Daniels, "The Kronstadt Revolt," *American Slavic and East European Review*, x, 246-47.

The sailors needed no outside encouragement to raise the banner of insurrection. For months their grievances had been accumulating: inadequate food and fuel, curtailment of leaves, bureaucratic administration of the fleet, reports from home of Bolshevik oppression. In January 1921, as we have seen, no fewer than 5,000 Baltic seamen had resigned from the Communist party in disgust with the policies of the regime. Desertion and absence without leave were on the increase. During furloughs, the sailors had a vivid glimpse of food requisitions and were themselves exposed to search and seizure by the ubiquitous roadblock detachments. By February 1921, therefore, Kronstadt was clearly ripe for a rebellion. What set it off were not the machinations of émigré conspirators and foreign intelligence agents but the wave of peasant risings throughout the country and the labor disturbances in neighboring Petrograd. And as the revolt unfolded, it followed the pattern of earlier outbursts against the central government from 1905 through the Civil War, against tsarist and Bolshevik regimes alike. A particularly striking forerunner of March 1921 was the mutiny at the Petrograd naval base in October 1918, which anticipated Kronstadt in its protest against grain requisitioning and against the appointment of political commissars from above, in its slogans of "free soviets" and "Down with the commissarocracy," and in the prominent role among its instigators of Left SR's, Maximalists, anarchists, and nonparty rebels of an ultra-radical stripe.

The Kronstadters themselves, both during the rising and afterwards in exile, indignantly rejected all government accusations of collaboration with counterrevolutionary groups either at home or abroad. They denied in particular any intention to restore the old order. "We are defenders of the power of all the toilers," declared the rebel *Izvestiia*, "and against the tyrannical authority of any single party."[47] Their

[47] *Pravda o Kronshtadte*, p. 120.

revolt, they insisted, had been completely spontaneous from start to finish. No agitators had been active in their midst before the explosion, no anti-Bolshevik literature had circulated through their ranks, no foreign money or assistance had reached them at any time. Such is the testimony of the survivors who fled to Finland during the final Bolshevik assault.[48]

Of particular interest are the statements of Petrichenko himself in exile. We Kronstadt sailors, he said, to paraphrase an article he wrote in 1925, far from being counterrevolutionaries, are the very guardians of the revolution. During the Civil War we fought with unstinting courage to defend Petrograd and Russia against the Whites, and in March 1921 our devotion to the cause remained undiminished. Cut off from the outside world, we could receive no aid from foreign sources even if we had wanted it. We served as agents of no external group: neither capitalists, Mensheviks, nor SR's. Our revolt, rather, was a spontaneous effort to eliminate Bolshevik oppression. We had no predetermined blueprint of action, but felt our way as circumstances dictated. It is possible that others may have drawn up their own plans for an insurrection—indeed, this usually happens in such situations. But this had nothing to do with the Provisional Revolutionary Committee. Throughout the rising the initiative never passed from our hands. And when we heard that right-wing elements were seeking to exploit our revolt, we immediately warned our supporters in an article called "Gentlemen or Comrades."[49]

The reference here is to the lead editorial in the rebel *Izvestiia* of March 6. It declared:

[48] Quarton to Secretary of State, April 23, 1921, National Archives, 861.00/8619. Cf. "Interv'iu s chlenami Vremennogo Revoliutsionnogo Komiteta," Hoover Library.

[49] Petrichenko, "O prichinakh Kronshtadtskogo vosstaniia," *Znamia Bor'by*, December 1925-January 1926, pp. 4-8.

You, comrades, are now celebrating a great and blood-
less victory over the Communist dictatorship, but your enemies are celebrating with you. However, the motives of
your joy and of theirs are completely opposite. Whereas you
are inspired by the burning desire to restore the real power
of the soviets and by the noble hope of giving the worker
free labor and the peasant the right to dispose of his land
and the products of his labor, they are inspired by the hope
of restoring the tsarist whip and the generals' privileges.
Your interests are different, and therefore they are no
fellow-travelers of yours. You wanted the overthrow of
Communist rule for the purpose of peaceful reconstruction
and creative work; they wanted it for the enslavement of
the workers and peasants. You are seeking freedom; they
want to shackle you again. Look sharp. Do not let the
wolves in sheeps' clothing approach the helmsman's
bridge.[50]

IF, THE Secret Memorandum notwithstanding, the Russian
émigrés neither organized nor inspired the rebellion, they
did not remain idle once it had broken out. The aims of the
insurgents, to be sure, were far removed from their own:
the sailors wanted a system of free soviets in which only
workers and peasants would be represented; no restoration
of the Constituent Assembly was envisioned, nor any freedoms or political rights for the landowners and middle
classes, who were to remain a dispossessed and outcast
minority. Nevertheless, the rising stirred new hope among
the expatriates. For Alexander Kerensky, the prime minister
of the ill-fated Provisional Government, it heralded the imminent collapse of Bolshevism.[51] Similarly, the Kadet leader
Miliukov, who had abandoned all faith in armed intervention,
welcomed the revolt as the beginning of an unconquerable

[50] *Pravda o Kronshtadte*, p. 61.
[51] *Golos Rossii*, March 13, 1921.

liberation movement by the mass of Russians themselves. In an interview with the Paris correspondent of the *New York Times*, he expressed optimism that the days of Lenin's regime were numbered and called on the American government to send food to the rebels, though he made no appeal for troops or weapons. His colleague Vinaver, however, was more cautious. "It is impossible to say yet what chances of success this particular movement has," he said. "The Bolsheviks may be able to break it for the time being, but they will not kill it."[52]

The National Center, for its part, was jubilant. What had happened in Kronstadt was precisely what the author of the Secret Memorandum had forecast just a few weeks before, even if it had happened sooner than expected. Now the immediate task was to gather aid for the rebels. "The rising in Kronstadt," states a confidential circular in the archives of the Center, "has found a response in all the hearts of the Russian exiles." We must send food and medicine at once, the document continues, under the flag of the Red Cross; beyond this, we must supply the insurgents with aircraft, motor launches, fuel, and clothing to assist in spreading the revolt to the mainland before the Bolsheviks can muster their forces.[53] On March 6 Burtsev's *Obshchee Delo,* the semi-official organ of the Center, issued a passionate appeal to all émigré groups to join forces in support of the rebellion lest the final chance to save Russia be missed:

> We are living through an hour that will not be repeated. To remain an idle witness of events is out of the question. We make an urgent appeal to all Russians— and through them to our allies—to afford the Kronstadt revolutionists active material support. Let the insurgents be given arms, let food be secured for Petrograd. The

[52] *New York Times*, March 9, 1921.
[53] Untitled manuscript, Columbia Russian Archive.

struggle against the Bolsheviks is our common cause! If we chatter our way through these terrible days, if we still cannot pull ourselves out of the quagmire of debates and resolutions, woe to us, woe to Russia! If Europe, which has already lost so many opportunities, loses this one as well, then woe to her, woe to the entire world![54]

Although the émigrés were too divided to be drawn into any genuine cooperative effort, Burtsev's appeal did not go unheeded. The very next day, March 7, the Russian Union of Commerce and Industry in Paris declared its intention to send food and other supplies to Kronstadt, and communicated this decision to its representatives in Helsingfors. At the same time, it sent a radiogram to the Kronstadt Revolutionary Committee (the radio operator of the *Petropavlovsk* was able to pick up messages transmitted through Reval) assuring the rebels of full support. The radiogram declared that an initial sum of two million Finnish marks had already been pledged to aid Kronstadt in "the sacred cause of liberating Russia," and, moreover, that the Provisional Government's ambassador in Paris, V. A. Maklakov, had secured from the French foreign minister a promise of help in providing the insurgents with food. On March 9 the Union of Commerce and Industry established a special committee to organize an effective supply line to Kronstadt and Petrograd. Other anti-Bolshevik groups quickly followed suit, and the next day a joint meeting was held to work out a common plan.[55]

Meanwhile, a committee was formed by the National Center branch in Helsingfors to channel supplies to the insurgents. Professor Grimm, Wrangel's chief representative in Finland, was elected chairman, and Professor Tseidler be-

[54] *Obshchee Delo*, March 6, 1921.

[55] *Rul'*, March 9, 11, and 12, 1921; *Poslednie Novosti*, March 9, 1921. In 1919, it is worth noting, the National Center in Viborg had raised money from the Union of Commerce and Industry to assist Yudenich's Northwest Army: *Arkhiv russkoi revoliutsii*, I, 296.

came its busiest member, hurrying to Paris, the financial center of the Russian emigration, to collect funds for the enterprise. From N. Kh. Denisov, the head of the Union of Commerce and Industry, he immediately obtained the sum of 100,000 francs. After Tseidler returned to Finland, Count V. N. Kokovtsov, who had served as Minister of Finance and prime minister under Tsar Nicholas II, and was now chairman of the International Bank in Paris, sent him 5,000 British pounds, and the Russian-Asiatic Bank contributed 225,000 francs. Additional funds were donated by other Russian banks, insurance companies, and financial concerns throughout Europe, and by the Russian Red Cross, which funneled all collections to Tseidler, its representative in Finland. By March 16 Kokovtsov was able to inform the Committee of Russian Banks in Paris that deposits for Kronstadt already exceeded 775,000 francs, or the two million Finnish marks originally pledged to the rebels by the Union of Commerce and Industry.[56]

Apart from their own energetic fund-raising campaign, the émigrés sought the assistance of the Entente powers. Representatives of the National Center telegraphed urgent appeals to President Harding and to Herbert Hoover, the American Secretary of Commerce, for the immediate dispatch of food to the Kronstadt sailors. Similar requests came from the Russian Parliamentary Committee in Paris and from General Wrangel in Constantinople, who also sent a message to Kozlovsky in Kronstadt, offering the assistance of his Russian Army as soon as it could be mobilized.[57] A

[56] *Rul'*, March 18, 1921; Grimm to Kartashev, March 11, 1921, Maklakov Archives, Series A, Packet 5, No. 13. One member of the Grimm committee had ties with Boris Savinkov's anti-Communist organization in Poland: Grimm to Giers, March 15, 1921, Giers Archives, File 88.

[57] General E. K. Miller, Paris, to National Center in Helsingfors, March 14, 1921, Miller Archives, File 5M, No. 5; *Obshchee Delo*, March 7, 1921; *Rul'*, March 9, 1921; *Za Narodnoe Delo*, March 15, 1921.

rump conference of the deposed Constituent Assembly, from its meeting place in Paris, wired Boris Bakhmetiev, the Provisional Government's ambassador in Washington, to try to persuade the Americans to intercede. But the United States government, loath to resume the interventionist policies of the Civil War, turned a deaf ear to all such appeals. The prospects of British aid were even dimmer, and apparently little effort was made by the émigrés to win support in London. At that very moment, indeed, a trade agreement between Britain and Soviet Russia was just around the corner, a reflection of the *modus vivendi* which had been in the making since the conclusion of hostilities the previous year.

The best hope of foreign support came from France, the most unyielding of the Allied nations in its opposition to the Bolshevik regime. It is known from archival documents that the National Center was in constant contact with the French foreign ministry throughout the uprising.[58] Kerensky's journal in Berlin reported that a French squadron had been ordered to sail for the Baltic port of Reval with the mission of aiding Kronstadt,[59] but there is no evidence to corroborate this. According to the Labourite *Daily Herald*, the insurgents received financial aid from the French. "I can state definitely," wrote the *Herald*'s diplomatic correspondent, "that the French Government is concerned in the Kronstadt affair, and that a large sum of money for the use of the mutineers has been sent by them to a certain professor [evidently Tseidler] in Viborg. Supplies are also being sent under cover of the Red Cross."[60]

It is possible, of course, that a portion of the large sums raised so quickly by the Paris émigrés and sent to Tseidler in

[58] See the correspondence between General Miller and the French foreign ministry in the Miller Archives, File 5M, No. 5.
[59] *Golos Rossii*, March 13, 1921.
[60] *Daily Herald*, March 14, 1921.

Viborg came from the French government. (The French, it should be noted, continued to feed Wrangel's forces in Turkey throughout this period.) On the other hand, France was already moving—although more slowly than Britain—towards an accommodation with the Soviet regime, and the likelihood of their furnishing any appreciable aid to the Kronstadters does not seem very great. According to the well-informed journal of Pavel Miliukov, the French refused to interfere either politically or militarily in the crisis, but confined themselves to requesting Finland to allow food to pass through its borders to feed the starving Kronstadt population. This tallies with a detailed and extremely valuable report from Harold Quarton, the American consul in Viborg, to the Secretary of State in Washington; while admitting that, of all the foreign powers, the French were the most likely to be involved, Quarton nevertheless concludes that little or no aid had in fact been provided.[61]

With regard to the involvement of the Red Cross, however, the Bolsheviks (and the *Daily Herald*) were on solider ground. For there can be no doubt that the National Center, in its efforts to organize a supply line to Kronstadt, used the Russian Red Cross as cover. This is admitted in the private correspondence of the Center's agents on the Baltic.[62] On the other hand, Soviet charges that the International Red Cross and the American Red Cross were also implicated are without foundation. Professor Tseidler hoped to use the food stores of the International Red Cross in Stettin and Narva to aid the rebels, and the Russian Red Cross in Paris tele-

[61] *Poslednie Novosti*, March 9, 1921; *Za Narodnoe Delo*, March 15, 1921; Quarton to Secretary of State, April 23, 1921, National Archives, 861.00/8619: "Analysis of Foreign Assistance Rendered to the Cronstadt Revolution."
[62] General Kliuev to General Miller, March 14, 1921, Miller Archives, File 5M, No. 5; Grimm to Giers, March 15, 1921, Giers Archives, File 88.

graphed Geneva for permission, but none was forthcoming. Tseidler also asked the Baltic Commissioner of the American Red Cross, Colonel Ryan by name, to release his stores in Viborg. (The National Center no doubt felt it had a special claim to this food, for it had originally been purchased by General Yudenich in 1919 to feed the population of Petrograd once the Bolsheviks had been evicted, and later turned over to the American Red Cross to aid Russian refugees in the Baltic area.)[63] Eager to help, Ryan went to Paris on March 11 to consult with his superiors at the European headquarters of the American Red Cross. The talks, however, were without result. As Ryan told a reporter from *Obshchee Delo*, two difficulties stood in the way: first, his organization was barred by its constitution from lending aid to any political or military group, and second, even if this could somehow be circumvented, the Finnish government would not allow any food to pass over its borders.[64] Despite Bolshevik accusations of Finland's complicity with the Whites, throughout the revolt, in the words of Harold Quarton, the Finns were "zealous in respecting the recently concluded peace treaty" (of October 14, 1920) with the Soviet government. The Finnish General Staff considered the rising premature and doomed to failure, and did not want to give the Bolsheviks any excuse for military reprisals. At best, as Tseidler himself noted afterwards, the Finns were willing

[63] *Poslednie Novosti*, March 15, 1921; *Novaia Russkaia Zhizn'*, March 12, 1921. See also the correspondence between National Center leaders in Paris and Finland (Kartashev, Kliuev, Miller, Grimm, Tseidler) in Maklakov Archives, Series A, Packet 5, No. 13, and in Miller Archives, File 5M, No. 5.

[64] *Obshchee Delo*, March 17, 1921. After the rebellion, in a letter to the president of the Russian Red Cross in Paris, Tseidler admitted that no help had been received from either the British or American Red Cross. Tseidler wrote that he would never forget the "triumphant tone" of one American Red Cross official (Hopkins by name), who told him: "It's a good thing we didn't give you our flour." Tseidler to B. E. Ivanitskii, March 20, 1921, Giers Archives, File 88.

to allow medical supplies through as a humanitarian gesture,[65] but nothing came of this offer.

In Paris, the National Center and its sympathizers were frantic over these unanticipated roadblocks. Prince G. E. Lvov, Kerensky's predecessor as prime minister of the Provisional Government, besought the Finnish ambassador to reconsider, then tried again to get the French to intervene. He also went to the headquarters of the American Red Cross with a plea to release the stores in Viborg, but all of his efforts were unavailing.[66] Meanwhile, time was running out. The food situation in Kronstadt was growing desperate—so desperate that on March 13 Petrichenko wired Professor Grimm and authorized him to petition Finland and other countries for assistance. According to Quarton, the Finnish General Staff was of the opinion (rightly, as events were to show) that the rebels' food supply could not last beyond the end of the month. Quarton nevertheless advised Washington against any American attempt to send supplies by sledge for fear that they might be intercepted.[67] The United States Commissioner in Berlin was of the same opinion, having been convinced by certain émigrés there that any intervention could only help Lenin out of his difficulties by uniting Russia against a new foreign invasion; hence, to grant the requests of the Paris exiles for assistance, he concluded, would, even on philanthropic grounds, be "premature and subject to misconstruction."[68] This message, incidentally, was forwarded by the Secretary of State to the national headquarters of the American Red Cross in Washington and perhaps affected

[65] Quarton to Secretary of State, March 11, 1921, National Archives, 861.00/8319; Chargé in Helsingfors to Secretary of State, April 22, 1921, *ibid.*, 861.00/8628; Tseidler, *O snabzhenii Peterburga.*

[66] *Poslednie Novosti*, March 8, 1921; *Rul'*, March 10, 1921; *Obshchee Delo*, March 17, 1921.

[67] Petrichenko to Grimm, March 13, 1921, Grimm Archives; Quarton to Secretary of State, March 11, National Archives, 861.00/8318.

[68] Dresel to Secretary of State, March 14, 1921, *ibid.*, 861.00/8323.

the organization's decision not to intervene. "The Red Cross," wrote its national secretary a few weeks after the revolt, "gave no assistance of any kind whatever to the rebels in Kronstadt, nor did it attempt to do so."[69]

The Russian Red Cross, on the other hand, did its utmost to get aid to the insurgents until the clock ran out. As head of its branch in Finland, Tseidler continued to gather money from sympathizers across the continent, but his chief concern now was to find some way to deliver the supplies to the besieged sailors. On March 16, as the rebellion approached its final act, Baron P. V. Vilken, an associate of Tseidler and Grimm, made his way across the ice to Kronstadt in the guise of a Russian Red Cross representative. Vilken, a former captain in the Imperial Navy, had served as commander of the *Sevastopol* and as head of the minelayer division of the Baltic Fleet. The Bolsheviks rightly call him a White agent, though he did not, as they claim, use the cover of the American or International Red Cross. His "secret mission," as Quarton termed it, was to offer the Provisional Revolutionary Committee food and medicine as soon as a supply route could be arranged.[70] In the past, such an approach would doubtless have met with a curt rebuff. But now the sailors were desperately short of food, and their medical supplies were completely exhausted. Any doubts about Vilken's motives (his officer background was known to the rebel leaders) were brushed aside, and the Revolutionary Committee accepted his offer. The Red Cross, explained Petrichenko, was "a philanthropic and not a political organization."[71]

[69] National Secretary, American Red Cross, to Secretary of State, May 21, 1921, *ibid.*, 861.00/8572. A second letter (May 24, 861.00/8627) noted that aid had been supplied only to the Kronstadt refugees in Finland.

[70] *Krasnyi Arkhiv*, 1927, No. 6, p. 93; Quarton to Secretary of State, April 23, 1921, National Archives, 861.00/8619; *Krasnaia Gazeta*, March 20, 1921; Pukhov, *Kronshtadtskii miatezh*, p. 59.

[71] *Znamia Bor'by*, December 1925-January 1926, p. 8.

But, as Petrichenko pointed out and the Communists themselves acknowledged, no outside aid ever reached the insurgents.[72] A few tons of flour and lard were brought over on sledges by Finnish smugglers, but even this inadequate consignment arrived too late and fell into Bolshevik hands.[73] Thus the enormous efforts of the Kadet émigrés to provision Kronstadt ended in total failure. No Red Cross food stores were ever released; access through Finland remained blocked; and attempts to obtain icebreakers and transport ships came to nothing. The final blow fell on March 16 with the signing of the Anglo-Soviet trade agreement, a "stab in the back," to quote *Obshchee Delo*'s bitter reaction,[74] which effectively discouraged Finland and other countries from reviewing their policy of neutrality. Nothing, in short, had been done to implement the Secret Memorandum, and the warnings of its author were fully borne out. Perhaps the necessary preparations would have been made had the revolt not broken out so early and caught the émigrés off balance. In any case, the only supplies which the rebels were destined to receive reached them in Finnish refugee camps after their insurrection had been suppressed.

DESPITE Burtsev's pleas for unity in the "common cause" of dislodging the Bolsheviks from power, the Russian expatriates remained hopelessly divided. Throughout the rebellion, the Mensheviks, the Socialist Revolutionaries, and the liberals of the National Center went their own separate ways; there was no cooperation among them, no pooling of energies and resources. The SR's, however, made their own plans—unsuccessful in the end—to supply the rebels.

The events in Kronstadt brought new life and vigor to the

---

[72] See Jane Degras, ed., *The Communist International, 1919-1943*, 3 vols., London, 1956-1965, I, 213-15.

[73] Chargé in Helsingfors to Secretary of State, April 22, 1921, National Archives, 861.00/8628.

[74] *Obshchee Delo*, March 18, 1921.

SR organization in exile. In Paris, Berlin, and Prague, the most renowned of the party's leaders—Alexander Kerensky, head of the Provisional Government, and Victor Chernov, chairman of the short-lived Constituent Assembly—threw themselves into the task of raising funds to purchase foodstuffs and other supplies needed to keep the insurrection alive. From private correspondence intercepted by Bolshevik intelligence agents and subsequently published by the Soviet government, we know that they were able to collect substantial amounts of money. Two letters from V. M. Zenzinov in Prague to a member of the SR Administrative Center in Paris (dated March 8 and 13) mention sums in excess of 100,000 French francs, plus $25,000 sent from New York by Boris Bakhmetiev, Kerensky's ambassador to the United States. The letters also indicate that some 50,000 poods of flour had been collected in Amsterdam for shipment to Kronstadt.[75]

All aid was to be channeled through Victor Chernov in the Baltic city of Reval, who played a role for the SR's analogous to that of Tseidler and Grimm for the Kadet National Center. During the first week of the rising, Chernov sent the following radiogram to the Provisional Revolutionary Committee:

> The chairman of the Constituent Assembly, Victor Chernov, sends his fraternal greetings to the heroic comrade sailors, Red Army men, and workers, who for the third time since 1905 are throwing off the yoke of tyranny. He offers to aid with men and to provision Kronstadt through the Russian cooperatives abroad. Inform us what and how much is needed. I am prepared to come in person and give my energies and authority to the service of the people's revolution. I have faith in the final victory of the laboring masses. Hail to the first to raise the banner of

[75] *Rabota eserov zagranitsei*, Moscow, 1922, pp. 66-70.

the people's liberation! Down with despotism from the left and the right![76]

The Revolutionary Committee held a special meeting to consider the offer. Only Valk voted in favor, while Perepelkin voted to reject it out of hand; the rest followed Petrichenko and Kilgast, who argued that the best course was to decline for the time being.[77] As a result, Chernov received the following reply: "The Provisional Revolutionary Committee of Kronstadt expresses to all our brothers abroad its deep gratitude for their sympathy. The Provisional Revolutionary Committee is thankful for Chernov's offer, but it declines for the moment, until further developments become clarified. Meanwhile, everything will be taken into consideration."[78] The tone of the reply was not unfriendly. Although the sailors, expecting their revolt to spread to the mainland, did not think outside aid necessary, neither did they want to shut the door if it should be needed later. In the end, however, no SR help was requested and none was ever to reach Kronstadt.

In contrast to the Kadets and SR's, the Mensheviks in exile held aloof from anti-Bolshevik conspiracies and made no attempt to aid the rebels. Ever since Lenin and his followers seized power, the Mensheviks had acted as a legal opposition party, seeking to win a share of political authority through free and unhampered elections to the soviets. During the Civil War, regarding the Whites as a greater evil than the Bolsheviks, they opposed armed insurrection against the regime and threatened to expel any member who joined the counterrevolution. (Ivan Maisky, the future Soviet diplomat, was ejected from the party after entering the militantly anti-Bolshevik SR government in Samara.) As late as 1921,

---

[76] *Revoliutsionnaia Rossiia*, 1921, No. 8, pp. 3-4; Berkman, *The Kronstadt Rebellion*, p. 16.

[77] *Pravda*, April 7, 1921.

[78] *Revoliutsionnaia Rossiia*, 1921, No. 8, pp. 3-4.

for all their denunciations of Bolshevik despotism and terror, the Mensheviks clung to the belief that armed struggle against Lenin's government could only benefit the counterrevolutionaries; and *Sotsialisticheskii Vestnik* [The Socialist Courier], the principal Menshevik organ abroad, while sympathizing with the Kronstadt sailors in their opposition to one-party dictatorship and the policies of War Communism, dissociated itself from the interventionist efforts of the Kadets and SR's. Our aim, the journal declared, is to combat Bolshevism not with guns but with the irresistible pressure of the working masses.[79]

IN SUMMARY, the Russians in exile (with the partial exception of the Mensheviks) rejoiced at the uprising and sought to assist the insurgents by every possible means. To this extent the Soviet charges against them are justified. But it is not true that the émigrés had engineered the rebellion. On the contrary, for all the intrigues in Paris and Helsingfors, the Kronstadt uprising was a spontaneous and self-contained movement from beginning to end. What the evidence shows is not that the revolt was the outcome of a conspiracy but that an incipient plot apparently existed within Russian circles abroad, and that the plotters, while sharing the enmity of the sailors towards the existing regime, played no role in the actual rising. The National Center anticipated the outbreak and laid plans to help organize it and, with French assistance, to supply its participants with food, medicine, troops, and military equipment. The Center's ultimate objective was to assume control of the rebellion and make Kronstadt the springboard of a new intervention to oust the Bolsheviks from power. As it turned out, however, there was no time to put these plans into effect. The eruption occurred too soon, several weeks before the basic conditions of the plot—the melting of the ice, the creation of a supply line, the se-

[79] *Sotsialisticheskii Vestnik*, March 18, 1921, pp. 1-3.

curing of French support, and the transportation of Wrangel's scattered army to a nearby staging area—could be fulfilled.

That the Kadets and SR's should attempt to turn the revolt to their own advantage is hardly surprising. But to the end it was the sailors and their Revolutionary Committee who called the tune. Not until the situation became desperate did they appeal for outside help, for they confidently expected that their own example would set off a mass revolt on the mainland. Nor did they ever receive any of the aid with which the émigrés were endeavoring to furnish them, and, apart from Baron Vilken's visit on March 16, scarcely any direct contact with their would-be supporters occurred during the course of the uprising. The available evidence, incidentally, reveals no links of any sort between the exiles and the former tsarist officers at Kronstadt, the most logical source of collaboration in any White conspiracy.

What can be shown, however, is that some sort of agreement was concluded between the rebels and the émigrés after the rising had been crushed and its leaders had fled to Finland. In May 1921 Petrichenko and several of his fellow refugees at the Fort Ino camp decided to volunteer their services to General Wrangel. At the end of the month they wrote to Professor Grimm, Wrangel's representative in Helsingfors, and offered to join forces in a new campaign to unseat the Bolsheviks and restore "the gains of the March 1917 Revolution." The sailors put forward a six-point program as the basis for any common venture: (1) all land to the peasants, (2) free trade unions for the workers, (3) full independence for the border states, (4) freedom of action for the Kronstadt fugitives, (5) the removal of shoulder epaulettes from all military uniforms, and (6) the retention of their slogan "all power to the soviets but not the parties." Surprisingly, however, the slogan was to be retained only as a "convenient political maneuver" until the Communists had been overthrown. Once victory was in hand, the slogan would be shelved and a temporary military dictatorship installed to prevent anarchy from engulfing the country. This last point, no doubt, was intended as a sop for Wrangel. The sailors, at any rate, insisted that in due course the Russian people must be "free to decide for themselves what kind of government they want."[80]

Grimm immediately agreed to these terms, and Wrangel himself sent a favorable reply several weeks later. The pact, moreover, appears to have been implemented. For during the summer of 1921, if reports of the Soviet secret police are to be credited, Petrichenko, in collaboration with Grimm and Baron Vilken, recruited a group of refugee sailors and smuggled them into Petrograd, which, at an appropriate time, they were to help seize as a new bridgehead against the Communists. Once inside the city, the sailors worked under the direction of the Petrograd Fighting Organization, an underground group affiliated with the National Center and headed by V. N. Tagantsev, a former professor of geography at Petrograd University. Eventually, it seems, the forces of General Wrangel were to come into play, but before this could happen the Fighting Organization was uncovered and liquidated.[81]

The refugees, however, did not lose heart. In June 1921 the Congress of National Union, summoned by the National Center to unite like-minded émigrés in an anti-Bolshevik crusade, received a message from a group of Kronstadters in

[80] Petrichenko et al. to Grimm, Fort Ino, May 31, 1921, and to Wrangel, May 31, 1921, Grimm Archives and Giers Archives, File 88.

[81] *Iz istorii Vserossiiskoi chrezvychainoi komissii, 1917-1921 gg.: sbornik dokumentov*, Moscow, 1958, pp. 433-36, 445-58; "O rasskrytom v Petrograde zagovorov protiv Sovetskoi vlasti," Vecheka Presidium, August 29, 1921, Columbia Russian Archive. Tagantsev was executed in August 1921. On the Petrograd Fighting Organization see also Vardin, *Revoliutsiia i men'shevizm*, pp. 141-54; Pukhov, *Kronshtadtskii miatezh*, pp. 117-18; *Krasnaia Letopis'*, 1931, No. 3, pp. 18-19; and *Voprosy Istorii*, 1968, No. 1, pp. 133-36.

Finland warmly endorsing their program.[82] Furthermore, in the archives of the National Center there is a confidential document of October 30, 1921, signed by Petrichenko and Yakovenko (as chairman and deputy chairman of the Provisional Revolutionary Committee), which authorizes one Vsevolod Nikolaevich Skosyrev to join the Russian National Committee in Paris as a representative of the refugees for "the coordination of active work with other organizations standing on a platform of armed struggle against the Communists."[83]

None of this, of course, proves that there were any ties between the Center and the Revolutionary Committee either before or during the revolt. It would seem, rather, that the mutual experience of bitterness and defeat, and a common determination to overthrow the Soviet regime, led them to join hands in the aftermath. The Bolsheviks persisted in denying the spontaneous nature of the rebellion, blaming it on a whole array of Russian opposition groups—ranging from monarchists on the Right to anarchists on the Left—in cooperation with the Allied espionage services. But no convincing proof has even been put forward to substantiate these charges. Lenin himself admitted as much when he told the Tenth Party Congress on March 15 that in Kronstadt "they do not want the White Guards, and they do not want our power either."[84] Although he insisted that the émigrés had an important role in the affair, Lenin recognized that the rising was not a mere repetition of the White movements of the Civil War. He looked upon it, rather, as a sign of the deep gulf which had come to divide his party from the Russian people. If the White Guards were involved, he said, "at the same time the movement amounts to a petty bourgeois counterrevolution, to petty bourgeois anarchistic spon-

[82] *Obshchee Delo,* June 13, 1921.
[83] "Mandat," October 30, 1921, Columbia Russian Archive.
[84] *Desiatyi s"ezd RKP(b),* p. 414.

taneity." By this he meant that, at bottom, the revolt reflected the discontent of the Russian peasantry, the small proprietors who had no use for the state and its controls but wanted to be left alone to use their land as they saw fit. "Without doubt," Lenin added, "this petty bourgeois counterrevolution is more dangerous than Denikin, Yudenich, and Kolchak put together. For we are dealing with a country in which peasant property has come to ruin, besides which the demobilization of the army has set loose vast numbers of potentially mutinous elements."[85]

His colleague Bukharin took a similar view. Far more serious than Kronstadt, he told the Tenth Congress, was the "petty bourgeois infection" which had spread from the peasantry to a segment of the working class. This, he said, was a much greater hazard than the fact that some general or other had raised a military mutiny at Kronstadt. A few months later Bukharin returned to the same theme. "The documents which have since been brought to light," he told the Third Comintern Congress in July 1921, "show clearly that the affair was instigated by purely White Guard centers, but at the same time the Kronstadt mutiny was a petty bourgeois rebellion against the socialist system of economic compulsion."[86]

By these remarks, Lenin and Bukharin, for all the invective of the official propaganda machine, succeeded in laying bare the true essence of the Kronstadt rebellion. The sailors' mutiny had less to do with White conspiracies than with the spontaneous peasant revolts and working-class unrest then sweeping the country. Taken together, these movements represented a mass protest against the Bolshevik dictatorship and its obsolete program of War Communism. It was a protest of the people against the government, and the rising at Kronstadt was its most eloquent and dramatic expression.

[85] *Ibid.*, pp. 33-34.
[86] *Ibid.*, pp. 224-25; N. Bukharin, *The New Policies of Soviet Russia*, Chicago, 1921, p. 56.

4. First Assault

*T*he *Bolsheviks*, faced with a staggering domestic crisis, were determined to end the revolt as quickly as possible. Their very existence as a government seemed at stake. For one thing, the title of "Provisional Revolutionary Committee," adopted by the rebel leaders on March 2, was itself a provocation and a challenge. But even more menacing was the initial demand of the *Petropavlovsk* resolution. By appealing for new elections to the soviets, "in view of the fact that the present soviets do not express the will of the workers and peasants," the insurgents in effect were questioning the legitimacy of Bolshevik rule. The theme was sounded again on March 3 in the first number of the Kronstadt *Izvestiia*. The Communist party, declared the lead editorial, had thoroughly alienated itself from the people. Only the common efforts of the toiling masses, operating through freely elected soviets, could rescue the nation from further misery and oppression.[1] Given the recent disturbances in Moscow and Petrograd, and the peasant revolts still raging along the peripheries, such pronouncements, in the eyes of the authorities, carried subversive overtones. Unless quick action were taken, Kronstadt, it was feared, might trigger a general upheaval.

Further cause for alarm was provided by the revival of hostile maneuvers among the Russians who had emigrated. After nearly three years of Civil War, the fear of counter-revolutionary conspiracies had become deeply ingrained in the Soviet leadership. Fed by an endless stream of rumors, a "White Scare" (comparable to "Red Scare" hysteria in the West) gripped the ranks of the party. To many Bolsheviks—especially during the first days of the rebellion when the situation was confused and reliable information hard to come by—Kronstadt smacked unmistakably of an anti-Soviet plot.

[1] *Pravda o Kronshtadte*, p. 45.

After a long series of White generals—Kornilov, Krasnov, Miller, Yudenich, Kolchak, Denikin, Wrangel—backed by the Entente and the Russian opposition, General Kozlovsky seemed to fit the familiar pattern. When news of the revolt first reached Petrograd, Zinoviev's brother-in-law awakened Victor Serge at the Hotel Astoria. "Kronstadt is in the hands of the Whites," he said in an agitated voice. "We are all under orders."[2]

Not that the Bolsheviks had any inkling of the National Center's Secret Memorandum, or they would surely have brought it to light in their propaganda war against the insurgents. Yet they did know that plans were afoot to provision Kronstadt and to send troops and equipment to bolster the rebellion. Soviet agents, as we have seen, intercepted the correspondence of the SR leaders. They also knew of Chernov's offer to aid the insurgents. Furthermore, the money-raising campaign of the Kadets and Octobrists was openly reported in the émigré press, and the activities of Tseidler and Grimm in Finland did not go unnoticed.[3] That the exiles in Paris, Berlin, and Helsingfors were alive with new hope and excitement undoubtedly heightened the sense of urgency in Moscow and Petrograd and strengthened the government's resolve to liquidate the revolt promptly and decisively.

It would seem, then, that Soviet charges of a counterrevolutionary plot were not mere fabrications designed solely as propaganda against the rebels, but rather that propaganda was mingled with genuine anxiety at the prospect of a White resurgence. In any event, the Bolsheviks sought in every way to discredit Kronstadt in the eyes of the people. They were particularly worried by the effect of the rising on the army. If Soviet troops should be needed to suppress the mutiny, it had to be depicted as a dangerous counterrevolutionary movement. Thus Kozlovsky was linked to the White generals

[2] Serge, *Memoirs of a Revolutionary*, p. 124.
[3] *Izvestiia Petrogradskogo Soveta*, March 16, 1921.

of the Civil War and labeled a "new Yudenich," menacing Petrograd from its Baltic approaches.[4] And a special circular to the Red Army charged the rebels with attempting to disrupt the peace negotiations with the Poles at Riga; but for Kronstadt, the soldiers were told, they might have been demobilized and allowed to return to their homes.[5]

The rising, moreover, was said to be "part of a great plan to provoke trouble within Soviet Russia to impair its international position."[6] The Whites were conspiring not only to bring about a renewed Polish intervention but to sabotage the new détente with the West. Specifically, they wanted to prevent any shift in American policy towards an accommodation with the Soviets. The new Republican president (Harding), according to the Bolshevik press, was disposed to resume commercial relations with Russia, a far-fetched belief which may have been encouraged by an enterprising American visitor, W. B. Vanderlip, whom Lenin took to be a wealthy businessman with influential connections in Washington. Similarly, Lev Kamenev warned the Tenth Party Congress that the counterrevolutionaries were bent on upsetting the imminent trade agreement with the British.[7] As Leonid Krasin, the Soviet emissary in London, put it, "certain sinister interests are working, at any rate, for a postponement, possibly a rupture, of the negotiations." Krasin was confident, however, that Kronstadt would meet the same fate as all previous White Guard plots: "When you remember the troubles the Soviet Government has faced successfully during the past three years, this Kronstadt affair is insignificant. And it will be dealt with in the usual manner."[8]

Of greater concern to the Bolsheviks was the determina-

[4] *Petrogradskaia Pravda*, March 4, 1921.

[5] "Prikaz voiskam Krasnoi Armii Moskovskogo garnizona," No. 226, March 3, 1921, Maklakov Archives, Series B, Packet 5, No. 5.

[6] *Pravda o Kronshtadte*, p. 71.

[7] *Desiatyi s"ezd RKP(b)*, p. 456.

[8] *Daily Herald*, March 7, 1921.

tion of the émigrés to gain access to Kronstadt and use it as a base for a landing on the mainland. This would have meant nothing less than a resumption of the Civil War, something which, in view of the general exhaustion of the country, the Soviet regime might not have been able to survive. What the authorities feared, in other words, was not so much the rebellion itself as what it might lead to. The real danger, Lenin told the Tenth Party Congress at its opening session, was that Kronstadt might serve as "a step, a ladder, a bridge" for a White restoration.[9] It was in this sense, primarily, that Lenin and his associates regarded the sailors as counterrevolutionaries. "Show us who your supporters are," they seemed to say, "and we shall tell you who *you* are." They spoke of the rebels themselves not as vicious enemies of the people but as wayward brothers, as much to be pitied as condemned. "We waited as long as possible," said Trotsky at a parade for the troops who had crushed the revolt, "for our blind sailor comrades to see with their own eyes where the mutiny led." And Bukharin addressed the Third Comintern Congress in a similar vein: "Who says the Kronstadt rising was White? No. For the sake of the idea, for the sake of our task, we were forced to suppress the revolt of our erring brothers. We cannot look upon the Kronstadt sailors as our enemies. We love them as our true brothers, our own flesh and blood."[10]

For foreign Communists in Russia, such as Victor Serge and André Morizet, statements like these were extremely disturbing. Having been led to believe that Kronstadt was merely a repetition of the anti-Bolshevik movements of the Civil War, they were "astonished and troubled" to find among the Soviet leaders none of the malice which had been

[9] *Desiatyi s"ezd RKP(b)*, p. 34.

[10] Isaac Deutscher, *The Prophet Armed*, New York, 1954, p. 514; Raphael R. Abramovitch, *The Soviet Revolution, 1917-1939*, New York, 1962, p. 203. Cf. André Morizet, *Chez Lénine et Trotski, Moscou 1921*, Paris, 1922, pp. 78-84.

felt for the White legions and their collaborators; their talk, rather, was punctuated by "sympathetic reticences" which to the visitors betrayed the party's troubled conscience. Yet these outsiders recognized the dilemma of their Bolshevik comrades: the dilemma of holding power while at the same time preserving their revolutionary ideals. After considerable soul-searching, and with "unutterable anguish," Serge declared himself on the side of the Communists against the insurrection, even though Kronstadt, he said, had right on its side—even though the party, swollen by the influx of power-seekers, inspired little confidence among the people. For if the Bolshevik dictatorship should fall, he reasoned, it was only a short step to chaos, to a general peasant revolt, a *Pugachevshchina* as of old, the massacre of the Communists, the return of the émigrés with their sterile and outmoded policies, and in the end another dictatorship, this time antiproletarian rather than antibourgeois. Still, Serge vowed personally not to take up arms against the famished workers and sailors who, he said, had been pushed to the limits of their endurance.[11]

IN THE END, arms were indeed employed to subdue the rebels. But was force really necessary? How seriously did the Bolsheviks try to reach a peaceful settlement before bringing their guns into action? By their own account, every effort was made to avoid bloodshed, but in fact they might have done much more. During the first week of the rebellion, it is true, numerous appeals were made to the insurgents to listen to reason; on March 1, as we know, both Kalinin and Kuzmin went to Kronstadt as peacemakers and spoke at the open-air meeting in Anchor Square, and Kuzmin spoke at the House of Education the next day. Yet they offered no concessions, such as had been granted, for example, to the striking workers in Petrograd. Although the situation plainly

---

[11] Serge, *Memoirs of a Revolutionary*, pp. 126-29.

called for tact and conciliation, these were conspicuously absent in the speeches of the two officials. Their manner was defiant, belligerent, unyielding, and their tone was so threatening that it could only provoke the excitable sailors still further. From the start, the attitude of the authorities was not one of serious negotiation but of delivering an ultimatum: either come to your senses or suffer the consequences.

This was unfortunate, indeed tragic, for the chances were good that the insurgents would have responded to a more sympathetic and flexible approach. But the Bolsheviks, faced with one of the gravest crises in their history, were in no mood for compromise. Their nerves were badly frayed. They feared the Poles, the émigrés, the Entente, and the possibility that Kronstadt might become the spearhead of a new interventionist campaign; they feared the spread of the revolt to the mainland, already seething with discontent and ablaze in several locations with peasant uprisings; they feared the loss of political power, followed by anarchy and then a White restoration. In such circumstances, negotiation with the rebels seemed too risky. Any hesitation, any sign of weakness in the face of defiance and subversion, might precipitate the general collapse of their authority. After seizing power and holding it through three years of bloody conflict, were they now to sacrifice everything to a mutiny of hotheaded and undisciplined sailors? Could they afford to play a game of waiting and hope for the revolt to peter out by itself? Time was not on their side. Before very long the thaw would come. We learn from the rebel *Izvestiia* of March 15 that the snow on the city streets in Kronstadt was already beginning to turn to slush.[12] In a matter of weeks the ice in the Gulf of Finland would melt, making an infantry assault on the fortress impossible. The warships frozen in Kronstadt harbor would be freed for action. What is more, even if Finland persisted in barring transit across its borders, supplies and reinforcements

[12] *Pravda o Kronshtadte*, p. 162.

could then come into Kronstadt by sea. To prevent all this from happening, the Bolsheviks realized they would have to act quickly. What government would long tolerate a mutinous navy at its most strategic base, a base which its enemies coveted as a stepping-stone for a new invasion? "We waited as long as possible," said Trotsky shortly after the rebellion was suppressed, "but we were confronted by the danger that the ice would melt away and we were compelled to carry out . . . the attack."[13]

AMONG the chief concerns of the authorities, two were perhaps the most immediate: that the rebellion might spread to the mainland, and that it might touch off mutinies in other units of the army and navy. Both of these fears were heightened by events in Oranienbaum on March 2. That afternoon emissaries from Kronstadt made their way across the ice with copies of the *Petropavlovsk* resolution, which they distributed in Petrograd and a few neighboring towns. At Oranienbaum the rank and file of the First Naval Air Squadron held a meeting at their club, unanimously endorsed the resolution, and, following Kronstadt's example, proceeded to elect their own Revolutionary Committee. Soon after this they met again in a nearby hangar and chose a three-man delegation to cross the ice and establish direct contact with the Kronstadters. In the middle of the night—apparently after the delegates from the Air Squadron arrived with their offer to join the movement—the Kronstadt Revolutionary Committee sent a party of 250 men to Oranienbaum, but they were met by machine-gun fire and forced to withdraw. The three envoys of the Air Squadron were arrested by the Cheka while attempting to return to their base. Meanwhile, the commissar of the Oranienbaum garrison, having learned of the incipient mutiny, called Zinoviev's Defense Committee with an urgent request for reinforcements. All Communists

[13] Deutscher, *The Prophet Armed*, p. 514.

at Oranienbaum were issued arms and given extra rations to allay any discontent which they themselves may have felt over the food situation. At 5 A.M. on March 3 an armored train with a detachment of *kursanty* and three batteries of light artillery arrived from Petrograd. The barracks of the Air Squadron were quickly surrounded and their occupants arrested. A few hours later, after intensive questioning, 45 men were taken out and shot, among them the chief of the Division of Red Naval Aviators and the chairman and secretary of the newly formed Revolutionary Committee.[14]

The suppression of the Oranienbaum mutiny came as the first major setback to the Kronstadt leaders. Confident that their revolt would spread to the mainland, thereby forcing the Bolsheviks to yield to their demands, they had refused to take the offensive, sending only a small force to Oranienbaum with disastrous results. (The Oranienbaum rebels, for their part, displayed the same naïve mentality, making no effort to arm themselves and to seize control of their own base.) Yet, if the attitude of the Air Squadron was any indication, Oranienbaum—as Kozlovsky and his colleagues insisted—could probably have been taken with slight resistance. Then the rebels could have marched on Petrograd, whose inhabitants might well have been encouraged to rise against the government. But all advice of this kind was stubbornly rejected. The sailors felt far more secure on their island bastion than off somewhere on the mainland in the unaccustomed role of foot soldiers. Fearing that their numbers were insufficient for an offensive, they preferred to shut themselves in their seemingly impregnable fortress, bristling with guns on every side, and wait until the government agreed to terms.

Henceforward every appeal that they should assume the initiative fell on deaf ears. When the "military specialists"

[14] *Pravda o Kronshtadte*, pp. 92-94; Petrichenko, *Pravda o Kronshtadtskikh sobytiiakh*, pp. 8-9.

proposed cutting the ice around Kotlin Island with artillery fire in order to make it invulnerable to an infantry attack, the Revolutionary Committee responded that there were not enough spare shells to do the job and that, in any case, the water would only freeze again in a very short time.[15] Thus, for the duration of the rising, no attempt was made to moat the fortress or to free the icebound warships, although outsiders assumed that such action must have been taken.[16] Similarly, when the specialists recommended barricading the streets in the eastern part of the city near the vulnerable Petrograd Gate (a foresighted suggestion, as it turned out), the Revolutionary Committee insisted that it lacked the men and materials for the task, though plenty of both were actually on hand. Kozlovsky later explained that the sailors refused to cooperate because of their congenital mistrust of officers and of higher authority in general. Scorning their obstinacy and lack of discipline, he complained that the revolt ought not to have occurred till the thaw had melted the ice of the Finnish Gulf. It was the impatience of the sailors to throw off the Communist yoke, he said, which precipitated the premature outbreak.[17]

Meanwhile, the rebellion had had little success in igniting the mainland. In only a few places—notably Oranienbaum, Peterhof, and Petrograd—did dissident movements emerge that were willing to espouse the rebel cause. But the Com-

[15] Report of Lieutenant R. Kelley, in Quarton to Secretary of State, April 23, 1921, National Archives, 861.00/8619. Stories in the émigré press (e.g. *Rul'*, March 8, 1921) that the *Ermak* was used by the rebels to break a path to Oranienbaum were erroneous. The vessel was in Petrograd, having gone there for fuel only a day before the outbreak of the rebellion.

[16] See, for example, Quarton to Secretary of State, March 9, 1921, *ibid.*, 861.00/8296: "Ice is thickly frozen on both shores but revolutionists have probably moated themselves and are protected by open water."

[17] *Novaia Russkaia Zhizn'*, March 19, 1921; London *Times*, March 21, 1921; *Sotsialisticheskii Vestnik*, April 5, 1921, pp. 5-6.

munists throughout the area had been put on the alert for seditious activity, and in every case where it occurred it was promptly snuffed out. In Petrograd, for instance, a delegation of Kronstadt sailors tried to win over the crew of the icebreaker *Truvor* (some sources say it was the *Ermak*), apparently with the aim of freeing the *Sevastopol* and *Petropavlovsk* and moating Kotlin Island against an infantry invasion, and perhaps too of opening a supply channel to the West. But Bolshevik troops were immediately dispatched to the ship, and the Kronstadters and their sympathizers were taken into custody.[18] Otherwise Kronstadt did little to spread the revolt. Of the 200 emissaries sent to distribute the *Petropavlovsk* resolution in the towns of Petrograd province, only a handful avoided capture; sailors bearing leaflets were intercepted as far south as Dno, a railway junction on the line from Petrograd to Vitebsk. The insurgents also tried using the telephone to explain their position to Petrograd and Krasnaya Gorka, but their efforts came to nothing. The authorities, on their side, telephoned the Revolutionary Committee and vainly attempted to convince it that its position was hopeless. At the same time, loyal Communists at Kronstadt made use of the open lines to report on the munitions, food, and morale of the rebels.[19]

For the most part, then, the rebels adopted a defensive strategy, a strategy which, so they thought, would enable them to hold out until the thaw had made their position impregnable. Meanwhile, they addressed themselves to administering the affairs of the island, and especially to strengthening its defenses. They hoped that the government would come to terms but did not rule out the possibility of an armed assault. "At any moment," warned the Provisional Revolu-

[18] "Prichiny, povody, techenie i otsenka Kronshtadtskikh sobytii," manuscript, Hoover Library; Pukhov, *Krasnaia Letopis'*, 1931, No. 1, p. 17.

[19] Petrichenko, *Pravda o Kronshtadtskikh sobytiiakh*, p. 12; Katkov, "The Kronstadt Rising," *St. Antony's Papers*, No. 6, p. 33.

tionary Committee on March 4, "we may expect an attack by the Communists with the aim of conquering Kronstadt and again subordinating us to their authority and reducing us to hunger, cold, and ruin."[20] For the first week, however, the rebellion remained a war of nerves rather than guns.

Why did the government wait so long before launching its attack? The delay, it would appear, was dictated as much —if not more—by the need to make adequate military preparations as by the desire to arrive at a peaceful settlement. During the first days of March the Bolsheviks hastened to secure the old capital as well as important strategic points in the surrounding area, particularly Krasnaya Gorka and Oranienbaum, and Lisy Nos and Sestroretsk on the Karelian coast. All Communist party members in Petrograd and its neighboring towns were mobilized and issued arms. By March 5 a militia some 4,000 strong had been collected, augmented by volunteers from the Young Communists and the local trade unions. In addition, hundreds of *kursanty* were called in from the immediate area as well as from such distant cities as Moscow, Orel, and Nizhni Novgorod, and special Cheka troops (*Vokhr*) and men from the roadblock detachments were pressed into service against the rebellion. A careful watch was placed on trains from Petrograd to mainland points in the direction of Kronstadt to prevent any contact with the insurgents. Soviet leaders, their concern aroused by the abortive revolt at Oranienbaum (and perhaps by memories of the anti-Bolshevik mutiny at Krasnaya Gorka in 1919), reinforced the garrisons of these strongpoints and made personal inspection trips to root out any seditious activity.

In Petrograd itself, although the strikes and demonstrations had all but ended, a mood of dark anticipation verging on panic persisted. One morning in early March, as Victor Serge was leaving the Hotel Astoria, he saw an old servant

[20] *Pravda o Kronshtadte*, p. 51.

quietly making her way out with several parcels. "Where are you off to like this, so early in the morning, grandmother?" he asked. "There's a smell of trouble about the town," she replied. "They're going to cut all your throats, my poor little ones, they're going to be looting everything all over again."[21] Threats against the Jews became widespread. Many of the city's factories and shops kept their gates shut because of incessant rumors of renewed outbreaks. On March 3 the Petrograd Defense Committee, now vested with absolute power throughout the entire province, took stern measures to prevent any further disturbances. The city became a vast garrison, with troops patrolling in every quarter. Notices posted on the walls reminded the citizenry that all gatherings would be dispersed and those who resisted shot on the spot. During the day the streets were nearly deserted, and, with the curfew now set at 9 P.M., night life ceased altogether.[22]

Zinoviev, in his triple role as party boss, chairman of the Petrograd Soviet, and chairman of the Defense Committee, made full use of the power concentrated in his hands. Throughout the emergency he continued to act with efficiency and dispatch, showing little of his reputed excitability or tendency to panic. On March 4 he summoned a special session of the Soviet, with Kronstadt as the main topic on the agenda. Aside from the regular members, representatives from other institutions—trade unions, factory committees, military units, youth organizations—were invited to attend. The anarchist leaders Alexander Berkman and Emma Goldman, still on friendly terms with the government, were present and left vivid descriptions of the proceedings, to which a few details can be added from contemporary press accounts.[23]

[21] Serge, *Memoirs of a Revolutionary*, p. 125.

[22] *Petrogradskaia Pravda*, March 3, 1921; *Izvestiia Petrogradskogo Soveta*, March 3, 1921.

[23] Berkman, *The Kronstadt Rebellion*, pp. 30-31; Goldman, *Living*

From start to finish the meeting was a stormy one. Zinoviev and Kalinin denounced the revolt as a White Guard plot, abetted by Mensheviks, SR's, and Entente intelligence agents, whereupon a man in the front row, a worker from the Arsenal factory, stood up and defended the insurgents. Pointing his finger at Zinoviev, he shouted: "It's the cruel indifference of yourself and of your party that drove us to strike and that roused the sympathy of our brother sailors, who had fought side by side with us in the Revolution. They are guilty of no other crime, and you know it. Consciously you malign them and call for their destruction." Cries of "counterrevolutionist," "traitor," and "Menshevik bandit"— Emma Goldman reports—turned the assembly into a bedlam, but the workman stood his ground, his voice rising above the tumult: "Barely three years ago Lenin, Trotsky, Zinoviev, and all of you were denounced as German spies. We, the workers and sailors, had come to your rescue and saved you from the Kerensky Government. Beware that a similar fate does not overtake you!"

At that point, a Kronstadt sailor rose to the speaker's defense. Nothing had changed in the revolutionary spirit of his comrades, he declared. They were ready to defend the revolution with their last drop of blood. Then he proceeded to read the *Petropavlovsk* resolution, and the meeting, says Goldman, became a pandemonium of shouting and confusion. Zinoviev, replying amid the commotion, demanded the immediate surrender of Kronstadt on penalty of death. Over the protest of several delegates, a resolution was adopted calling on the sailors to abandon their folly and restore authority to the Kronstadt Soviet, where it properly belonged. If blood is spilled, the resolution declared, it will rest on your own consciences. "Decide at once. Either you are with

---

My Life, pp. 879-81; *Krasnaia Gazeta*, March 5, 1921; *Izvestiia TsIK*, March 6, 1921. See also Kornatovskii, ed., *Kronshtadtskii miatezh*, pp. 40-42; and *Pravda o Kronshtadte*, pp. 165-66.

us against the common enemy, or you will perish in shame and disgrace together with the counterrevolutionaries."[24]

One figure who had been expected to attend the meeting was Trotsky, the government's most talented troubleshooter in times of crisis, but he did not arrive on time. The outbreak of the rebellion had found him in western Siberia, the scene of widespread peasant disturbances. On hearing the news he returned at once to Moscow to consult with Lenin, then hurried north to Petrograd, reaching the old capital on the 4th or 5th of March. His first act was to issue a harsh ultimatum (published on March 5) demanding the immediate and unconditional capitulation of the mutinous sailors:

The Workers' and Peasants' Government has decreed that Kronstadt and the rebellious ships must immediately submit to the authority of the Soviet Republic. Therefore, I command all who have raised their hands against the socialist fatherland to lay down their arms at once. The obdurate will be disarmed and turned over to the Soviet authorities. The arrested commissars and other representatives of the government must be liberated at once. Only those who surrender unconditionally may count on the mercy of the Soviet Republic. At the same time, I am issuing orders to prepare to quell the mutiny and subdue the mutineers by force of arms. Responsibility for the harm that may be suffered by the peaceful population will fall entirely upon the heads of the counterrevolutionary mutineers. This warning is final.[25]

If this was a sincere attempt to avoid an armed clash, it was obviously bound to fail. Taking no account of the mood of the sailors, it could only make them more unbending than

---

[24] Kornatovskii, ed., *Kronshtadtskii miatezh*, p. 42.

[25] Trotskii, *Kak vooruzhalas' revoliutsiia*, III, part 1, 202. The co-signers of the ultimatum were S. S. Kamenev, commander in chief of the Red Army, and M. N. Tukhachevsky, commander of the Seventh Army in Petrograd.

ever in their determination to hold out until reforms had been granted. "That it should have fallen to Trotsky to address such words to the sailors," noted his biographer, Isaac Deutscher, "was another of history's ironies. This had been his Kronstadt, the Kronstadt he had called 'the pride and the glory of the revolution.' How many times had he not stumped the naval base during the hot days of 1917! How many times had not the sailors lifted him on their shoulders and wildly acclaimed him as their friend and leader! How devotedly had they followed him to the Tauride Palace, to his prison cell at Kresty, to the walls of Kazan on the Volga, always taking his advice, always almost blindly following his orders! How many anxieties they had shared, how many dangers they had braved together!" But the times were now different, and the Provisional Revolutionary Committee replied to Trotsky's ultimatum with a warning of its own: "The ninth wave [that is, the culminating wave of a storm at sea] of the Toilers' Revolution has risen and will sweep from the face of Soviet Russia the vile slanderers and tyrants with all their corruption—and your clemency, Mr. Trotsky, will not be needed."[26]

On the same day, March 5, a separate leaflet was issued by the Petrograd Defense Committee and dropped over Kronstadt by airplane. If anything, its language was even more provocative than that of Trotsky's ultimatum. Behind the SR's and Mensheviks, it read, the White officers are showing their fangs. The real leaders of the rebellion are General Kozlovsky and his aides, Captain Burkser, Kostromitinov, Shirmanovsky, and other White Guards, who are deceiving you with promises of democracy and freedom. In actuality, they are fighting for a restoration of tsarism, for a new Viren [commander of the Kronstadt naval base until his murder in February 1917] to sit on your necks. That Petrograd, Siberia, and the Ukraine are behind you is an insolent lie. The truth

[26] Deutscher, *The Prophet Armed*, p. 512; *Pravda o Kronshtadte*, p. 68.

is that you are surrounded on all sides, your position is hopeless. The leaflet concluded with a prophetic warning: at the last minute, the Kozlovskys and Petrichenkos will leave you in the lurch and flee to Finland. What will you do then? If you follow them, do you think you will be fed in Finland? Haven't you heard what happened to Wrangel's men, who are dying like flies of hunger and disease? The same fate awaits you too, unless you surrender within 24 hours. If you do, you will be pardoned; but if you resist, "you will be shot like partridges."[27]

Although the threat to shoot the rebels "like partridges" has often been attributed to Trotsky, the true perpetrator was Zinoviev's Defense Committee. The sailors, in any event, were roused to a violent fury. Trotsky and Zinoviev became their archvillains and the symbols of all that was malevolent and odious within the Soviet regime. (Lenin, who remained in the background for the moment, was not exposed to Kronstadt's wrath until the following week, and even then never with the same venom as his two colleagues.) Indignation reached fever pitch when the authorities in Petrograd ordered the families of the Kronstadters arrested as hostages. A system of hostages had been inaugurated by Trotsky during the Civil War as a warning to the "military specialists," the ex-tsarist officers, who might be tempted to betray the Red forces under their command. "Let the turncoats know," read Trotsky's order of September 30, 1918, "that they are at the same time betraying the members of their own families—fathers, mothers, sisters, brothers, wives, and children."[28] In the case of Kronstadt, however, the decision to take hostages was not made by Trotsky, as a number of accounts suggest, but by the Petrograd Defense Committee before Trotsky's arrival in the city. The Defense Committee demanded the immediate release of the three Communist

[27] Kornatovskii, ed., *Kronshtadtskii miatezh*, pp. 188-89.
[28] Trotskii, *Kak vooruzhalas' revoliutsiia*, I, 151.

officials who had been imprisoned by the sailors on March 2: "If but a hair falls from the head of a detained comrade, it will be answered by the heads of the hostages."[29] The announcement was made on March 5, the same day that the government issued its ultimatum to the rebels. On March 7 the Kronstadt *Izvestiia* responded with a demand that the hostages be liberated within 24 hours: "The Kronstadt garrison declares that Communists here enjoy full liberty and their families are absolutely safe. The example of the Petrograd Soviet will not be followed here, as we consider such methods most shameful and vicious, even if prompted by desperate fury. Never before has history witnessed such acts."[30] Nothing, however, came of this appeal.

Meanwhile, Alexander Berkman and Emma Goldman, having learned of the Bolshevik ultimatum, resolved to do what they could to prevent a bloodbath. On March 5, with two of their comrades, they sent a letter to Zinoviev, proposing that an impartial commission be formed to mediate the dispute. The commission, which would consist of five persons, two of them anarchists, would go to Kronstadt and try to work out a peaceful settlement. It was hunger and cold, said the letter, combined with the absence of any outlet for their grievances, that had driven the sailors to open protest, but genuine counterrevolutionaries might try to exploit the situation unless an immediate solution were found—not by force of arms but by amicable agreement. Resorting to violence would only aggravate matters and serve the cause of the Whites. At the same time, the use of force by a Workers' and Peasants' government against the workers and peasants themselves would have a profoundly demoralizing effect upon the international revolutionary movement.[31]

---

[29] *Pravda* and *Izvestiia TsIK*, March 5, 1921.

[30] *Pravda o Kronshtadte*, p. 73.

[31] Berkman, *The Bolshevik Myth*, pp. 301-302; Goldman, *Living My Life*, pp. 882-83. The letter was drafted by Berkman.

There is a good chance that some such conciliatory step, coming after the failure of the sailors to win support on the mainland, might have soothed their anger and forestalled the tragedy which followed. Although Berkman's appeal went unanswered, the next day, March 6, the Petrograd Soviet telegraphed the Revolutionary Committee, asking if a delegation of both party and nonparty members of the Soviet might visit Kronstadt to look into the situation. Whether prompted by the anarchists or not, this was the first constructive and conciliatory gesture made by the Bolsheviks since the outbreak of the rebellion. It is unfortunate, therefore, that it should have been rejected. Full of bitterness against a government which had just arrested their wives and children, the rebels answered that they did "not trust the nonparty status of your nonparty representatives." Instead, they demanded that the Petrograd population send true nonparty workers, soldiers, and sailors, chosen in the presence of Kronstadt observers, plus a maximum of 15 percent of Communist delegates to be appointed by the Petrograd Soviet.[32] This reply, abrupt and unyielding, effectively stifled the proposal. Afterwards there were no further efforts by the government to reach an accommodation with the insurgents.

BY MARCH 7 the clock had run out. The 24-hour ultimatum of March 5, extended by another 24 hours the next day, had expired with neither side modifying its position. And now the government was ready to use force. During the period of grace, a steady stream of men and equipment had been flowing into Petrograd and its neighboring strongholds. Each day saw the arrival of additional *kursanty* and Cheka detachments, and the most reliable units of the Red Army, drawn from various sectors of the country. In addition, some of the most prominent "military specialists" and Red Commanders were called in to draw up a plan of attack. On

[32] *Pravda o Kronshtadte*, pp. 73-74.

March 5 M. N. Tukhachevsky, a gifted and an experienced officer in spite of his youth, was put in charge of the Seventh Army and of all other troops in the Petrograd Military District, replacing D. N. Avrov, whose seat he took on Zinoviev's Defense Committee. Born of a noble family in Penza province, Tukhachevsky had been a page in the Imperial Cadet Corps and a lieutenant in the tsarist army during the First World War, but after the October Revolution he had shifted his loyalties to the Bolsheviks, becoming one of the outstanding military leaders of the Civil War. In 1920, at the age of 27, he had commanded the Red forces on the northern Polish front and nearly succeeded in capturing Warsaw before being turned back by Marshal Pilsudski.[33]

Tukhachevsky now faced a task as difficult as any in his career. The Seventh Army had been stationed in the Petrograd area throughout the Civil War (blocking Yudenich's advance in 1919) and was now in a "demobilization mood."[34] With the fighting over, the men longed to return to their homes. They were mostly of peasant origin and, sharing the discontents of the countryside, saw little to criticize in the rebel program—indeed, the slogans of Kronstadt struck a sympathetic chord among them. Moreover, the workers' demonstrations in Petrograd had affected their morale. Obviously, then, to send such men to fight their own brethren, the proverbial "pride and glory" of the revolution, involved considerable risk. They might well refuse to fire on the rebels or even go over to their side. Thus Tukhachevsky sought to bolster their spirits, taking pains to feed and outfit them as well as he could. But to lead the assault he relied mainly on the military cadets, the special forces of the Cheka, and the picked Communist units brought in from other areas.

[33] On Tukhachevsky's role in the suppression of Kronstadt, see L. V. Nikulin, *Tukhachevskii*, Moscow, 1964, pp. 134-50.
[34] Kornatovskii, ed., *Kronshtadtskii· miatezh*, p. 44; S. E. Rabinovich, "Delegaty 10-go s"ezda RKP(b) pod Kronshtadtom v 1921 godu," *Krasnaia Letopis'*, 1931, No. 2, pp. 26-31.

Kronstadt, meanwhile, girded itself for the attack. A key strategic outpost, it boasted a sizable garrison and excellent defenses. The rebels numbered some 13,000 sailors and soldiers, with perhaps 2,000 additional men recruited from the civilian population. Kotlin Island was surrounded by numerous forts and batteries, most of them built in the late nineteenth century from the plans of General E. I. Totleben, an outstanding Russian military engineer. On the northern side were Forts Totleben and Krasnoarmeets and a chain of seven numbered forts extending towards the Karelian coastline. On the south were Forts Peter, Paul, Konstantin, and Alexander, and two numbered forts. All the batteries and forts were thickly armored and equipped with heavy guns in turrets. The city proper was encircled by a thick wall and defended by several gun emplacements. All told, Kronstadt had 135 cannon and 68 machine guns mounted on the forts and ships. The *Petropavlovsk* and *Sevastopol* were each armed with a dozen 12-inch guns and sixteen 120-milimeter guns. Constructed on the eve of the First World War, they were thoroughly modern men-of-war, among the first dreadnoughts in the Imperial Russian Navy. The *Petropavlovsk* had been seriously damaged by a British torpedo boat in 1919 but had since been repaired and restored to service. Frozen side by side in the harbor, however, the two battleships were obviously not as effective as they might have been. Some of the ice around them had been chopped away, but there was still inadequate space to maneuver, and to some extent the large ships obstructed each other's fire. Nevertheless, their guns far outclassed those of Krasnaya Gorka, the most powerful fort on the mainland. Only four of the latter's 12-inch cannon were in operating order, since the heavy damage suffered during the June 1919 mutiny had not yet been fully repaired. The rest of the fort's artillery was of insufficient caliber to harm distant Kronstadt. Thus, in the event of an artillery duel, as the author of the Secret Memorandum had pointed out, Krasnaya Gorka was no match for the island fortress and its ships, which boasted twenty-four 12-inch guns in working order, as well as twelve 11-inch and five 10-inch guns. Besides the *Petropavlovsk* and *Sevastopol*, moreover, eight other warships lay in the Kronstadt harbor and repair docks, including a battleship and three heavy cruisers as well as fifteen gunboats and twenty tugs. Because no ice-breaker was available, however, none of these vessels could be brought into action.[35]

To reduce the fortress, then, was no easy task. In addition to its excellent defenses, Kronstadt benefited from the wide expanse of ice which separated it from the Bolshevik strongholds on the mainland. It was five miles to Oranienbaum and a dozen to Krasnaya Gorka on the southern shore of the Gulf, and seven miles to Lisy Nos and eleven to Sestroretsk on the northern or Karelian coast. Thus an attacking army would have to cross a terrifying stretch of open ice, unprotected from the murderous fire of artillery and machine guns concealed behind steel and concrete bunkers. It was this nightmare more than anything else—more than war-weariness or any sympathy for the defenders—which undermined the morale of the Communist forces gathered on the shores of the Finnish Gulf awaiting orders to advance.

Yet, however impregnable the fortress might have appeared, it had some serious weaknesses. Among other things, the stores of ammunition were insufficient to sustain a prolonged siege; the defenders lacked warm clothing and winter shoes; and, owing to the general shortage of fuel, the *Petropavlovsk* had only 300 tons left (40 tons were consumed on an average day) and the *Sevastopol* none at all. Worse still, food supplies were dwindling rapidly. Although the in-

---

[35] The data on Kronstadt's defenses have been gleaned from Pukhov, *Kronshtadtskii miatezh*, pp. 80-81; Kornatovskii, ed., *Kronshtadtskii miatezh*, pp. 43, 95; *Pravda o Kronshtadte*, pp. 24, 90; *Bol'shaia sovetskaia entsiklopediia*, 1st edn., xxxv, 223; *Rul'*, March 12, 1921; and London *Times*, March 16 and 30, 1921.

habitants had some potatoes which they had grown themselves, stocks of canned goods and of horsemeat were precariously low. There was no flour on hand and only a little bread, of poor quality, enough (according to well-informed estimates) to last another two weeks at a daily ration of half a pound.[36] One thing was abundantly clear: both sides would suffer before the rebellion had run its course.

MILITARY operations began on March 7. At 6:45 in the evening the Communist batteries at Sestroretsk and Lisy Nos on the northern shore opened fire on Kronstadt. The barrage, directed chiefly at the outlying forts, was intended to soften up the rebel defenses for an infantry assault. When the forts replied in kind, the cannon of Krasnaya Gorka on the opposite coast chimed in, answered in turn by the 12-inch guns of the *Sevastopol*. A full-scale artillery duel was under way. In Petrograd, Alexander Berkman was crossing the Nevsky Prospect when he heard the distant rumble of gunfire rolling towards him. Kronstadt was under attack! The sounds had a shattering effect on the anarchist leader, destroying the last remnants of his faith in the Bolshevik regime. "Days of anguish and cannonading," he recorded in his diary. "My heart is numb with despair; something has died within me. The people on the street look bowed with grief, bewildered. No one trusts himself to speak. The thunder of heavy guns rends the air."[37]

March 7 was the anniversary of Women Workers' Day. Amid the noise of exploding shells, the Kronstadt radio sent greetings to the working women of the world. Denouncing the Communists as "the enemies of the toiling people," the rebels called for an end to tyranny and despotism of every kind. "May you soon accomplish your liberation from every form

---

[36] Report of Lieutenant R. Kelley, in Quarton to Secretary of State, April 23, 1921, National Archives, 861.00/8619.

[37] Berkman, *The Bolshevik Myth*, p. 303.

of violence and oppression. Long live the free revolutionary working women! Long live the Worldwide Social Revolution!"[38]

The exchange of cannon fire did not last long; a combination of snow and dense fog reduced visibility to zero, causing both sides to break off their barrage. Damage to Kronstadt was slight, and only two defenders were injured. Nonetheless, the Revolutionary Committee expressed its outrage. The first shots have been fired, declared the Kronstadt *Izvestiia* the next morning, but we shall sink the approaching "pirate ship" of the Bolsheviks. "All power to the soviets! Keep your hands off this power, hands stained with the blood of those who have fallen in the cause of freedom, in the struggle with the White Guards, the landlords, and the bourgeoisie!"[39]

In keeping with Tukhachevsky's plan, the artillery bombardment was followed by an attempt to take the fortress by storm. The attack, carried out by Communist forces from both the northern and southern shores of the mainland, came the next morning before dawn. In a blinding snowstorm Tukhachevsky's troops started across the ice, shrouded in white coveralls to blend with the snow covering the Finnish Gulf. Out in front were detachments of military cadets, followed by picked Red Army units, with Cheka machine gunners bringing up the rear to discourage any would-be deserters. The defenders were ready and waiting. As the troops approached, they were met by a murderous barrage of artillery and machine-gun fire from the forts and batteries around the island. Some of the exploding shells cracked open the ice, plunging scores of attackers into a watery grave. It was the beginning, as Serge noted, of a ghastly fratricide.[40] After the Gulf had swallowed its first victims, some of the Red soldiers, including a body of Peterhof *kursanty*, began to

---

[38] *Pravda o Kronshtadte*, p. 80.
[39] *Ibid*.
[40] Serge, *Memoirs of a Revolutionary*, p. 130.

defect to the insurgents. Others refused to advance, in spite of threats from the machine gunners at the rear who had orders to shoot any waverers. The commissar of the northern group reported that his troops wanted to send a delegation to Kronstadt to find out about the insurgents' demands. The night before, it appears, Bolshevik soldiers had already gone across in small numbers to exchange literature with the defenders.[41] In the end, only a fraction of the assault troops succeeded in reaching the outermost forts, but even they were compelled to withdraw under a thick blanket of fire.

By dawn the snowstorm had subsided, revealing a broad expanse of ice littered with corpses on every side. With visibility restored, the Communist batteries resumed their pounding of the fortress, while the heavy guns of Kronstadt returned their fire, damaging a section of railway between Oranienbaum and Peterhof and setting a number of buildings aflame. An occasional probing action by Soviet infantry failed to yield any results. During the afternoon Communist airplanes flew over the Gulf to bomb Kronstadt's fortifications, the first air attack on the island since Yudenich's Baltic campaign in 1919. Although the raids continued sporadically throughout the rest of the day, they caused little harm. About 6 P.M. one bomb landed inside the city itself, damaging a house and slightly wounding a thirteen-year-old boy. Throughout the revolt Bolshevik air attacks were never very effective, thanks to heavy ground fire and frequently poor visibility.[42]

The fighting on March 8 had scarcely begun when the Petrograd Soviet triumphantly announced that the rebels were already "in full rout." The same day, Lenin, addressing the opening session of the Tenth Party Congress in Moscow, was

[41] Petrichenko, *Pravda o Kronshtadtskikh sobytiiakh*, p. 12; Mett, *La Commune de Cronstadt*, p. 51.

[42] For additional details of the March 8 assault, see Kornatovskii, ed., *Kronshtadtskii miatezh*, pp. 44-46, 67-68; Petrichenko, *Pravda o Kronshtadtskikh sobytiiakh*, pp. 14-15; and *Pravda o Kronshtadte*, pp. 23, 90, 106, 180.

equally confident of the outcome. "I do not yet have the latest news from Kronstadt," he said, "but I have no doubt that this uprising, behind which looms the familiar figure of the White Guard general, will be liquidated within the next few days, if not hours."[43] These declarations, as it turned out, were premature. Actually, the assault of March 8 proved· an unmitigated failure. The Communists lost hundreds of men without even breaching Kronstadt's defenses.[44] In their haste to suppress the revolt, they had deployed an insufficient force—perhaps 20,000 in all—and had made inadequate preparations for a successful storming of the powerful fortress. Troops chosen for their reliability had faltered at the crucial moment, partly out of reluctance to fire on ordinary sailors and soldiers like themselves, but mainly for fear of crossing the open ice without protection of any kind, exposed to the devastating crossfire of Kronstadt's batteries and forts.

That evening a party of Bolsheviks approached Kronstadt from the south, carrying a flag of truce. Two members of the Provisional Revolutionary Committee, Vershinin and Kupolov, went out on horseback to meet them. According to a *kursant* in the Bolshevik party, Vershinin, a sailor from the *Sevastopol*, shouted an appeal for joint action against the Jewish and Communist oppressors, and called for the election of a true revolutionary authority in the form of free soviets.[45] In any event, Vershinin was seized on the spot, but Kupolov managed to gallop to safety.

The rebels were incensed at this treachery, but their feelings of outrage were tempered by compassion for the fallen Bolshevik soldiers. In an· editorial entitled "Let the Whole

[43] *Izvestiia Petrogradskogo Soveta*, March 8, 1921; *Desiatyi s"ezd RKP*(b), p. 33.

[44] A well-informed source estimates Bolshevik losses as 500 dead and 2,000 wounded: "Kak nachalos' vosstanie v Kronshtadte," March 12, 1921, Miller Archives, File 5M, No. 5.

[45] Kornatovskii, ed., *Kronshtadtskii miatezh*, pp. 95-96. Cf. *Pravda o Kronshtadte*, pp. 94-98, 129.

World Know," the Revolutionary Committee bitterly accused "Field Marshal" Trotsky of responsibility for the bloodshed. To avoid further violence, the committee again proposed that a nonparty delegation be sent to Kronstadt to learn the true facts about their movement. "Let the toilers of the whole world know that we, the defenders of soviet power, are guarding the conquests of the Social Revolution. We shall win or perish beneath the ruins of Kronstadt, fighting for the just cause of the laboring masses. The toilers of the world will be our judges. The blood of the innocent will fall upon the heads of the Communist fanatics, drunk with power. Long live the power of the soviets!"[46]

[46] *Pravda o Kronshtadte*, p. 82.

5. The Kronstadt Program

The Kronstadt rebellion lasted only a little more than two weeks. Yet, during this short time, a revolutionary commune of a remarkable type was established under the leadership of the Provisional Revolutionary Committee, whose members, while having no long-term strategy to speak of, displayed considerable gifts of improvisation and self-organization. The committee, as we have seen, had been created on March 2 from the five-man presidium of the conference in the House of Education. But it soon became clear that a larger body would be needed to handle the administration and defense of the city and garrison. Thus, on the evening of March 4, some 200 delegates from Kronstadt's factories and military units—presumably the same delegates who had met in the House of Education two days before—gathered after work in the Garrison Club and, amid cries of "Victory or death!," elected an enlarged Revolutionary Committee of 15 members.[1]

To facilitate the task of directing Kronstadt's civilian and military affairs, the new committee moved its headquarters from the battleship *Petropavlovsk* to the House of the People, located in the city proper. And to assist Petrichenko, the committee's chairman, Yakovenko and Arkhipov were chosen as deputy chairmen and Kilgast as secretary. Each of the remaining members was assigned a specific area of responsibility: civic affairs were administered by Valk and Romanenko, justice by Pavlov, and transportation by Baikov (whose regular job in Kronstadt had been transport chief of the fortress construction department), while Tukin was in charge of food supply and Perepelkin of agitation and propaganda.[2]

In keeping with Point 9 of the *Petropavlovsk* resolution,

[1] *Pravda o Kronshtadte*, pp. 56-57.
[2] *Novaia Russkaia Zhizn'*, March 11, 1921; Pukhov, *Kronshtadtskii miatezh*, p. 76.

differential food rationing was abolished. Special rations were given only to hospitals and children's homes, and extra food might also be dispensed to the sick on the written prescription of a doctor. Otherwise food in Kronstadt was issued on an equal basis in exchange for coupons. Distribution was handled by two existing agencies, Gorkommuna and Gorprodkom, under the Revolutionary Committee's close supervision. From time to time the points of distribution were announced in the rebel newspaper, the daily *Izvestiia* of the Provisional Revolutionary Committee. The committee also used the radio of the *Petropavlovsk* to broadcast special announcements to the town population and to communicate with the outside world.[3]

In the first days of the uprising, an 11 P.M. curfew was imposed and movement in and out of the city placed under strict control. Schools were closed until further notice. At the same time, the Revolutionary Committee issued a series of edicts affecting Kronstadt's political structure. Following Point 7 of the *Petropavlovsk* resolution, it abolished the political department of the fortress and launched a new educational program at the Garrison Club. The local Workers' and Peasants' Inspectorate was replaced by a commission of trade union delegates, intended, one suspects, as a model for the "itinerant bureau of control" specified in Point 14 of the *Petropavlovsk* charter. Furthermore, in every public institution, trade union, factory, and military unit, a revolutionary troika was elected—without Communist members—to carry out the orders of the Revolutionary Committee at the local level.[4]

Alongside of the Revolutionary Committee, the conference of delegates which convened in the House of Education on

---

[3] *Pravda o Kronshtadte*, pp. 52-54, 77-78; Berkman, *The Kronstadt Rebellion*, pp. 20-21. All fourteen issues of *Izvestiia* are reproduced in *Pravda o Kronshtadte*, which thus constitutes the most valuable source on the program and activities of the insurgents.

[4] *Pravda o Kronshtadte*, p. 177.

March 2 remained in existence for the duration of the rebellion, with a membership that fluctuated between two and three hundred sailors, soldiers, and workingmen. The conference met on March 4 to enlarge the Revolutionary Committee, and again on March 8 and 11, when, among other things, it created a new Kronstadt Trade Union Council, free from the domination and control of the Communist party. Not surprisingly, however, its agenda was chiefly occupied with questions of defense and of food and fuel supply.[5] As described by one authority, the conference was Kronstadt's own distinctive form of parliament,[6] but more accurately, perhaps, it served as a kind of interim Soviet, a prototype of the "free soviets" for which the insurgents had risen in revolt.

It was the sailors, the most militant element of the Kronstadt population, who were the driving force behind this activity. In matters of organization, planning, and propaganda, the bluejackets took the initiative from the first, and continued to play a dominant role in the movement throughout its brief history. Not a single soldier (much less an officer) held a seat on the Provisional Revolutionary Committee, and civilian workmen and employees formed only a small minority of its membership. But if the sailors took the lead, the Kronstadt garrison—the "military specialists" and the Red Army troops who manned the surrounding forts and batteries—soon fell into line; and the townspeople too, always susceptible to the influence of the seamen, with whom their occupations brought them into close contact, offered their active support. For a fleeting interval Kronstadt was shaken out of its listlessness and despair. A Finnish journalist who visited the island at the height of the rebellion was struck by the "enthusiasm" of its inhabitants, by their renewed sense of purpose and mission.[7]

---

[5] *Ibid.*, pp. 56-57; *Revoliutsionnaia Rossiia*, 1921, No. 7, p. 22.
[6] Pukhov, *Kronshtadtskii miatezh*, p. 85.
[7] *Za Narodnoe Delo*, March 15, 1921.

Kronstadt's mood, it has often been noted,[8] was a throwback to the ebullience and high excitement of 1917. For the sailors, who styled themselves "Communards," 1917 was the Golden Age, and they longed to recapture the spirit of the revolution, when the trammels of discipline were discarded and their ideals were as yet uncontaminated by the exigencies of power. Four years before, when they cast their lot with the Bolsheviks, they thought they shared the same objectives; the Bolsheviks, by all appearances, were fellow revolutionaries of the extreme Left, apostles of a mass upheaval that would eliminate coercion and injustice and usher in a toilers' republic of free soviets. "Socialism," Lenin himself declared in November 1917, "is not created by orders from above. State-bureaucratic automatism is alien to its spirit; socialism is alive, creative—the creation of the popular masses themselves."[9] The succeeding months, however, saw the emergence of a centralized dictatorship, and the sailors felt betrayed. They felt that the democratic principles for which they had struggled had been abandoned by a new privileged elite. During the Civil War they remained loyal to the Bolsheviks but were determined to restore the revolution to its original path. And once the danger of the Whites had been eliminated, they rose to redeem the pledges of October.

As a political movement, then, the Kronstadt revolt was an attempt by disillusioned revolutionaries to throw off the "nightmare rule" of the Communist dictatorship, as the rebel *Izvestiia* described it,[10] and restore the effective power of the soviets. Historically, the soviet was traceable to the village commune, the traditional Russian institution of local self-government. As Emma Goldman observed, it was nothing

[8] See, for example, Voline, *La Révolution inconnue*, p. 462; Berkman, *The Kronstadt Rebellion*, p. 18; and Katkov, "The Kronstadt Rising," *St. Antony's Papers*, No. 6, p. 70.

[9] Lenin, *Polnoe sobranie sochinenii*, xxxv, 57.

[10] *Pravda o Kronshtadte*, p. 55.

but "the old Russian *mir* in an advanced and more revolutionary form. It is so deeply rooted in the people that it sprang naturally from the Russian soil as flowers do in the fields."[11] For Lenin, however, free soviets, independent of party control, had always been anathema. He instinctively distrusted the spontaneous action of the people. Organs of local democracy, he feared, might serve as a potential bridge for reaction or lead to economic and social chaos. Nevertheless, when the revolution came and local soviets sprang up everywhere, he recognized their value as a force to destroy the old order and as a means to acquire power. "All power to the soviets" became one of his party's principal watchwords. After the October coup, however, Lenin reverted to his original centralism by imposing a revolutionary dictatorship upon the anarchic and undisciplined masses. And although the soviet system continued to be upheld as a new and higher form of government, as the "proletarian dictatorship" envisioned by Marx, the soviets were progressively subjected to party control, so that by 1921 they had become mere rubber stamps for the emerging bureaucracy.

It was against this perversion of the revolution that the sailors rose in protest. The conflict, as they saw it, was between the popular ideal of a "toilers' republic" and a "proletarian dictatorship" that was in fact a dictatorship of the Bolsheviks. Opposed to the exclusive rule of any single party, they aimed at breaking up the Communist monopoly of power by securing freedom of speech, press, and assembly for the workers and peasants, and by holding new elections to the soviets. The sailors, as Berkman noted, were the staunchest supporters of the soviet system; their battle-cry was the Bolshevik slogan of 1917: "All power to the soviets."[12] But, in contrast to the Bolsheviks, they demanded free and unfettered soviets, representing all left-

---

[11] Avrich, *The Russian Anarchists*, p. 252.
[12] Berkman, *The Kronstadt Rebellion*, pp. 24-25.

wing organizations—SR's, Mensheviks, anarchists, Maximalists—and reflecting the true aspirations of the people. Thus the motto on the masthead of the rebel *Izvestiia* had a new twist: "All power to the soviets but not the parties." "Our cause is just," declared the *Petropavlovsk* radio on March 6. "We stand for power to the soviets but not the parties, for the freely elected representation of the toilers. The soviets that have been captured and manipulated by the Communist party have always been deaf to all our demands and needs; the only reply we have ever received has been shooting."[13]

But if the rebels called for free soviets, they were not democrats in the sense of advocating equal rights and liberties for all. Like the Bolsheviks whom they condemned, they maintained a rigorous class attitude towards Russian society. When they spoke of freedom, it was freedom only for the workers and peasants, not for the landlords or middle classes. This, indeed, was what they meant by a "toilers' republic"—the exercise of the general will of the laboring masses over their former oppressors and exploiters. There was no place in their program for a liberal parliament on West European lines, and it is symbolic that a Kronstadt seaman should have led the dispersal of the Constituent Assembly in January 1918. Three years later the sailors remained firmly opposed to the Assembly or to any similar institution. In their eyes, a national parliament would inevitably be dominated by a new privileged minority, if not by the very same elements which had been driven to flight by the revolution. They had no use for representative government, but wanted direct mass democracy of and by the common people through free soviets. "The soviets and not the Constituent Assembly are the bulwark of the toilers," proclaimed the organ of the Provisional Revolutionary Com-

[13] *Ibid.*, p. 19; *Pravda o Kronshtadte*, p. 65.

mittee.[14] For the rebels, in short, parliament and the soviets were antithetical forms of government, the one entailing the supremacy of the bourgeoisie, the other of the toilers. But they feared, too, that any new Assembly would become merely another tool of the Bolsheviks in their quest for absolute power. After the fall of Kronstadt, a Soviet reporter asked a group of survivors why they had not called for the restoration of the Constituent Assembly. "Party lists mean Communists" (*A raz spiski—znachit kommunisty*), one of them replied with a wry smile. What we want, he said, is genuine self-determination of the workers and peasants, and it is only through the soviets that this can be achieved.[15]

IN ITS economic content, the Kronstadt program was a broadside aimed at the system of War Communism. It reflected the determination of the peasantry and working class to sweep away the coercive policies to which they had been subjected for nearly three years. The Kronstadters (following an age-old Russian practice) charged the government—and the government alone—with all the ills that afflicted the country. Little blame was attached to the chaos and destruction of the Civil War itself, to the inescapable ravages of contending armies, to the Allied intervention and blockade, to the unavoidable scarcity of fuel and raw materials, or to the difficulties of feeding the hungry and healing the sick in the midst of famine and pestilence. All the suffering and hardship, rather, was laid at the door of the Bolshevik regime: "Communist rule has reduced all of Russia to unprecedented poverty, hunger, cold, and other privations. The factories and mills are closed, the railways on the verge of breakdown. The countryside has been fleeced to the bone.

[14] *Pravda o Kronshtadte*, p. 132.
[15] *Ibid.*, p. 31.

We have no bread, no cattle, no tools to work the land. We have no clothing, no shoes, no fuel. The workers are hungry and cold. The peasants and townsfolk have lost all hope for an improvement of their lives. Day by day they come closer to death. The Communist betrayers have reduced you to all this."[16]

The sailors, like the peasants from whom most of them sprang, severely condemned the "new serfdom" of the Bolshevik regime, particularly the seizure of food by armed collection detachments. "The peasant was right," declared the Kronstadt *Izvestiia*, "who told the Eighth Congress of Soviets: 'Everything is just fine—the land is ours but the grain is yours, the water ours but the fish yours, the forests ours but the wood yours.' "[17] Any villagers who balked at the government's depredations, the journal added, were denounced as "kulaks" and "enemies of the people," regardless of how impoverished and desperate they might be. *Izvestiia* further decried the establishment of state farms on some of the best gentry land, a practice which not only deprived the peasants of what they considered their rightful possession but also entailed the use of hired labor as in tsarist times. This, as the insurgents saw it, violated the essential spirit of the revolution, which had abolished "wage slavery" and exploitation in every form. *Izvestiia* upheld the right of the peasants to carry on small-scale cultivation by their own efforts and for their own benefit. State farms were nothing but "the estates of the new landlord—the state. This is what the peasants have received from the socialism of the Bolsheviks, instead of the free use of their newly won lands. In exchange for requisitioned grain and confiscated cows and horses, they got Cheka raids and firing squads. A

[16] *Ibid.*, pp. 164-65.

[17] *Ibid.*, pp. 82-84, 163. No record of this statement appears in the official minutes of the Congress, but it could have been made at a closed session, such as the one discussed in Chapter 1 which Lenin attended.

fine system of exchange in a workers' state—lead and bayonets for bread!"[18]

In industry, by the same token, the rebels wanted freedom for the workers and small handicrafts producers to control their own destiny and enjoy the products of their labor. They did not, however, favor "workers' control,"· as is often supposed. The mere supervision of production by local factory committees was, as they saw it, at once inadequate and inefficient: inadequate because, instead of allowing the workers to run the factories themselves, it left the former managers and technicians in key positions of responsibility; and inefficient because it did not provide for necessary coordination with other enterprises. Nor did they approve of the nationalization of industry with state control of production by appointed managers and technical specialists. "Having disorganized production under 'workers' control,'" declared the Kronstadt *Izvestiia*, "the Bolsheviks proceeded to nationalize the factories and shops. From a slave of the capitalist the worker was transformed into a slave of the state enterprises." At the same time, the trade unions had become a "centralized Communist edifice," reduced to useless paperwork instead of running the factories and assisting in the educational and cultural advancement of the workers. Only new elections could convert the unions into free institutions for the "broad self-determination" of the workers. As for artisans and craftsmen, they should be given complete freedom provided they did not employ hired labor. "Revolutionary Kronstadt," proclaimed the Provisional Committee, "is fighting for a different kind of socialism, for a Soviet Republic of the toilers, in which the producer himself will be the sole master and can dispose of his products as he sees fit."[19]

The dominant note of the rebellion, then, was disillusionment with Communist rule. The Bolsheviks, said the rebel

[18] *Ibid.*, pp. 172-74.   [19] *Ibid.*, pp. 92, 173-74.

Izvestiia, were only afraid of losing power, and so deemed "every means permissible—slander, violence, deceit, murder, vengeance upon the families of the rebels."[20] The meaning of the revolution had been caricatured, the workers and peasants subdued, the whole country silenced by the party and its secret police, the prisons filled not with counterrevolutionaries but with laborers and intellectuals. "In place of the old regime," lamented *Izvestiia*, "a new regime of arbitrariness, insolence, favoritism, theft, and speculation has been established, a terrible regime in which one must hold out one's hand to the authorities for every piece of bread, for every button, a regime in which one does not belong even to oneself, where one cannot dispose of one's labor, a regime of slavery and degradation. . . . Soviet Russia has become an all-Russian concentration camp."[21]

What, then, was to be done? How could the revolution be returned to its original path? Until March 8, when the Bolsheviks launched their initial assault, the insurgents continued to hope for peaceful reform. Convinced of the righteousness of their cause, they were confident of gaining the support of the whole country—and Petrograd in particular —in forcing the government to grant political and economic concessions. The Communist attack, however, marked a new phase in the rebellion. All chance of negotiation and compromise came to an abrupt end. Violence remained the only course open to both sides. On March 8 the sailors proclaimed a new slogan: they appealed to the entire Russian population to join them in a "third revolution" to finish the job begun in February and October 1917: "The workers and peasants steadfastly march forward, leaving behind them both the Constituent Assembly, with its bourgeois regime, and the dictatorship of the Communist party,

[20] *Ibid.*, p. 83. The last phrase, of course, is a reference to the seizure of hostages in Petrograd.
[21] *Ibid.*, pp. 128, 165.

with its Cheka and its state capitalism, whose hangman's noose encircles the necks of the laboring masses and threatens to strangle them to death. . . . Here in Kronstadt has been laid the first stone of the third revolution, striking the last fetters from the laboring masses and opening a broad new road for socialist creativity."[22]

REPEATED attempts have been made by Western as well as Soviet historians to trace the Kronstadt program to one or another of the anti-Bolshevik parties of the Left. To what extent are such comparisons valid? On a number of points the rebel demands did indeed coincide with those of the left-wing political opposition. Mensheviks, Socialist Revolutionaries, and anarchists had all been protesting against the Bolshevik monopoly of power and the system of War Communism. They had all been calling for free soviets and trade unions, for civil liberties for workers and peasants, and for an end to the terror and the release of socialists and anarchists under arrest. And the demand for a coalition government in which all socialist parties would be represented had been made by SR's and Mensheviks as early as October 1917—to which even an outspoken group of Bolsheviks had lent their support: "We take the stand that it is necessary to form a socialist government of all parties in the Soviet. We assert that other than this there is only one path: the preservation of a purely Bolshevik government by means of political terror. We cannot and will not accept this. We see that this will lead . . . to the establishment of an irrespon-

[22] *Ibid.*, pp. 83-84. The hopes and demands of the rebels, summarized above, are most clearly set forth in three documents: the *Petropavlovsk* resolution of February 28-March 1, and two long editorials in the rebel journal, "What We Are Fighting For," published on March 8, and "Socialism in Quotation Marks," which appeared in the very last issue of March 16. Taken together, these documents present the fullest and most eloquent statement of the Kronstadt program. The *Petropavlovsk* resolution is printed in Chapter 2, and the two editorials appear in the Appendixes.

sible regime and to the ruin of the revolution and the country."[23]

The rebels shared one notable feature with the Socialist Revolutionaries, namely an overriding preoccupation with the needs of the peasant and small producer and a corresponding lack of concern for the complexities of large-scale industry. But they refused, on the other hand, to endorse the central SR demand for the restoration of the Constituent Assembly or to accept the assistance offered them by the respected SR leader Victor Chernov. From this alone it is plain that the SR's did not exert a dominant influence within the rebel movement. The same was true of the Mensheviks. The Mensheviks, to be sure, had been the foremost champions of the soviets since their first appearance in 1905, and the Kronstadt idea of a nonpartisan conference of workers, soldiers, and sailors recalls a similar proposal by the Menshevik leader Akselrod, which had formed the theoretical basis for the establishment of the original Petersburg Soviet. Nevertheless, Menshevik influence had never been very great in Kronstadt, a traditional stronghold of the extreme Left. A number of active Mensheviks were to be found among the artisans and workingmen in the town and shipyards (the two members of the Revolutionary Committee whom Soviet sources identify as Mensheviks, Valk and Romanenko, were both workmen), yet the Kronstadt program paid comparatively little attention to questions affecting the industrial proletariat. Moreover, the number of Mensheviks among the sailors—the backbone of the insurrection—was negligible. It is also worth noting that throughout the course of the revolt the Menshevik leadership in Petrograd and abroad refrained from endorsing the overthrow of the Bolsheviks by force of arms.

The influence of the anarchists, by contrast, had always been fairly strong within the fleet, and they have sometimes

[23] Daniels, *The Conscience of the Revolution*, p. 66.

been charged with inspiring the uprising. But this is largely untrue. For one thing, the most prominent Kronstadt anarchists of recent years were no longer on the scene: Anatoli Zhelezniakov, the fierce young sailor who had dispersed the Constituent Assembly, had been killed in action against the Whites;[24] I. S. Bleikhman, a popular Anchor Square orator in 1917, had died a few months before the revolt; and his comrade Efim Yarchuk, a leading figure in the Kronstadt Soviet during the revolution, was now in Moscow, and, when not in prison, was kept under close watch by the Cheka. Yarchuk's own history of Kronstadt assigns no outstanding role to the anarchists in 1921, nor does any other anarchist source of the period. A thorough listing of anarchists who died in the Civil War or fell victim to Soviet persecution during the early 1920's includes Zhelezniakov, Yarchuk, and Bleikhman but no other Kronstadters.[25] Only one member of the Provisional Revolutionary Committee (Perepelkin) has ever been linked with the anarchists, and then only indirectly. Moreover, the journal of the movement mentions the anarchists only once, when publishing the text of the *Petropavlovsk* manifesto, which demanded "freedom of speech and press for workers and peasants, anarchists and left-wing socialist parties."[26]

Still, the spirit of anarchism, so powerful in Kronstadt during 1917, had by no means dissipated. Perepelkin may

[24] Avrich, *The Russian Anarchists*, p. 198. A statue of Zhelezniakov stands today in the city of Kronstadt: *Kronshtadt: kratkii putevoditel'*, p. 116.

[25] *Goneniia na anarkhizm v Sovetskoi Rossii*, Berlin, 1922.

[26] Dan, *Dva goda skitanii*, p. 156; *Pravda o Kronshtadte*, p. 46. Cf. Katkov, "The Kronstadt Rising," *St. Antony's Papers*, No. 6, pp. 59-62. According to the prominent anarchist Volin (*La Révolution inconnue*, pp. 469-70), the Provisional Revolutionary Committee sent emissaries to Petrograd to bring Yarchuk and himself to Kronstadt to assist in the rebellion, unaware that they had been imprisoned by the Bolsheviks. Volin adds that Petrichenko had anarchist sympathies, but I have found no evidence to confirm these claims.

have been the only reputed anarchist among the rebel leaders, but as coauthor of the *Petropavlovsk* resolution and head of agitation and propaganda, he was in a good position to propagate his libertarian views. Some of the key slogans of the movement—"free soviets," "third revolution," "Down with the commissarocracy"—had been anarchist slogans during the Civil War, and "All power to the soviets but not the parties" also had an anarchist ring. On the other hand, most anarchists would have balked at any appeal for "power," and the sailors, for their part, never called for the complete elimination of the state, a central plank in any anarchist platform.

In any case, anarchists throughout Russia were elated by the rising. They hailed Kronstadt as "the Second Paris Commune,"[27] and angrily denounced the government for sending troops against it. At the height of the insurrection, an anarchist leaflet appeared in the streets of Petrograd; it criticized the population for turning its back on the rebels, for remaining silent while the thunder of artillery sounded in the Finnish Gulf. The sailors have risen for you, the people of Petrograd, the leaflet declared. You must shake off your lethargy and join the struggle against the Communist dictatorship, after which anarchism will prevail.[28] Other anarchists, meanwhile, such as Berkman and Goldman, were vainly seeking to mediate the conflict and avert a bloodbath.

The rebellion, in short, was neither inspired nor engineered by any single party or group. Its participants were radicals of various stripes—SR's, Mensheviks, anarchists, rank-and-file Communists—who possessed no systematic ideology nor any carefully laid plan of action. Their credo, compounded of elements from several revolutionary strains, was vague and ill-defined, more a list of grievances, an outcry of protest against misery and oppression, than a coherent

[27] Avrich, *The Russian Anarchists*, p. 230.
[28] Kornatovskii, ed., *Kronshtadtskii miatezh*, pp. 164-66

and constructive program. In place of specific proposals, particularly in agriculture and industry, the insurgents preferred to rely on what Kropotkin called "the creative spirit of the masses," operating through freely elected soviets.

Their ideology, perhaps, may best be described as a kind of anarcho-populism, whose deepest urge was to realize the old *Narodnik* program of "land and liberty" and "the will of the people," the ancient dream of a loose-knit federation of autonomous communes in which peasants and workers would live in harmonious cooperation, with full economic and political liberty organized from below. The political group closest to the rebels in temperament and outlook were the SR Maximalists, a tiny ultra-militant offshoot of the Socialist Revolutionary party, occupying a place in the revolutionary spectrum between the Left SR's and the anarchists while sharing elements of both. On nearly every important point the Kronstadt program, as set forth in the rebel *Izvestiia*, coincided with that of the Maximalists, lending credence to the Soviet claim that the editor of the journal was a Maximalist (Lamanov by name).[29] The Maximalists preached a doctrine of total revolution. They opposed the restoration of the Constituent Assembly and called instead for a "toilers' soviet republic" founded on freely elected soviets, with a minimum of central state authority. Politically, this was identical with the objective of the Kronstadters, and "Power to the soviets but not the parties" had originally been a Maximalist rallying-cry.

The parallels in the economic sphere are no less striking. In agriculture the Maximalists denounced grain requisitioning and the establishment of state farms, demanding that all the land be turned over to the peasants for their unhindered

---

[29] Slepkov, *Kronshtadtskii miatezh*, p. 33; Pukhov, *Kronshtadtskii miatezh*, p. 77. Although there is no mention of him in the sources for the 1921 rebellion, A. Lamanov was in fact an active Maximalist agitator during the Revolution of 1917.

use. In industry they rejected workers' control over bourgeois administrators in favor of the "social organization of production and its systematic direction by representatives of the toiling people." For the Maximalists, as for the rebels, this did not mean the nationalization of the factories and a centralized system of state management; on the contrary, they warned repeatedly that centralization leads directly to "bureaucratism," reducing the laborer to a mere cog in a vast impersonal machine. "Not state management and workers' control, but workers' management and state control" was their motto, with the government performing the tasks of planning and coordination. It was essential, in short, to transfer the means of production to the people who used them. This was the message of every Maximalist slogan: "All land to the peasants," "All factories to the workers," "All bread and products to the toilers."[30]

THAT the mentality of the rebellion was essentially anarcho-populist is clear from the language and myths of its participants. Propaganda in Kronstadt was conducted by men whose emotions and rhetoric were close to the peasants' and workers' own feelings. Expressed in simple slogans and catchphrases, it possessed a rough folk eloquence which captured the mood of the people at large. Rebel agitators wrote and spoke (as an interviewer later noted)[31] in a homespun language free of Marxist jargon and foreign-sounding expressions. Eschewing the word "proletariat," they called, in true populist fashion, for a society in which all the "toilers"—peasants, workers, and the "toiling intelligentsia"—would play a dominant role. They were inclined to speak of a "social" rather than a

[30] Soiuz S-R Maksimalistov, *Trudovaia sovetskaia respublika*, Moscow, 1918, and *O rabochem kontrole*, Moscow, 1918; G. Nestroev, *Maksimalizm i bol'shevizm*, Moscow, 1919; *Maksimalist*, No. 2, August 25, 1918, pp. 5-9 and No. 16, April 15, 1921, pp. 15-16.

[31] "Beseda s Kronshtadtsami," *Revoliutsionnaia Rossiia*, 1921, No. 8, pp. 6-8.

"socialist" revolution, viewing class conflict not in the narrow sense of industrial workers versus bourgeoisie, but in the traditional *Narodnik* sense of the laboring masses as a whole pitted against all who throve on their misery and exploitation, including politicians and bureaucrats as well as landlords and capitalists. Western ideologies—Marxism and liberalism alike—had little place in their mental outlook. Their distrust of parliamentary government was deeply rooted in the populist and anarchist heritage: Herzen, Lavrov, and Bakunin had all rejected parliament as a corrupt and alien institution, a "talking-shop" to safeguard the interests of the upper and middle classes against the claims of the rejected and outcast, for whom the path to salvation lay in local self-rule based on the traditional Russian commune.

The Kronstadters, moreover, exhibited a powerful streak of Slavic nationalism, which, in view of their predominantly peasant origins, is not surprising. Although self-proclaimed internationalists, the sailors showed little concern for the worldwide revolutionary movement. Their talk, rather, centered on the Russian people and their destiny, and their theme of a "third revolution" bears a messianic quality akin to the "third Rome" doctrine of sixteenth-century Muscovy: "The autocracy has fallen. The Constituent Assembly has departed to the region of the damned. The commissarocracy is crumbling. The time has come for the true power of the toilers, the power of the soviets."[32] At times, however, their peasant nativism was curiously mingled with elements from the European revolutionary tradition, as when an Orthodox funeral ceremony for the fallen rebels, performed in the Seamen's Cathedral on Anchor Square, ended with the strains of the "Marseillaise."[33] But the populist character of the move-

[32] *Pravda o Kronshtadte*, p. 128. The "third Rome" doctrine proclaimed: "Two Romes have fallen, but the third stands, and a fourth there will not be."

[33] Petrichenko, *Pravda o Kronshtadtskikh sobytiiakh*, p. 18.

ment predominated, manifesting itself not only in the religious services of the participants and in their social creed, but also in the traditional folk myths which run like scarlet threads through the ideological fabric of the rebellion.

One such myth, deeply embedded in peasant psychology, was that of the centralized state as an artificial body forcibly grafted upon Russian society, an alien growth weighing heavily on the people and responsible for their suffering. Popular hatred for the government and its functionaries had deep roots in Russian history, dating back to the Cossack and peasant revolts of the seventeenth and eighteenth centuries.[34] For Stenka Razin and Pugachev the ruling gentry did not belong to the Russian folk, the *narod*, but formed a class apart, a breed of parasites sucking the blood of the peasants. Theirs was a Manichaean vision in which the forces of good, embodied in the common people, were pitted against the forces of evil, embodied in the state and its officials. The sailors of Kronstadt were direct descendants of these primitive rebels, heirs to the tradition of spontaneous revolt (*buntarstvo*) against bureaucratic despotism. They were as ready to fight the "commissars and bureaucrats" as Razin and Pugachev had been to fight the "boyars and officials." The misdeeds of the nobility became the misdeeds of the new ruling stratum, the Communist party, to which all popular misfortunes— from famine and civil war to slavery and exploitation—were attributed.

This age-old sense of alienation from state officialdom was succinctly expressed in the title of a rebel editorial, "We and They," published immediately after the first Bolshevik assault across the ice. It was also expressed in the term "commissarocracy," the sailors' favorite epithet for the Soviet regime: "Lenin said, 'Communism is Soviet power plus electrification.' But the people are convinced that the Bolshe-

---

[34] These myths will be treated at length in a separate work, *Russian Rebels, 1600-1800*, now in progress.

vik form of Communism is commissarocracy plus firing squads."[35] Bolshevik officialdom was assailed as a new privileged caste of self-seekers who enjoyed higher pay, larger food rations, and warmer living quarters than the rest of the people. Recall the attacks on Kalinin, who was driven from Anchor Square with shouts of "You manage to keep warm enough" and "Look at all the jobs you've got—I'll bet they bring you plenty." Again and again the party officials were accused of stealing the fruits of the revolution and imposing a new form of slavery over the "body and soul" of Russia. "Such is the shining kingdom of socialism to which the dictatorship of the Communist party has brought us," complained the last number of the rebel *Izvestiia*. "We have obtained state socialism with soviets of functionaries who vote obediently according to the dictates of the party committee and its infallible commissars. The slogan 'He who does not work shall not eat' has been twisted by the new 'soviet' order into 'Everything for the commissars.' For the workers and peasants and laboring intelligentsia there remains only cheerless and unremitting toil in a prison environment."[36]

Not unexpectedly, the principal targets of Kronstadt's wrath were Zinoviev and Trotsky, who "sit in their soft armchairs in the lighted rooms of tsarist palaces and consider how best to spill the blood of the insurgents."[37] Zinoviev incurred the sailors' loathing as the party boss of Petrograd who had suppressed the striking workers and who now stooped to taking their own families as hostages. But the *bête noire* of rebel fury was Trotsky. Commissar for War and chairman of the Revolutionary War Council, Trotsky was responsible for the harsh ultimatum of March 5 and for ordering the attack which followed three days later. A whole ar-

---

[35] *Pravda o Kronshtadte*, pp. 79-80, 90. For Lenin's speech (to the Eighth Congress of Soviets) see *Vos'moi vserossiiskii s"ezd sovetov*, p. 30.

[36] *Pravda o Kronshtadte*, pp. 172-74.

[37] *Ibid.*, p. 106.

senal of epithets was aimed at him: "bloody Field Marshal Trotsky," "this reincarnation of Trepov," "Maliuta Skuratov . . . head of the Communist *oprichnina*," "the evil genius of Russia" who "like a hawk swoops down on our heroic city," a monster of tyranny "standing knee-deep in the blood of the workers." "Listen Trotsky," declared the Kronstadt *Izvestiia* on March 9, "the leaders of the Third Revolution are defending the true power of the soviets against the outrages of the commissars."[38]

The rebels, true to their populist mentality, drew a sharp line between Trotsky and Zinoviev on the one hand and Lenin on the other—between the traitorous boyars and the tsar from whom they concealed the people's suffering. Traditionally, the Russian lower classes had turned their anger not against the ruler himself, whom they venerated as their anointed father, but against his corrupt and scheming advisors, in whom they saw the embodiment of all that was pernicious and evil. It was not the remote autocrat who oppressed the poor: "God is high in the heavens," went the old proverb, "and the tsar is far away." Rather, it was the landlord and official on the spot who fleeced the peasants and townsfolk, keeping them in misery and degradation.

Interestingly enough, Lenin's behavior in the Kronstadt rebellion tended to support this image. During the first week, while Trotsky and Zinoviev were on the scene in Petrograd, issuing threats and preparing an offensive against the insurgents, Lenin remained in Moscow, involving himself only to the extent of signing the order of March 2 which outlawed Kozlovsky and his alleged accomplices. Not once was his name mentioned in the Kronstadt newspaper, which, in characteristic language, was busy denouncing the "gendarmes"

[38] *Ibid.*, pp. 80-82, 91, 120. Trepov was a notorious chief of police under Nicholas II. Maliuta Skuratov was the murderous head of Ivan the Terrible's secret police, the *oprichniki*, who conducted a reign of terror in the sixteenth century.

Trotsky and Zinoviev for "concealing the truth" from the people.[39] On March 8, however, at the opening session of the Tenth Party Congress, Lenin emerged from the background and condemned the revolt as the work of White Guard generals and of petty-bourgeois elements of the population. After this speech the Kronstadt Revolutionary Committee criticized him for the first time. The peasants and workers, said the rebel *Izvestiia*, had "never believed a word of Trotsky and Zinoviev" but had not expected Lenin to associate himself with their "hypocrisy." A poem in *Izvestiia* wryly spoke of him as "Tsar Lenin," and the journal now denounced "the firm of Lenin, Trotsky, and Co." where earlier it had spoken only of "bloodthirsty Trotsky and Co."[40]

Yet even now Lenin was treated with a degree of sympathy which set him apart from his associates. According to the rebel *Izvestiia* of March 14, Lenin had told his colleagues during a recent discussion of the trade union question: "All of this bores me to death. Even without my illness I would be glad to throw it all up and flee no matter where." "But," commented *Izvestiia*, "Lenin's cohorts would not let him flee. He is their prisoner, and he must utter slanders just as they do."[41] Here, in purest form, we have the ancient legend of the benevolent tsar as a helpless captive of his treacherous boyars. Lenin continued to be venerated as something of a father-figure. Accordingly, when portraits of Trotsky and other Bolshevik leaders were torn from Kronstadt's office walls, those of Lenin were allowed to remain.[42] The same attitude persisted even after the rebellion had been drowned in blood. In a Finnish internment camp, Yakovenko, deputy chairman of the Provisional Revolutionary Committee, dis-

[39] *Ibid.*, p. 158.

[40] *Ibid.*, pp. 89, 162, 179.

[41] *Ibid.*, pp. 150-52. Cf. Katkov, "The Kronstadt Rising," *St. Antony's Papers*, No. 6, pp. 49-50.

[42] *Za Narodnoe Delo*, March 17, 1921; *Novaia Russkaia Zhizn'*, March 19, 1921.

tinguished sharply between Lenin and his colleagues. A bearded sailor, tall and powerfully built, Yakovenko had fought on the Bolshevik side in the October Revolution and was incensed at the party's betrayal of its ideals and promises. His face red with anger, he lashed out at "murderer Trotsky" and "scoundrel Zinoviev." "I respect Lenin," he said. "But Trotsky and Zinoviev pull him along with them. I'd like to take care of those two with my own hands."[43]

Trotsky in particular was the living symbol of War Communism, of everything the sailors had rebelled against. His name was associated with centralization and militarization, with iron discipline and regimentation. On the trade union question he had taken a hard and dogmatic line, in contrast to Lenin's tactful and conciliatory approach. He had small regard for the peasantry as a revolutionary force, while Lenin had always realized that the cooperation of the rural population was essential if power were to be won and maintained, an attitude which his orthodox contemporaries scorned as a survival of the *Narodnik* heresy. Where Trotsky was intolerant, flamboyant, and supercilious, where he exhibited what Lenin in his famous "Testament" was to call a "too far-reaching self-confidence," Lenin himself was esteemed for his simple habits of life and lack of personal pretension.

Lenin, moreover, was a Great Russian from the middle Volga, the heart of peasant Russia. Frugal, unostentatious, austere, he was looked upon as a simple son of Russia who shared the people's anxieties and was accessible to them in their time of suffering. Trotsky and Zinoviev, by contrast, were of Jewish origin and identified with the internationalist wing of the Communist movement rather than with Russia itself. Zinoviev, in fact, was president of the Comintern. And Trotsky, according to the Kronstadt Revolutionary Committee, was responsible during the Civil War for the death of thousands of innocent people "of a nationality different from

[43] *Revoliutsionnaia Rossiia*, 1921, No. 8, p. 6.

his own."[44] Although the rebels, in the same breath, denied any anti-Semitic prejudice, there is no question that feelings against the Jews ran high among the Baltic sailors, many of whom came from the Ukraine and the western borderlands, the classic regions of virulent anti-Semitism in Russia. For men of their peasant and working-class background, the Jews were a customary scapegoat in times of hardship and distress. Traditional nativism, moreover, led them to distrust "alien" elements in their midst, and, the revolution having eliminated the landlords and capitalists, their hostility was now directed against the Communists and Jews, whom they tended to identify with one another.

The sailors, incidentally, were well aware of Trotsky's and Zinoviev's Jewish origins, if only from the flood of anti-Semitic propaganda released by the Whites during the Civil War in an effort to link Communism with a Jewish conspiracy. "Bronstein (Trotsky), Apfelbaum (Zinoviev), Rosenfeld (Kamenev), Steinberg—all of them are alike unto thousands of other true sons of Israel," ran a White leaflet accusing the Jewish Bolsheviks of plotting to take over the world.[45] That fantasies like this circulated within the Baltic Fleet is evident from the memoirs of a seaman stationed at the Petrograd naval base at the time of the Kronstadt rising.[46] In a particularly vicious passage he attacks the Bolshevik regime as the "first Jewish Republic"; and the "wicked boyar" theme, so prominent in Russian popular myth, clearly emerges when he labels the Jews a new "privileged class," a class of "Soviet princes." The author reserves his worst venom for Trotsky and Zinoviev (or Bronstein and Apfelbaum, as he often refers to them), calling the government ultimatum to Kronstadt "the ultimatum of the Jew Trotsky." These sentiments, he

[44] "Interv'iu s chlenami Vremennogo Revoliutsionnogo Komiteta," manuscript, Hoover Library.

[45] Norman Cohn, *Warrant for Genocide*, London, 1967, p. 120.

[46] "K vospominaniiam matrosa sluzhby 1914 goda," manuscript, Columbia Russian Archive.

asserts, were widely shared by his fellow sailors, who were convinced that the Jews and not the Russian peasants and workers were the real beneficiaries of the revolution: Jews held the leading posts within the Communist party and Soviet state; they infested every government office, especially the Food Commissariat, seeing to it that their fellow Jews did not go hungry; and even the roadblock detachments— that hated institution—though 90 percent manned by true Russians, were almost always commanded by Jews. Such beliefs, no doubt, were as prevalent in Kronstadt as in Petrograd, if not more so. Witness the appeal of Vershinin, a member of the Revolutionary Committee, when he came out on the ice on March 8 to parley with a Soviet detachment: "Enough of your 'hoorahs,' and join with us to beat the Jews. It's their cursed domination that we workers and peasants have had to endure."[47]

ALTHOUGH the rebels had only contempt for Communist officialdom, they were not hostile towards the rank and file of the party or to the ideals of Communism as such. True, some of the members of the Provisional Revolutionary Committee, when interviewed afterwards in Finland, spoke with bitterness of the Communists who "took away the people's rights."[48] But their antagonism had been sharpened by the bloody suppression of the revolt, and in any case they had the party's leadership in mind rather than its ordinary adherents. Indeed, more than a few insurgents, including Petrichenko and Kilgast, the chairman and secretary of the Revolutionary Committee, were themselves former Communists who felt that the ideals of the revolution had been contaminated and who were bent on restoring their original purity. Characteristic of their thought was the assertion of one sailor, still a party member, that Russia had been transformed

---

[47] Kornatovskii, ed., *Kronshtadtskii miatezh*, pp. 95-96.
[48] *Revoliutsionnaia Rossiia*, 1921, No. 8, pp. 6-8.

into a "frightful swamp" by a "tiny circle of Communist bureaucrats, who, beneath the Communist mask, have built themselves a cozy nest in our republic."[49]

For all their animosity towards the Bolshevik hierarchy, the sailors never called for the disbandment of the party or its exclusion from a role in Russian government and society. "Soviets without Communists" was not, as is often maintained by both Soviet and non-Soviet writers, a Kronstadt slogan. Such a slogan did exist: it had been trumpeted by peasant bands in Siberia during the Civil War, and Makhno's partisans in the south had similarly declared themselves "For the soviets but against the Communists."[50] But the sailors never appropriated these watchwords. That they did so is a legend which seems to have originated with the exiled Kadet leader Miliukov, who in Paris summed up the aims of the insurgents in the slogans "Soviets instead of Bolsheviks" (*Sovety vmesto Bol'shevikov*) and "Down with the Bolsheviks, long live the soviets." The sailors, he wrote, wanted power to pass from the existing one-party dictatorship to a coalition of socialists and nonparty radicals, acting through soviets from which the Communists had been banished. Such an arrangement, he said, would leave ample room for a restoration of the Constituent Assembly on the national level.[51] This, however, was a far from accurate description of the Kronstadt program, which explicitly rejected the Constituent Assembly and which did allow a place for the Bolsheviks in the soviets, alongside the other left-wing political organizations. In practice, it is true, Communists were excluded from the local *revtroiki* established during the insurrection, but they participated in strength in the elected conference of delegates, which was the closest thing Kronstadt ever had to the free soviets of its dreams.

[49] *Pravda o Kronshtadte*, p. 66.
[50] Trifonov, *Klassy i klassovaia bor'ba v SSSR*, pp. 106-107.
[51] *Poslednie Novosti*, March 11, 1921.

The object of the insurgents, then, was not to eliminate Communism outright, but to reform it, to purge it of the dictatorial and bureaucratic tendencies which had been thrown into relief during the Civil War. In this respect, Kronstadt resembled the opposition movements within the party —the "fleet opposition," the Democratic Centralists, and the Workers' Opposition—with which it shared similar discontents and a similar outlook of left-wing idealism. Like the "fleet opposition," to which some of them had undoubtedly belonged, the rebels objected to the heavy-handed and arbitrary methods of the political commissars in their midst. Like the Democratic Centralists, they opposed the increasing authoritarianism of the Bolshevik leadership and called for "democratization" both of the party and of the soviets. And like the Workers' Opposition, they protested against the "militarization" of labor, a term embracing one-man management and iron discipline in the factories, the subjugation of the trade unions, and the return of "bourgeois specialists" to their former position of authority. Finally, in common with all the opposition groups, the Kronstadters deplored the growing isolation of the party from the people and attacked the Bolshevik leaders for violating the essential spirit of the revolution—for sacrificing its democratic and egalitarian ideals on the altar of power and expediency.[52]

These parallels, however, must not be pushed too far. For one thing, where the rebels displayed a close affinity for the peasantry, both the Workers' Opposition and the Democratic centralists were urban groups made up of factory workers and intellectuals who paid little attention to the needs of the peasants. Even more important, in sharp contrast to the rebels, they sought to preserve the Bolshevik monopoly of power, condoning the use of terror wherever necessary to accomplish this. They limited their demands to internal party

[52] Cf. Daniels, *The Conscience of the Revolution*, pp. 145-46; and Schapiro, *The Origin of the Communist Autocracy*, pp. 305-306.

reform, and never advocated sharing political authority with the other socialist organizations. Still, the points of similarity between the Kronstadt program and their own were a source of embarrassment to the opposition leaders, and they bent over backwards to dissociate themselves from the mutineers. This was particularly true of the Workers' Opposition, whose spokesmen at the Tenth Party Congress, Shliapnikov and Kollontai, angrily disavowed any connection with the uprising and attributed it to the influence of "petty-bourgeois anarchist spontaneity," echoing Lenin's remarks at the opening session. Challenged from the floor, Kollontai declared that the Workers' Oppositionists were among the first volunteers to go to the front and fight the rebels.[53] A third leader, Yuri Lutovinov, was in Berlin at the time of the revolt, serving as deputy chief of the Soviet trade delegation. In a public interview he denounced the insurgents, repeating the official story of a White Guard plot assisted by Menshevik and SR counterrevolutionaries. If the government had delayed using force to crush the rebellion, he said, it was only to spare the civilian population of the city, but "the liquidation of the Kronstadt adventure is a matter of an extremely short time."[54]

Meanwhile, in Kronstadt itself, the local Communist organization had been infected by the virus of opposition. The rebellion, as Trotsky admitted, "attracted into its ranks no small number of Bolsheviks," some for fear of reprisal but most out of genuine sympathy with the rebel program. More precisely, Trotsky estimated that 30 percent of the Kronstadt Communists took an active part in the revolt while 40 percent occupied a "neutral position."[55] This, of course, was merely the climax of a great wave of defections which had reduced

[53] *Desiatyi s"ezd RKP(b)*, pp. 72, 300.
[54] "Beseda s Iu. Kh. Lutovinovym," *Novyi Mir*, March 13, 1921.
[55] Leon Trotsky, *The Revolution Betrayed*, New York, 1937, p. 96; *Desiatyi s"ezd RKP(b)*, p. 253.

party membership from 4,000 to 2,000 between September 1920 and March 1921, a dramatic index of the rebellious mood which had set in at the end of the Civil War. During the course of the uprising what remained of the Kronstadt party organization quickly fell to pieces: some 500 members resigned, not to mention nearly 300 candidates, while the remainder, as one of them testified, were badly demoralized and responded to the revolt with wavering and indecision.[56]

The rising tide of disaffection was reflected in the long lists of resignations from the party, published from time to time in the Kronstadt *Izvestiia*. In two issues alone more than 200 names filled the journal's columns. A leading cause of these defections was the Bolshevik assault of March 7 to 8. "I shudder to think," wrote a Kronstadt schoolmistress after the first bombardment, "that I may be considered an accomplice in spilling the blood of innocent victims. I feel that I can no longer believe in and propagate that which has disgraced itself by this savage act. Therefore, with the first shot, I have ceased to regard myself as a candidate member of the Communist party."[57] Thereafter, the heavier the cannonade from the Bolshevik forts on the mainland, the greater the exodus of party members in Kronstadt. Each day the pages of the rebel *Izvestiia* carried letters from local Communist groups, condemning the government for its use of violence and endorsing the countermeasures of the Revolutionary Committee. Those who publicly announced their withdrawal from the party did not renounce the ideals of Communism but attacked the party's leaders for perverting those ideals for their own interests. A Kronstadt schoolmaster, for example, decried the influx of careerists into the party who had "sullied with filth the beautiful idea of Communism."[58] Another letter came from a Red Commander in the Kronstadt

[56] Kornatovskii, ed., *Kronshtadtskii miatezh*, pp. 13-15, 86; Pukhov, *Kronshtadtskii miatezh*, pp. 50, 95.

[57] *Pravda o Kronshtadte*, p. 108.

[58] *Ibid.*, p. 133.

garrison, the son of a Populist who had been condemned to exile in the celebrated "Trial of the 193" during the 1870's. "I have come to realize," he wrote, "that the policies of the Communist party have led the country into a blind alley from which there is no exit. The party has become bureaucratized. . . . It refuses to listen to the voice of the masses, on whom it wishes to impose its will. . . . Only freedom of speech and greater opportunity to participate in the reconstruction of the country by means of revised election procedures can bring our country out of its lethargy. . . . I refuse henceforth to consider myself a member of the Russian Communist party. I wholly approve of the resolution passed by the citywide meeting on March 1, and I hereby place my energies and abilities [at the disposal of the Revolutionary Committee]."[59]

Throughout the rebellion there was no serious opposition from the Kronstadt Communist organization. On March 2 a band of party loyalists, some 200 strong, met at the Higher Party School and armed themselves against the rebels but soon decided that the situation was hopeless and fled across the ice to Krasnaya Gorka.[60] During the early stages other party stalwarts quit the island for the mainland or went to the surrounding forts in a vain attempt to rouse them against the insurgents. Meanwhile, the Revolutionary Committee began to take the principal Bolshevik leaders into custody. The first to be arrested—at the March 2 conference in the House of Education—were Kuzmin, commissar of the fleet; Vasiliev, chairman of the defunct Soviet; and Korshunov, commissar of the Kronstadt battleship squadron. The following day E. I. Batis, head of *Pubalt*, was seized by a rebel patrol while making his way across the ice to Fort Totleben.[61] Among the

[59] *Ibid.*, p. 59.
[60] Kornatovskii, ed., *Kronshtadtskii miatezh*, p. 31; Petrichenko, *Pravda o Kronshtadtskikh sobytiiakh*, p. 8.
[61] *Pravda o Kronshtadte*, p. 58.

others to be imprisoned was Dr. L. A. Bregman, a veteran Kronstadt Bolshevik and secretary of the district party committee.

A number of officials avoided arrest by collaborating with the rebels. On March 2 a "Provisional Bureau of the Kronstadt Organization of the Russian Communist Party" was formed by three local Bolsheviks, Ia. Ilyin, the commissar of food supply, F. Pervushin, a former leader of the Soviet, and A. Kabanov, chairman of Kronstadt's Trade Union Council. The Bureau issued a declaration on March 4, recognizing the need for new elections to the soviets and calling on all Kronstadt Communists to remain on the job and obey the orders of the Revolutionary Committee. It warned, moreover, against "malicious rumors," concocted by Entente agents, to the effect that Communists were preparing to overthrow the rebellion or, on the other hand, that party members would be shot by the insurgents.[62] Ilyin's cooperation, as it turned out, was a deception, an effort to gain time until help could come from the mainland. On the sly, he was telephoning reports on Kronstadt's food supply to his superiors at Krasnaya Gorka. The ruse, however, was soon discovered. Ilyin was arrested and his Bureau apparently dissolved, for nothing more is heard of it in the remaining days of the revolt.[63]

All told, some 300 Communists were arrested during the course of the insurrection, most of them local officials, together with a few caught trying to flee or otherwise considered dangerous by the Revolutionary Committee. While this was by no means a trifling figure, representing as it did about a fifth of the total membership in Kronstadt, it is remarkable that so many were left free and unmolested when the authorities, for their part, had executed forty-five seamen at Orani-

[62] *Ibid.*, pp. 50-51.
[63] *Ibid.*, p. 130; Kornatovskii, ed., *Kronshtadtskii miatezh*, p. 228; *Krasnaia Gazeta*, March 18, 1921.

enbaum and taken the relatives of the Kronstadters hostage. Perhaps the latter move, while arousing the fury of the insurgents, tempered their behavior by raising the prospect of retaliation. At any rate, Kronstadt was noteworthy for its humane treatment of its adversaries during a period of high emotion and growing tension. No harm whatever came to the 300 Bolshevik prisoners; there were no executions, no tortures, no beatings. The revolt, after all, was not against the Whites, whom the sailors passionately hated and would have slaughtered without the slightest remorse, but against fellow revolutionaries whose ideals they shared and whose practices they were merely seeking to reform. One may wonder, however, about the fate of a Trotsky or a Zinoviev had they fallen into the rebels' hands.

In any case, even the most unpopular officials emerged unscathed. Reports that Kuzmin had been brutally handled and had barely escaped summary execution lacked any basis in truth. Victor Serge ran into him at Smolny after the revolt, and Kuzmin, looking hale and hearty, confessed that such stories were mere "exaggerations," that he and his comrades had been treated correctly. Ilyin was also spared, though Petrichenko was incensed at his treachery.[64] And when the Revolutionary Committee heard that relatives of Communists were being boycotted or dismissed from their jobs, it cautioned the population against vengeful behavior: "In spite of all the outrageous acts of the Communists, we shall have enough restraint to confine ourselves only to isolating them from public life so that their malicious and false agitation will not hinder our revolutionary work."[65]

Nevertheless, the fate of the prisoners aroused no little

[64] Serge, *Memoirs of a Revolutionary*, pp. 126-27; *Pravda o Kronshtadte*, p. 130.

[65] *Pravda o Kronshtadte*, pp. 75, 84. On the relations between the rebels and the local Communists, see Katkov, "The Kronstadt Rising," *St. Antony's Papers*, No. 6, pp. 45-48.

concern within the Bolshevik government. After the first wave of arrests, the authorities responded by taking hostages and warning that any harm to the Communists would have grave consequences. The prisoners themselves, by their own testimony, lived in constant fear of being shot.[66] Nor was their situation improved when 50 Communists at Fort Krasno-armeets made a break for the Karelian coast and were intercepted. On other occasions loyalists signaled to the shore with flashlights and fired flares to illuminate targets at night. As a result, especially after the March 8 attack, the rebels began to deal more strictly with the Bolsheviks in their midst. On March 10 all Communists were ordered to turn in their arms and flashlights. Soon after this, the Revolutionary Committee told the population to look out for traitors signaling to the enemy. "Justice will be meted out on the spot," warned *Izvestiia*, "without any court, according to the laws dictated by the moment." There were cases of minor harassment, for example when two party members were accused of hoarding food; and at the March 11 conference of delegates, it was revealed that 280 pairs of boots had been taken from the Bolshevik prisoners for the use of the defenders stationed on the ice, the owners being provided with bast sandals in return. The announcement was greeted with applause and shouts of "Quite right! Take their coats too!" And this apparently was done, for one captive later testified that both his overcoat and boots had been confiscated.[67]

"OUR REVOLT is an elemental movement to get rid of Bolshevik oppression; once that is done, the will of the people will manifest itself." Thus did Petrichenko, in an interview with an American journalist in Finland, characterize the

[66] See the interview with Vasiliev in *Krasnaia Gazeta*, March 18, 1921.

[67] *Pravda o Kronshtadte*, pp. 96, 101, 122, 130, 138, 156; Pukhov, *Kronshtadtskii miatezh*, p. 99; Kornatovskii, ed., *Kronshtadtskii miatezh*, p. 77.

March uprising.[68] In a single sentence he conveyed the spirit of the rebellion, for the distinguishing feature of Kronstadt was its spontaneity, a feature it shared with the peasant insurrections and worker disturbances of the same period. Regarded as a single phenomenon, these movements constituted a revolt of the masses in the tradition of Razin and Pugachev, with the sailors filling the role of the Cossacks and *strel'tsy*, whose proclivity for sudden outbursts against organized despotism they had inherited in full measure. This same tradition had also expressed itself in 1917, a new edition of the classic "Russian revolt, blind and pitiless," as Pushkin described the *Pugachevshchina* of the eighteenth century. For the anarchists, Maximalists, and other left-wing extremists, the "social revolution" had arrived at last. They threw in their lot with the Bolsheviks, whose slogans, some of them borrowed from the syndicalists and SR's, suited their own mood and aspirations. "Land to the peasants! Down with the Provisional Government! Control of the factories to the workers!" As a revolutionary program, this was closer to *narodnichestvo* than to Marxism, and had strong appeal to the anarcho-populist instincts of the untutored elements of the Russian population.

After October, however, Lenin and his party, bent on consolidating their power and rescuing the country from social chaos, tried to divert the revolution from below into centralist and authoritarian channels. Their efforts ran contrary to the urges of the peasantry and working class, for whom the revolution was the very negation of centralization and authoritarianism. What the people clearly wanted was a decentralized society founded on local initiative and self-determination. To be left alone by the government and its agents, after all, had been the perennial dream of the lower classes. Thus it was not for nothing that the peasants distinguished

---

[68] Quarton to Secretary of State, April 9, 1921, National Archives, 861.00/8470.

between the "Bolsheviks," who eliminated the nobles and gave them the land, and the "Communists," who established state farms and sent requisitioning teams into the country-side; in 1917 the Bolsheviks promised an anarcho-populist millennium but once in power reverted to their original statist axioms.

There were, broadly speaking, two fundamentally opposed trends within the Russian revolutionary tradition. One was the centralist trend, represented by Lenin and his party and aiming to replace the old order with a revolutionary dictatorship; the other, pursued by the anarchists and SR's, was towards decentralized self-rule, the absence of strong governmental authority, and trust in the democratic instincts of the people. Kronstadt, with its roots in peasant particularism and spontaneous rebellion, belonged squarely in the second category. Opponents of centralized despotism in all its forms, the sailors turned against their former Bolshevik allies and their elitist brand of state socialism. They went so far, indeed, as to deny that the Bolshevik program was socialism at all. For the rebels, as for Bakunin before them, socialism without personal liberty and self-determination—for the lower classes at least—was nothing but a new form of tyranny, worse in some ways than the one it had replaced.

It was this divergence of outlook that lay at the root of the conflict of March 1921. An essential feature of Bolshevism was its distrust of mass spontaneity. Lenin believed that, left to their own devices, the workers and peasants would either content themselves with partial reforms or, worse still, fall victim to the forces of reaction. In his view, therefore, the masses must be led "from without," by a dedicated revolutionary vanguard. This was a basic tenet of his political philosophy, and he applied it to the situation in Kronstadt. We must weigh with care, he told the Tenth Party Congress, the political and economic lessons of this event. "What does it signify? The transfer of political authority to some nondescript conglomeration or alliance of ill-assorted elements, giving the appearance of being just a bit to the right of the Bolsheviks, or perhaps even to the left of the Bolsheviks—one cannot tell, so amorphous is that combination of political groups which in Kronstadt are attempting to take power in their own hands." Although he blamed the revolt on a White Guard plot, he was fully alive to its true significance. The movement, he said, was a counterrevolution of "petty-bourgeois anarchistic spontaneity," that is, a mass revolt closely linked to the peasant and worker unrest of the same moment. As such, it was extremely dangerous to the survival of Bolshevism, more dangerous than Denikin, Kolchak, and Yudenich put together.[69]

More than anything else, Lenin feared the outbreak of a new *Pugachevshchina*. He feared that the same anarcho-populist tide which had carried the Bolsheviks to power would now engulf them. What made the sailors particularly dangerous was the fact that, in contrast to the Whites, they had revolted in the name of the soviets. The rebels, as Victor Serge remarked, belonged body and soul to the revolution.[70] They voiced the suffering and will of the people, and thus pricked the conscience of the Bolshevik leadership more than any other opposition movement could. Lenin understood the mass appeal of the rebellion. He attacked it as "petty bourgeois" and "semi-anarchist" in the same way that he had attacked the Populists a quarter-century earlier for their romantic dream of a bygone era of communes and handicrafts cooperatives. Such a vision was anathema to the Bolshevik temperament; it was not merely primitive and inefficient but reactionary as well, and could not survive in the twentieth cen-

[69] *Desiatyi s"ezd RKP(b)*, pp. 33-34. On another occasion Lenin sought to minimize the dangers of Kronstadt, saying that it posed a "smaller threat to Soviet power than the Irish Army to the British Empire." *Polnoe sobranie sochinenii*, XLIII, 129.

[70] Serge, *Memoirs of a Revolutionary*, p. 131.

tury, when the centralized state and the centralized industrial machine were everywhere triumphant.

This is why, for Lenin, Kronstadt was more hazardous than the White armies of the Civil War. It stood for an ideal which, however unattainable, corresponded to the deepest urges of the Russian lower classes. But if Kronstadt had its way, Lenin reasoned, it would mean the end of all authority and cohesion and the breakup of the country into a thousand separate fragments, another period of chaos and atomization like 1917, but this time directed against the new order. Before long, some other centralized regime—of the Right rather than the Left—would fill the vacuum, for Russia could not endure in a state of anarchy. Thus for Lenin the course was clear: whatever the cost, the rebels must be crushed and Bolshevism restored in Kronstadt.

6. Suppression

On *March 9*, the day after the abortive assault on the rebel stronghold, the Bolshevik leader Kamenev addressed the Tenth Party Congress in Moscow. The military situation in Kronstadt, he said, had become "more protracted" than anyone had expected, so that the liquidation of the mutiny would not be accomplished "at an early hour."[1] The first attack had been premature. In their anxiety to crush the rebellion before it could receive outside help or spread to the mainland, the authorities had acted too hastily, making faulty preparations and using an insufficient quantity of troops and equipment, with the result that the assault was repulsed with heavy losses.

But now time was even more pressing, for before long the ice would begin to melt. Thus Tukhachevsky, the Bolshevik commander, urgently prepared for a second attack in much greater strength than before. Artillery and aircraft were rushed to the theater of operations. On both coasts facing Kotlin Island a rapid buildup took place, with fresh troops pouring in from all parts of the country. Low morale having played a part in the disaster of March 8, the men were chosen with particular care. Whole battalions of military cadets and Young Communists arrived from towns as remote as Smolensk and Vitebsk, Riazan and Nizhni Novgorod, singing the "Internationale" as a token of their revolutionary fidelity.[2] Picked Communist detachments and special Cheka units made up a very high proportion of the new assault force. In addition, loyal regiments were called in from the Ukraine and from the Polish front, augmented by Chinese, Tatar, Bashkir, and Lettish troops who might have fewer qualms than Great Russians about firing on the insurgents. As one

[1] *Desiatyi s''ezd RKP(b)*, p. 167.

[2] *Grazhdanskaia voina, 1918-1921*, I, 365; Pukhov, *Kronshtadtskii miatezh*, p. 150; *V ogne revoliutsii*, Moscow, 1933, p. 56.

observer put it, it was the Communists and non-Russians (*inorodtsy*) against the people.[3]

From the General Staff Academy such seasoned military leaders as Fedko, Uritsky, and Dybenko were summoned to help direct the assault. Dybenko, himself a former crew member of the *Petropavlovsk* and a prominent Bolshevik in the fleet during the Revolution, addressed a leaflet to his "Old Comrade Sailors of Kronstadt," denouncing Petrichenko as a "Poltava kulak" and calling on the rebels to lay down their arms.[4] At the same time, the government did all it could to convince its troops that the sailors were counterrevolutionaries. The press and radio insisted that the mutineers of "White Kronstadt" were acting at the behest of the émigrés and their Allied accomplices. "Damn the Kronstadt traitors," ran the headline of one Petrograd journal, "Kronstadt will be Red."[5]

Meanwhile, an uneasy calm had settled on the old capital. To prevent new disturbances from breaking out while final military preparations were being made, Zinoviev granted further concessions to the population, promising, among other things, to summon a citywide conference of nonparty workers and to curb "bureaucratism" within the party and government.[6] In Moscow the rebellion was a matter of growing concern. On March 10 Trotsky returned with a grim report on the situation and presented it to a closed session of the Tenth Party Congress. That evening some 300 delegates volunteered for the front, over a quarter of the total attendance and a dramatic measure of the gravity with which the rising was viewed ten days after its outbreak. To prove their loyalty, members

[3] Dan, *Dva goda skitanii*, pp. 154-55; *New York Times*, March 12, 1921; *Novaia Russkaia Zhizn'*, March 22, 1921; "Prichiny, povody, techenie i otsenka Kronshtadtskikh sobytii," manuscript, Hoover Library.

[4] Kornatovskii, ed., *Kronshtadtskii miatezh*, pp. 226-27.

[5] *Krasnaia Gazeta*, March 10, 1921.

[6] *Petrogradskaia Pravda*, March 11, 1921.

of the Workers' Opposition and Democratic Centralist factions were among the first to step forward.[7]

One of the volunteers, a Democratic Centralist named M. A. Rafail, has left an account of the role of the delegates in the final storming of the fortress. Arriving in Petrograd on March 11, they were hurriedly distributed among the troops concentrated on the mainland to the north and south of Kronstadt. Rafail and his party were sent to Oranienbaum, singing the "Internationale" as they went.[8] Although some were to take part in the actual fighting, their chief task was to boost the morale of the soldiers, to overcome their hesitancy to fire on the rebels by convincing them that they were defending the revolution against its enemies. They sought, moreover, to still the fears of the troops of crossing the open ice without protection; after the debacle of March 8, the men were filled with terror at the prospect of being mowed down by machine guns or of drowning under a hail of cannon shells. Another function of the delegates was to try to induce the rebels to give up their struggle. "Free soviets," they declared in a leaflet to Kronstadt, would in fact mean a restoration of the "bourgeoisie, landlords, generals, admirals, and noblemen, the princes and other parasites"; the slogan was merely a smokescreen for "the overthrow of Soviet power, the power of the exploited, and the restoration of the power of the capitalist exploiters." So make your choice now: "either with the White Guards against us, or with us against the White Guards."[9]

At first, however, the delegates had little success. The

[7] The minutes of the congress contain an incomplete list of 279 volunteers, including such prominent figures as K. E. Voroshilov, A. S. Bubnov (a Democratic Centralist), V. P. Zatonsky, and G. L. Piatakov: *Desiatyi s"ezd RKP(b)*, pp. 765-67.

[8] M. Rafail, *Kronshtadtskii miatezh (Iz dnevnika politrabotnika)*, Kharkov, 1921, pp. 4-6. Cf. Pukhov, *Kronshtadtskii miatezh*, p. 152.

[9] Rabinovich, "Delegaty 10-go s"ezda RKP(b) pod Kronshtadtom," *Krasnaia Letopis'*, 1931, No. 2, pp. 50-54.

morale of the Communist troops remained weak, while the spirits of the defenders, on the other hand, showed no sign of flagging. For this state of affairs Soviet military strategy was partly to blame: the Bolsheviks, to the surprise of the American consul in Viborg, had not "learned the futility of small attacks."[10] On March 9 new probes were launched across the ice, only to be driven back by the watchful defenders. The following day Soviet airplanes bombed the fortress, and after nightfall the batteries on both sides of the mainland pounded the rebel defenses with a merciless cannonade. This was followed, in the early hours of the 11th, by an invasion attempt from the southern coast, which was repulsed with heavy casualties. The rest of the day was quiet, a thick fog having moved in over the Finnish Gulf, preventing further military operations. Visibility was so poor that a Communist pilot, flying from Oranienbaum to Petrograd, mistakenly landed at Kronstadt. Seeing his error, he revved up his engines and managed to take off amid heavy gunfire, making it safely to Petrograd.[11]

Despite these repeated setbacks, the Soviet commanders, determined to crush the mutiny before the ice broke up, refused to suspend offensive operations until they were better prepared. On March 12 the air and artillery bombardment was resumed, continuing sporadically throughout the day but causing only minor damage. According to an émigré source, one Bolshevik plane was shot down by Kronstadt ground fire and crashed into the Finnish Gulf,[12] the only loss of its kind during the rebellion. The next morning the pattern of the past few days was repeated as the bombardment was succeeded by a predawn raid from the southern shore. Though camouflaged in white overalls, the assailants did not get very far before being driven back by crossfire

[10] Quarton to Secretary of State, March 11, 1921, National Archives, 861.00/8318.

[11] *Izvestiia Petrogradskogo Soveta*, March 11, 1921.

[12] *Za Narodnoe Delo*, March 18, 1921.

from the outlying rebel forts. But the assaults kept coming. On the morning of the 14th, under cover of darkness, fresh Bolshevik detachments advanced into a hurricane of artillery and machine-gun fire and were forced to withdraw, leaving scores of dead and wounded on the ice. This, however, was the last of the small-scale attacks. For the next 72 hours, though air and artillery operations continued as before, all ground activity ceased as the Communists prepared an all-out effort to take the rebel citadel by storm.

ON TOP of their military reverses, the Bolsheviks had other serious troubles to contend with. It was reported, for example, that the railway workers at Krasnoe Selo, a junction southwest of Petrograd, refused to transport troops being sent against Kronstadt. In another case, a Young Communist from Moscow noted that his train stopped again and again during the short trip from Petrograd to Oranienbaum, and although the engineer complained of bad fuel, the volunteers suspected foul play.[13] Much more serious was an incident on March 16, the very eve of the final assault. At Oranienbaum riflemen of the 27th Omsk Division, who had distinguished themselves against the Whites in the Civil War, started a mutiny with an appeal "to go to Petrograd and beat the Jews." Loyal troops under I. F. Fedko, one of the military experts from the General Staff Academy, quickly sealed off the base, surrounded the barracks of the Omsk mutineers, and arrested the ringleaders. But the virus of disenchantment was a potent one, from which not even the reliable *kursanty* were immune: at about the same time, an anti-Bolshevik conspiracy was unearthed among the cadets of the Peterhof Command School, several of whom were arrested and taken under guard to Petrograd.[14]

[13] *New York Times,* March 16, 1921; *V ogne revoliutsii,* p. 58.
[14] Kornatovskii, ed., *Kronshtadtskii miatezh,* pp. 100-101; Pukhov, *Kronshtadtskii miatezh,* pp. 147-48.

Yet, despite these instances of disaffection, a marked improvement in the morale of the Red forces occurred during the last two days before the decisive attack. Much of the credit must go to the delegates from the Tenth Party Congress, armed with a powerful new weapon: on March 15 the Congress in Moscow voted to replace forced requisitions with a tax in kind. When Lenin announced the new program before the assembly, a speaker from Siberia declared that "it is only necessary to tell all Siberia about this decree in order to stop the peasant disorders."[15] The delegates at the front, informed of the news, hastened to communicate it to the troops. The effect was remarkable. All at once, recalled one Bolshevik commissar, there occurred a "radical change in the mood" of the soldiers, most of whom were of peasant background.[16] The concession marked the beginning of the end of War Communism, and its announcement had a decisive influence on the performance of the Red forces in the final battle.

At about this time a shift was also occurring in the mood at Kronstadt, but in the opposite direction. Until the middle of March the morale of the rebels ran high, despite the overwhelming odds against them. "Today is the anniversary of the overthrow of the autocracy and the eve of the fall of the commissarocracy," boasted the Kronstadt *Izvestiia* of March 12.[17] A courier from the American consulate in Viborg, who visited the fortress that day, took note of the "good discipline and spirit among the garrison and population." And in a similar report an SR correspondent wrote that complete order and calm prevailed throughout the city and that workshops remained in operation. "We want to begin the work of liberating Russia," Petrichenko told him.

[15] *Desiatyi s"ezd RKP(b)*, pp. 430, 468.

[16] Rabinovich, "Delegaty 10-go s"ezda RKP(b) pod Kronshtadtom," *Krasnaia Letopis'*, 1931, No. 2, p. 32.

[17] *Pravda o Kronshtadte*, p. 126.

"We are striving to draw the population of Petrograd to our side. . . . We shall achieve the genuine power of the soviets."[18] Kronstadt was still sustained by the belief that its cause was just and that the revolt would soon spread to the mainland. On March 11 *Izvestiia* appealed to the rest of Russia to join the struggle against Bolshevik oppression: "Kronstadt is fighting for you, the hungry, the cold, the naked. . . . Comrades, the Kronstadters have raised the banner of rebellion, and they are confident that tens of millions of workers and peasants will respond to their call. It cannot be that the dawning which has begun here should not become a bright day for the whole of Russia and first of all Petrograd."[19]

Meanwhile, the Revolutionary Committee endeavored to strengthen the island's defenses against the imminent attack. Lights out was ordered after dark to make things more difficult for the enemy gunners and bombardiers. So far, despite the intensive bombardment, casualties were remarkably light; outsiders who visited Kronstadt reported little injury and only minor damage to buildings and installations. Through March 10, by the defenders' own reckoning, only 14 persons had been killed and 4 wounded (2 sailors, a soldier, and a civilian). On March 12 the rebel *Izvestiia* thought it noteworthy that a 14-year-old boy had been wounded while out on patrol (nothing could stop him, the journal explained, for his father, a peasant, had been shot by the Bolsheviks last year in his village).[20]

But matters were taking a turn for the worse. Contrary to expectations, Petrograd showed little sign of joining the

[18] Quarton to Secretary of State, March 13, 1921, National Archives, 861.00/8319; London *Times*, March 17, 1921; *Volia Rossii*, March 15, 1921.

[19] *Pravda o Kronshtadte*, pp. 120-21.

[20] *Ibid.*, pp. 122, 132; *New York Times*, March 16, 1921. Another source puts the number of wounded from Kronstadt and its forts at 60: "Kak nachalos' vosstanie v Kronshtadte," March 12, 1921, Miller Archives, File 5M, No. 5.

rebellion. A few copies of the Kronstadt *Izvestiia* were pasted on factory walls, and on one occasion a truck drove through the streets of the city scattering leaflets from the rebels. On March 7 the workers of the Arsenal factory endorsed the Kronstadt resolution and sent delegates to other enterprises to urge a general strike in support of the insurgents.[21] But all such efforts came to nothing, and the city, appeased by concessions and cowed by the presence of troops, remained quiet. The sailors felt betrayed, a feeling which rankled long after their movement was subdued. Refugees in Finland later complained that they had thought the Petrograd workers "meant business" and that the strikes would develop into a full-fledged revolution. Similarly, captured sailors whom Dan encountered in prison accused the workers of selling out to the government "for a pound of meat."[22]

No help, in fact, was forthcoming from any quarter. Kronstadt remained alone and isolated, subject to frequent air attacks and the pounding of the heavy guns from the mainland. Owing to the nocturnal sallies of Bolshevik raiding parties, the defenders had to do with little sleep; and, amid raging snowstorms, rebel patrols walked the ice in sandals for lack of boots. As fuel supplies dwindled, the Kronstadt *Izvestiia* appealed to the besieged population to use electricity as sparingly as possible. Ammunition was also getting low. On March 11 the defenders were ordered not to fire at Communist airplanes with rifles or machine guns, a futile action that only wasted precious cartridges. At the same time, the "military specialists" complained that artillery shells were being fired indiscriminately over long distances at doubtful targets. And the number of rebel casualties, though far from heavy, was mounting steadily. Around the middle of the month medical supplies ran out, and the death rate increased

[21] Mett, *La Commune de Cronstadt*, p. 46.
[22] Quarton to Secretary of State, April 23, 1921, National Archives, 861.00/8619; Dan, *Dva goda skitanii*, p. 153.

sharply. On March 14 collective funeral rites were performed at the Kronstadt Naval Hospital, and another ceremony took place in the Seamen's Cathedral on the 16th, as Communist artillery pounded the city. That evening rebel morale was badly shaken when a 12-inch shell from Krasnaya Gorka struck the deck of the *Sevastopol*, killing 14 seamen and wounding 36.[23]

In such circumstances, as a member of the Revolutionary Committee recalled, it was hopeless to maintain the initial enthusiasm generated by the revolt.[24] The repeated attacks, the lack of food and fuel, the long sleepless nights spent on guard in the cold, as Berkman noted, were sapping the vitality of the rebel stronghold.[25] With growing anxiety the defenders awaited the assault they knew had to come, and the strain and suspense began to tell on their nerves. Of primary concern was the state of Kronstadt's provisions, a problem which the author of the Secret Memorandum had foreseen weeks before the rebellion erupted. How long could the island, cut off from the outside world, feed its 50,000 inhabitants? By the end of the first week the initial daily ration of a half-pound of bread and a quarter-can of preserved food could not be maintained. On March 8 each person received a small quantity of oats to last four days. On the 9th a quarter-pound of black biscuit made of flour and dried potatoes was distributed. The following day the Kronstadt metal workers agreed to place their special allotment of canned horsemeat at the disposal of the community. Other than this, during the whole course of the insurrection there was distributed only one tin of condensed milk per person, an

[23] *Pravda o Kronshtadte*, pp. 75, 138; Quarton to Secretary of State, April 23, 1921, National Archives, 861.00/8619; Petrichenko, *Pravda o Kronshtadtskikh sobytiiakh*, p. 18.

[24] "Interv'iu s chlenami Vremennogo Revoliutsionnogo Komiteta," manuscript, Hoover Library.

[25] Berkman, *The Kronstadt Rebellion*, p. 36. Cf. Goldman, *Living My Life*, p. 884.

occasional tin of meat preserves, and, to children only, a half-pound of butter. By March 15 flour was gone and bread all but exhausted, and only a small quantity of canned goods remained on hand.[26]

The people were hungry, and, as the Petrograd Soviet noted, "hunger is often the main factor in the capitulation of fortresses in wars between peoples."[27] Kronstadt's hope that it could hold out alone until the ice melted was fading, and the rebel leaders began to have second thoughts about receiving outside help. Chernov's overtures during the early days of the rising had been politely refused. But when Baron Vilken arrived on March 16 with an offer of food and medicine in the name of the Russian Red Cross, it was gratefully accepted.

As we know, however, no aid ever came. For it was on March 16, too, that Tukhachevsky regrouped his army for the final storming of the rebel bastion. There were two attacking forces, the larger one deployed on the southern shore of the Finnish Gulf, the smaller along the northern or Karelian coastline. The total number of Communist troops has been variously estimated from 35,000 to 75,000 men, pitted against some 15,000 well-entrenched defenders.[28] The actual figure was probably around 50,000 (twice the number used in the first assault of March 8), of whom some 35,000 made up the Southern Group. Some of the best Bolshevik commanders were on hand to lead the assault. Many had proved their ability in the Civil War, including Fedko and Dybenko

---

[26] Mett, *La Commune de Cronstadt*, pp. 77-78; *Volia Rossii*, March 15, 1921; "Prichiny, povody, techenie i otsenka Kronshtadtskikh sobytii," manuscript, Hoover Library.

[27] *Izvestiia Petrogradskogo Soveta*, March 14, 1921.

[28] *New York Times*, March 18, 1921; *Novaia Russkaia Zhizn'*, March 22, 1921; "Prichiny, povody, techenie i otsenka Kronshtadtskikh sobytii," Hoover Library; Tseidler to president of Russian Red Cross, March 20, 1921, Giers Archives, File 88.

from the General Staff Academy and Vitovt Putna, who was put in charge of the mutinous 27th Omsk Division. For all the government's accusations that Kronstadt was a conspiracy of White Guard generals, ex-tsarist officers played a much more prominent role in the attacking force than among the defenders. The commanders of the Northern and Southern Groups, E. S. Kazansky and A. I. Sediakin, as well as their superiors, Tukhachevsky and S. S. Kamenev (no relation to the party leader L. B. Kamenev), had all been officers in the Imperial Army.

The morale of the rank and file was now much higher than before, owing to their reinforced numerical strength, the outstanding quality of their officers, and the tireless agitation of the party delegates. "We have suffered three years of hunger, lack of fuel, and the like. And now this betrayal. We'll settle their hash!"[29] Such was the tone of the Soviet propaganda machine, and it found a response in the new determination of the soldiers to crush the revolt once and for all. The men, outfitted in their white smocks and winter boots, were supplied with ample ammunition and special clippers for the barbed wire protecting Kronstadt's forts and batteries. Each soldier was issued a two-day ration of bread and two tins of preserved meat to forestall any grumbling about food. However, one commander in the Northern Group, in a recommendation hardly calculated to boost morale, advised his men not to eat before going into combat because stomach wounds were more likely to be serious after a meal.[30]

Tukhachevsky's plan called for a prolonged bombardment followed by a concerted infantry assault from three sides, the Northern Group striking at the northern end of Kotlin Island and the Southern Group at the southern and eastern ends. The cannonade began at 2 P.M. on March 16 and continued

[29] *Krasnaia Gazeta*, March 17, 1921.
[30] Kornatovskii, ed., *Kronshtadtskii miatezh*, p. 89.

throughout the day. Shells fell in Kronstadt near the cemetery where burial rites were being performed for the dead defenders. The insurgents replied with a heavy barrage from their forts and batteries and from the two dreadnoughts in the harbor. During the exchange a Communist shell crashed through the deck of the *Sevastopol*, causing only minor damage to the ship but killing or injuring 50 seamen. To avoid the same fate, the *Petropavlovsk* sent up a protective smokescreen, but the following day it too was to receive a full hit, killing 5 men and wounding 7.[31] In addition to the coastal barrage, aircraft were sent across the Gulf to bomb the fortress and its network of defenses. Yet the combined bombardment from the shore and air caused little physical damage and claimed relatively few rebel casualties. Its main effect was psychological, depressing still further the sinking morale of the defenders.

At nightfall the bombardment ceased. Mindful of the pattern of the past week, the rebels expected an attack to follow. Every man was at his post, though many had gone without relief for two or three days. For a long time there was complete silence, as searchlights from Kronstadt's forts and vessels scanned the ice for signs of movement. Finally, at 3 A.M. on the 17th the advance began. Protected by the dark and by a dense curtain of fog hanging over the Gulf, the Northern Group, made up largely of military cadets from the Petrograd area, proceeded in two columns from Sestroretsk and Lisy Nos, the one against Forts Totleben and

[31] Petrichenko, *Pravda o Kronshtadtskikh sobytiiakh*, p. 18; *New York Times*, March 19, 1921. Details of the assault have been gleaned chiefly from contemporary press reports and from the recollections of participants. See especially Kornatovskii, ed., *Kronshtadtskii miatezh*, pp. 45-51, 89-91; Pukhov, *Kronshtadtskii miatezh*, pp. 162-70; *Grazhdanskaia voina*, I, 367-73; Rafail, *Kronshtadtskii miatezh*, pp. 20-26; and K. E. Voroshilov, "Iz istorii podavleniia Kronshtadtskogo miatezha," *Voenno-Istoricheskii Zhurnal*, 1961, No. 3, pp. 15-35. Unfortunately, I have not been able to locate *Voennoe Znanie*, 1921, No. 8, which is devoted to the subject.

Krasnoarmeets and the other against the seven numbered forts strung out between Kotlin Island and the Karelian mainland. At the head of each column were volunteer shock troops to clear the way for the attack. Every effort was made to avoid detection. Conversation was forbidden, and orders were given in hushed tones. Communication was also achieved by flashlight signals carefully prepared in advance. Otherwise darkness was maintained and smoking prohibited.

At 5 A.M. the left-hand column from Lisy Nos, five battalions strong, sighted Forts 5 and 6, the outermost rebel strongpoints, looming ahead of them. Ordered on all-fours, the men crept the remaining distance along the ice, the water on its surface soaking through their white overalls. They reached the thick barbed wire barrier, and were cutting their way through, when they were suddenly illuminated by rebel flares and searchlights. The light was so intense, one soldier recalled, that "night was transformed into day." Fort 6 shouted for them to surrender. "We are your friends. We are for soviet power. We won't shoot you."[32] Ignoring these pleas, the *kursanty* rushed the forts with bayonets and grenades but were driven back with heavy losses by a murderous hail of machine-gun fire. Again and again the cadets, with cries of "Hoorah," returned to the attack, finally breaking through the rebel defenses, and after a fierce struggle the two forts were taken.

During the morning the fog lifted, and March 17 became a bright and sunny day. The Communists, now without cover, pressed their attack against the remaining forts. Both sides fought fanatically, suffering heavy loss of life. Shells from the rebel artillery broke up the ice, forming small lakes that became graves for scores of advancing troops. In one Communist battalion, according to S. P. Uritsky, a commander from the General Staff Academy, there were only 18 sur-

[32] Kornatovskii, ed., *Kronshtadtskii miatezh*, pp. 90, 105.

vivors.[33] But resistance was gradually overcome, and by mid-afternoon all the numbered forts had been taken and the *kursanty* had advanced to the northeast wall of the city of Kronstadt. Meanwhile, the right-hand column, consisting of only two companies, was trying unsuccessfully to capture Fort Totleben. Despite their exhaustion, the defenders fought with savage desperation, beating off their assailants repeatedly, with frightful casualties on both sides. With the onrush of infantry the big guns of the fort became useless, but the rebel machine guns and grenades took a heavy toll. One group of cadets blundered onto a minefield, and many were drowned when the explosions shattered the ice. At length, the attackers penetrated the fort, and hand-to-hand combat continued throughout the day. It was not until 1 A.M. on the 18th that Fort Totleben finally surrendered, whereupon nearby Krasnoarmeets followed suit.

In the meantime, the Southern Group had launched its attack against the southern and eastern ends of the city. Leaving Oranienbaum at 4 A.M. on the 17th, about an hour after the departure of the Northern Group, a large force, pulling their machine guns and light artillery with them, advanced in three columns towards Kronstadt's military harbor, while a fourth column made for the Petrograd Gate, the city's most vulnerable point of entry. It was still dark when advance units of the 79th Infantry Brigade approached the heavy gun emplacements defending the harbor. Searchlights threw out shafts of light, but the darkness and fog concealed the camouflaged troops from the defenders. Reaching the southern end of the city, Communist shock detachments quickly overpowered the crews of several outer batteries. Then, as they pressed forward, they were met by a heavy barrage of machine-gun and artillery fire from the surrounding rebel strongpoints. Shells and grenades tore holes in the ice, while thousands of ricocheting bullets sent tiny puffs of

---

[33] *Grazhdanskaia voina*, I, 370.

snow into the air. Facing this hurricane of death out in the open, the approaching formations displayed remarkable courage, trying desperately to resume their advance. They were also urged on by exhortations and threats from the rear. Not surprisingly, however, some of the men panicked and refused to proceed any further. When two soldiers, seized with fear, took shelter in an ice-bound barge, their commander shot them on the spot, then led the others forward.[34] The issue was decided, however, when several truckloads of rebel reinforcements arrived on the scene and, mounting a counterattack, drove the Communists to retreat. In the course of the battle more than half of the 79th Brigade were killed or wounded, including a number of delegates from the Tenth Party Congress.[35]

At the eastern end of the city the picture for the attackers was more encouraging. Just before daybreak, the 32nd Infantry Brigade, supported by the 95th and 96th Infantry Regiments, succeeded in breaching the wall north of the Petrograd Gate and fought their way into the town. About the same time, the 187th Infantry Brigade, commanded by Fedko and headed by a shock regiment of military cadets, forced an entry through the Gate itself, closely followed by the 167th and 80th Brigades. By this time the attackers had already suffered heavy losses, but once within the walls, in the words of a contemporary, "they encountered a veritable hell."[36] Machine guns and rifles seemed to fire at them from every window and every roof. On the sidewalks patches of red soon covered the ice and snow. The dead and wounded piled up on both sides, as the battle proceeded from street to street and house to house. Yet the rebels, even in the midst of this fratricidal bloodshed, when most of the forts

[34] Alexander Barmine, *One Who Survived*, New York, 1945, p. 95.
[35] Kornatovskii, ed., *Kronshtadtskii miatezh*, pp. 246-47.
[36] "Khod sobytii v Petrograde vo vremia Kronshtadtskogo vosstaniia," manuscript, March 19, 1921, Columbia Russian Archive.

had been taken and the battle was raging within the city itself, took no vengeance on their Communist prisoners. Near the Petrograd Gate a government rescue party hurried to the jail where their comrades were being kept and, breaking a window, handed in weapons to the inmates, who liberated themselves and immediately joined the fight.[37]

Throughout the day the fighting continued without letup. According to some accounts, the women of Kronstadt threw themselves into the struggle, carrying ammunition to the defenders and removing the injured under heavy fire to first-aid stations in the city's hospitals.[38] At 4 P.M. the insurgents launched a sudden counterattack which sent the Bolsheviks reeling and threatened to drive them back onto the ice. But at this critical moment the 27th Cavalry Regiment and a detachment of party volunteers from Petrograd arrived to save the day. Just before sundown, artillery from Oranienbaum was brought into the city and opened fire on the rebels with devastating effect. As the battle raged, men on both sides fell from wounds and sheer exhaustion. During the evening the *kursanty* of the Northern Group penetrated the city from the northeast and seized the staff headquarters of the fortress, taking many prisoners. They then linked up with their comrades of the Southern Group, who by that time had fought their way from the Petrograd Gate to the center of the town. By midnight the fighting had begun to die down. One by one the last forts were taken. Victory was now clearly in sight.

On March 5, before any blood had been shed in Kronstadt, the Petrograd Defense Committee had warned the insurgents that at the last moment their ringleaders, "the Kozlovskys and Petrichenkos," would abandon them to their fate and flee

[37] Kornatovskii, ed., *Kronshtadtskii miatezh*, pp. 78, 88.

[38] Petrichenko, *Pravda o Kronshtadtskikh sobytiiakh*, p. 21; Voline, *La Révolution inconnue*, p. 499; "Khod sobytii v Petrograde," Columbia Russian Archive.

to Finland.[39] This prediction was now fulfilled. On the evening of March 17, when all appeared lost, 11 members of the Revolutionary Committee (including Petrichenko) escaped across the ice to Terijoki. (Valk, Pavlov, and Perepelkin had been taken prisoner during the battle, and Vershinin, it will be recalled, had been seized on the ice during the first assault of March 8.) Kozlovsky, Solovianov, and other collaborating "military specialists" also fled. Shortly before midnight some 800 refugees, including the bulk of the rebel leadership, reached the Finnish coast. Having the most to fear from capture, they were the first to leave the island, except for a group from the numbered forts close to the Karelian shoreline. No doubt the prospect of summary execution had played a key part in their decision to evacuate. In any event, their departure was a signal for a mass exodus of defenders from Kotlin Island and its surrounding fortifications. During the next 24 hours a steady stream of refugees, mostly sailors, crossed the Finnish frontier. In all, some 8,000 fled, or more than half the total rebel strength. Some 400 horses were taken over the ice, and 2,500 discarded rifles were picked up near the coast by Finnish border guards.[40]

It has been noted that the Communist bombardment, while continuing on and off for 11 days, had done surprisingly little damage to Kronstadt's defenses. But now the retreating sailors, in a last gesture of defiance, removed the breech-locks from the guns of the forts and batteries, and destroyed dynamos, searchlights, machine guns, and other equipment. At the northern forts only a few of the weapons were in working order when the Communists returned.[41] On the night of March 17 the commanders of the *Petropavlovsk* and *Sevastopol* instructed their crews to blow up the vessels, but the men, learning that their leaders had fled,

[39] Kornatovskii, ed., *Kronshtadtskii miatezh*, p. 189.
[40] *Novaia Russkaia Zhizn'*, March 22 and 24, 1921.
[41] London *Times*, March 30, 1921.

refused to carry out the order. Instead, they arrested the officers in charge and sent word to the Soviet command that they were ready to surrender. At 11:50 P.M. Communist headquarters at Kronstadt was able to send a victory message to the Petrograd Defense Committee: "The counterrevolutionary nests on the *Petropavlovsk* and *Sevastopol* have been liquidated. Power rests in the hands of sympathizers with Soviet authority. Military activity aboard the *Petropavlovsk* and *Sevastopol* has ceased. Urgent measures are being taken to stop the officers who have fled towards the Finnish frontier."[42] During the early hours of March 18 detachments of *kursanty* occupied the two dreadnoughts. Meanwhile, except for a few pockets of diehards, the remaining insurgents were also surrendering, so that by noon on the 18th the forts and ships and nearly all of the town were in government hands. It only remained to mop up the isolated groups of defenders still holding out. During the afternoon the last resistance was overcome, and the guns of Kronstadt fell silent.

In its ferocity the battle of Kronstadt matched the bloodiest episodes of the Civil War. Losses were very heavy on both sides, but the Communists, forced to attack across the open ice against strongly entrenched defenders, paid much the greater cost. For the period from March 3 to 21, according to official health reports, the hospitals of Petrograd contained more than 4,000 wounded and shock cases, while 527 more died in their beds. These figures, of course, do not include the large number who had perished in the fighting. After the battle so many bodies were strewn over the ice that the Finnish government asked Moscow to remove them for fear that when the thaw came they would be washed ashore and create a health hazard.[43] A low estimate by official

[42] Kornatovskii, ed., *Kronshtadtskii miatezh*, p. 243.

[43] Mett, *La Commune de Cronstadt*, p. 56; London *Times*, March 31, 1921.

sources places total Communist dead at about 700, with 2,500 wounded or shell-shocked, but a Bolshevik participant noted that these figures were much too small, judging by what he alone had witnessed at Fort Number 6. Another estimate puts Red losses at 25,000 killed and wounded. However, according to Harold Quarton, the well-informed American consul in Viborg, total Soviet casualties amounted to about 10,000, which seems a reasonable calculation of all the dead, wounded, and missing taken together.[44] Some 15 delegates from the Tenth Party Congress lost their lives in the campaign. Together with the other fallen Bolsheviks, they were buried with military honors in a mass funeral held in Petrograd on March 24.[45]

Losses on the rebel side were fewer but by no means inconsiderable. No reliable figures are available, but one report puts the number of killed at 600, with more than 1,000 wounded and about 2,500 taken prisoner during the fighting.[46] Among the dead, more than a few were massacred in the final stages of the struggle. Once inside the fortress, the attacking troops took revenge for their fallen comrades in an orgy of bloodletting. A measure of the hatred which had built up during the assault was the regret expressed by one soldier that airplanes had not been used to machine gun the rebels fleeing across the ice to Finland. Trotsky and S. S. Kamenev, his commander in chief, sanctioned the use of chemical warfare against the insurgents, and if Kronstadt had resisted much longer, a plan to launch a gas attack with

[44] Kornatovskii, ed., *Kronshtadtskii miatezh*, p. 107; Pukhov, *Kronshtadtskii miatezh*, p. 169; "Khod sobytii v Petrograde," Columbia Russian Archive; Quarton to Secretary of State, March 19, 1921, National Archives, 861.00/8372. Lt. Kelley's figure of 25 to 30 thousand, however, is far too high: Quarton to Secretary of State, April 23, 1921, 861.00/8619.

[45] *Petrogradskaia Pravda*, March 25, 1921.

[46] Pukhov, *Kronshtadtskii miatezh*, p. 168; *Grazhdanskaia voina*, I, 372.

shells and balloons, devised by cadets of the Higher Military Chemical School, would have been carried out.[47]

NEWS of the suppression spread rapidly, evoking a variety of responses in different quarters. In Western Europe the Russian expatriates were desolate. They bemoaned their failure to deliver aid to the rebels and denounced Great Britain for signing its trade agreement with the Bolsheviks in the very midst of the struggle. One émigré journal, however, refused to despair. In an editorial on "The Lessons of Kronstadt," it declared that the fight for Russia's liberation would continue until victory had been achieved. Similarly, Professor Grimm wrote to a colleague that if a new outbreak should occur in Petrograd their group must not again be caught unawares.[48]

Inside Russia the Bolsheviks exulted in their hard-won triumph. But mingled with their exultation was a note of regret for their "erring sailor comrades." Sharing these feelings were the Communist visitors from abroad, who continued to support the regime, however uncertain they might be about the course it was taking; for Bolshevik Russia, they reasoned, with all its shortcomings, was the first socialist state in history, the first country in which the landlords and bourgeoisie had been driven from their entrenched power. Next to this, in their eyes, other considerations were of secondary importance. But some foreign Communists, like Victor Serge, were deeply troubled by what had happened. And for anarchists like Emma Goldman and Alexander Berkman the suppression of Kronstadt had a shattering effect. On the night of March 17, recalled Goldman in her memoirs, when the thunder of cannon came to a stop, the stillness that

[47] V. Pozdnyakov, "The Chemical Arm," in *The Red Army*, ed., B. H. Liddell Hart, New York, 1956, pp. 384-85. Colonel Pozdnyakov had been one of the students who drew up the plan.

[48] *Za Narodnoe Delo*, March 19, 1921; Grimm to Giers, March 31, 1921, Giers Archives, File 88.

fell over Petrograd was more fearful than the incessant firing of the preceding days. During the final hours, Berkman, "the last thread of his faith in the Bolsheviki broken," wandered helplessly through the streets, while Goldman sat in unbelieving agony in their hotel, "unutterable weariness in every nerve." As she sat, peering into the darkness, Petrograd seemed "a ghastly corpse" hung in a black pall, the street-lamps flickering yellow "like candles at its head and feet." The next morning, March 18, the Petrograd newspapers carried banner headlines commemorating the fiftieth anniversary of the Paris Commune. Bands played military tunes and Communists paraded in the streets, singing the "Internationale." "Its strains," noted Goldman, "once jubilant to my ears, now sounded like a funeral dirge for humanity's flaming hope." Berkman made a bitter entry in his diary: "The victors are celebrating the anniversary of the Commune of 1871. Trotsky and Zinoviev denounce Thiers and Gallifet for the slaughter of the Paris rebels."[49]

In Kronstadt, meanwhile, the Bolsheviks made every effort to eliminate the traces of the rising. Pavel Dybenko was appointed commander of the fortress, endowed with absolute powers to purge the city of dissident elements and disloyal ideas. In place of the Kronstadt Soviet, which was not revived, a *revtroika* consisting of Vasiliev, Bregman, and Gribov, three of Kronstadt's most trusted Bolshevik leaders, was established to assist the new commander. On March 18 a new journal, *Red Kronstadt*, began to appear in the city. The battleships *Petropavlovsk* and *Sevastopol* were rechristened the *Marat* and *Paris Commune*, while Anchor Square became the Square of the Revolution. Party reregistration was at once carried out, during which some 350 members were excluded or failed to appear. And a "surgical

[49] Goldman, *Living My Life*, p. 886; Berkman, *The Bolshevik Myth*, p. 303. Thiers was premier of France and Gallifet the general who subdued the Communards.

operation," as one writer put it, was performed on the Soviet Navy: unreliable Baltic sailors were scattered to the Black Sea, the Caspian, and the Aral, and to the Amur River flotilla in the Far East, while all naval units were purged of alleged *Ivanmory*—some 15,000 in all—within their ranks.[50] The Red Army soldiers who participated in the final assault were also dispersed to remote locations around the country. Only a month later their leader, Tukhachevsky, took command of the punitive expedition sent to crush Antonov's guerrillas in the Tambov region.[51]

Finally, it remains to describe the fate of the Kronstadt survivors. None of the captured rebels received a public hearing. From more than 2,000 prisoners taken during the struggle, 13 were chosen to be tried *in camera* as ringleaders of the mutiny. To bolster the case for a counterrevolutionary conspiracy, the Soviet press took pains to emphasize their social backgrounds: 5 were ex-naval officers of noble birth, 1 a former priest, and 7 of peasant origin.[52] Their names are unfamiliar: none belonged to the Revolutionary Committee, four of whose members—Valk, Pavlov, Perepelkin, and Vershinin—are known to have been in government custody, nor were any from among the "military specialists" who played an advisory role in the uprising. All the same,

---

[50] Kornatovskii, ed., *Kronshtadtskii miatezh*, p. 15; Pukhov, *Kronshtadtskii miatezh*, pp. 176-80. Cf. G. A. Cheremshanskii, "Kronshtadtskoe vosstanie, 28 fevralia-18 marta 1921," manuscript, Columbia Russian Archive. Cheremshansky was among the Baltic sailors transferred to the Amur.

[51] Fedko also took a leading part in suppressing Antonov. See M. N. Tukhachevskii, "Bor'ba s kontrrevoliutsionnymi vosstaniiami," *Voina i Revoliutsiia*, 1926, No. 8, pp. 3-15; A. I. Todorskii, *Marshal Tukhachevskii*, Moscow, 1963, pp. 71-73; and Nikulin, *Tukhachevskii*, pp. 151-56.

[52] *Krasnaia Gazeta*, March 23, 1921; *Petrogradskaia Pravda*, March 23, 1921; Kornatovskii, ed., *Kronshtadtskii miatezh*, pp. 247-49. According to the charges, the accused were responsible for the death or injury of "several thousand" Red troops, which tends to bear out Quarton's estimate of Bolshevik losses.

the 13 "ringleaders" were tried on March 20 and condemned to execution.

Of the remaining prisoners, several hundred are said to have been shot at once in Kronstadt. The rest were removed by the Cheka to its prisons on the mainland. In Petrograd the jails were filled to overflowing, and over a period of several months hundreds of rebels were taken out in small batches and shot. These included Perepelkin, whom Fyodor Dan had met while exercising in his prison courtyard. Before his execution he drafted a detailed account of the rising, but what became of it Dan did not know.[53] Others were sent to concentration camps, such as the notorious Solovki prison in the White Sea, condemned to forced labor, which for many meant a slow death from hunger, exhaustion, and illness.[54] In some cases, the families of the insurgents suffered a similar fate. Kozlovsky's wife and two sons, who had been taken as hostages in early March, were sent to a concentration camp; only his 11-year-old daughter was spared.[55]

What became of the rebels who fled to Finland? Some 8,000 escaped across the ice and were interned in refugee camps at Terijoki, Viborg, and Ino. Nearly all the fugitives were sailors and soldiers, with only a sprinkling of male civilians, women, and children.[56] The American and British

[53] Dan, *Dva goda skitanii*, pp. 153-57.

[54] Maximoff, *The Guillotine at Work*, p. 168; David Dallin and Boris Nicolaevsky, *Forced Labor in Soviet Russia*, New Haven, 1947, p. 170. According to a recent Soviet work, however, the majority of captured sailors were subsequently pardoned, "severe punishment" (i.e., execution) being meted out only to the ringleaders and implacable enemies of Soviet authority: Sofinov, *Istoricheskii povorot*, p. 36n.

[55] Dan, *Dva goda skitanii*, p. 158. Another contemporary source, probably in error, says that both sons were shot: "Svedeniia iz Petrograda ot 12 aprelia: Kronshtadt i otgoloski ego vosstaniia," manuscript, Hoover Library.

[56] The largest camp, at Fort Ino, contained 3,597 internees, of whom there were 3,584 men, 10 women, and 3 children. Only 25 of the men were nonmilitary: *Novaia Russkaia Zhizn'*, March 27, 1921.

Red Cross supplied them with food and clothing. Some were given employment in road construction and other public works. But life in the camps was bleak and depressing, and the refugees, who at first were allowed no contact with the local population, found it very difficult to adjust. The Finnish government appealed to the League of Nations to help settle them in other countries, while the Bolsheviks demanded their repatriation with their weapons. Lured by a promise of amnesty, many returned to Russia, only to be arrested and shipped off to concentration camps. In May and June groups of them passed through Dan's prison en route to a future of forced labor and early death.[57]

Despite the prevailing gloom and bitterness, Petrichenko continued to enjoy the respect of his fellow fugitives. His biggest mistake, they said, was his failure to shoot the Communist leaders in Kronstadt. Petrichenko himself had no regrets on this score. But he did admit, when interviewed at Terijoki by an American reporter, that the rebellion had been premature and poorly organized. "We are defeated," he said, "but the movement will proceed because it comes from the people themselves. . . . There are [millions] like me in Russia, not reactionary Whites and murderous Reds, and from these plain people will come the overthrow of the Bolsheviki."[58] Little is known of Petrichenko's subsequent life in exile. A Soviet collection of documents and memoirs pertaining to the Kronstadt rising contains what purports to be a letter from the rebel leader to a friend in Russia, dated November 17, 1923, in which he acknowledges his mistakes

[57] London *Times*, March 30, 1921; Dan, *Dva goda skitanii*, p. 159. Later in the year, according to some reports, a band of Kronstadt refugees organized the "Plekhanov Battalion" and, together with Finnish partisans, fought against the Bolsheviks in Eastern Karelia. See C. Jay Smith, *Finland and the Russian Revolution, 1917-1922*, Athens, Ga., 1958, pp. 193-97.

[58] Quarton to Secretary of State, April 5, 1921, National Archives, 861.00/8446; *New York Times*, March 31, 1921.

and indicates that he has applied for readmission to his homeland.[59] The letter, however, is of doubtful authenticity. An article published by Petrichenko in an SR journal in December 1925 shows not the slightest repentance for his role in the rebellion, which he continues to uphold as a spontaneous outbreak against the dictatorship of the Communist party, or rather of its leaders.[60]

The official Soviet history of the Civil War mistakenly records that Petrichenko soon left Finland and resettled in Czechoslovakia. In fact, he remained in Finland for nearly a quarter-century. In the aftermath of defeat, as we have seen, he was ready to cooperate with émigré circles in Western Europe, with whom he shared a desire to liberate Russia from Bolshevik rule. Later, however, he joined pro-Soviet groups in Finland. During the Second World War these activities got him into trouble with the Finnish authorities, and in 1945 he was repatriated to Russia, where he was immediately arrested. He died in a prison camp a year or two later.[61]

[59] Kornatovskii, ed., *Kronshtadtskii miatezh*, pp. 163-64.

[60] Petrichenko, "O prichinakh Kronshtadtskogo vosstaniia," *Znamia Bor'by*, December 1925-January 1926, pp. 4-8.

[61] *Grazhdanskaia voina*, I, 362; Serge, *Memoirs of a Revolutionary*, p. 132n; Unto Parvilahti, *Beria's Gardens*, New York, 1960, pp. 21, 285.

7. Epilogue

Kronstadt fell. The insurgents had fought with determination and courage. But their prospects for success had been dim from the start. The rising, as its leaders themselves acknowledged, had been badly timed and ill-prepared. The sailors had no invasion force, nor any outside help, while the Bolsheviks, having won the Civil War, were free to concentrate the best of their armed might against them. Moreover, the ice on the Finnish Gulf was still frozen solid, enabling the government to mount a large-scale infantry attack against the isolated rebel stronghold. Compared with the anti-Soviet movements of the Civil War, then, Kronstadt was an affair of modest proportions. If the Bolsheviks had been able to defeat Denikin, Kolchak, and Yudenich, and to turn back the legions of Pilsudski, then Kronstadt could not in itself have posed a serious military threat.

What really alarmed the Bolsheviks was the possibility that it might touch off a general revolt on the mainland or become the spearhead of a new intervention. The country, they knew, was in a state of turmoil verging on mass rebellion. So far, they had been able to keep their opponents isolated; but Kronstadt, though involving fewer numbers than, say, the peasant revolts in Siberia and Tambov, was well-fortified and manned by trained military personnel, and, situated as it was in the Baltic rather than the remote interior, could serve as a stepping-stone for an invading army.

Nevertheless, a rebel victory is hard to imagine. The Russian people, however embittered, were war-weary and demoralized, and with all their grievances against the government, they still feared a White restoration more than they hated the Communists. Moreover, the strikes in Petrograd, on which the sailors pinned their hopes, had already passed their climax. As for outside support, the Western powers had abandoned their policy of intervention and were shifting towards an accommodation with the Bolsheviks. The rebellion failed to upset the Anglo-Soviet trade agreement, as the Whites had hoped and the Communists feared; the pact was signed in London on March 16, only hours before the final assault on Kronstadt. On the same day, moreover, a friendship treaty with Turkey was concluded in Moscow. Nor did Kronstadt hinder negotiations with the Poles, who had no desire to renew the struggle with their old-time adversary. The treaty of Riga was signed on March 18, while Communist troops were mopping up the last pockets of rebel resistance. Finland, too, turned its back on the insurgents and prevented any aid from passing across its borders. Finally, the Russian émigrés remained as divided and ineffectual as before, with no prospect of cooperation in sight. General Wrangel, his troops dispersed and their morale sagging, was in no position to help; months would have been needed merely to mobilize his men and transport them from the Mediterranean to the Baltic. Or if a second front were attempted in the south, it would have meant almost certain disaster.

For the rebels the only hope of success lay in an immediate offensive on the mainland. Had they followed the advice of the "military specialists" and seized a bridgehead at Oranienbaum, there was a good chance that units of Red Army, and perhaps civilians as well, would have rallied to their standard. A rebellion against the state, as Alexander Berkman observed, must assume the initiative and strike with determination, allowing the government no time to muster its forces. Once it isolates itself or plays a waiting game, it is doomed to certain defeat. In this respect, noted Berkman, Kronstadt repeated the fatal error of the Paris Commune: just as the latter rejected an immediate attack on Versailles while the government of Thiers was disorganized, Kronstadt failed to march on Petrograd before the authorities could ready their defenses.[1] In March 1908, Lenin, in an article commemorating the Commune, had made a similar observation when he decried "the excessive magnanimity of the proletariat: instead of annihilating its enemies, it endeavored to exercise moral influence on them; it neglected the importance of purely military activity in the civil war, and instead of crowning its victory in Paris by a determined advance on Versailles, it delayed long enough for the Versailles government to gather its dark forces in preparation for the bloody week of May."[2] A fitting epitaph for the Kronstadt commune of 1921.

THUS it is difficult to escape the conclusion that, short of an invasion of the mainland, it was only a matter of time before the rebels would be crushed. In all likelihood this was true even if they had held out until the ice had melted and aid had reached them from the west. Protected by open water and replenished with food, medicine, and ammunition, they might have survived a few weeks longer and taken a heavier toll of Bolshevik lives, but sooner or later they were bound to succumb, if not to military pressure alone, then to the same combination of force and economic concessions which sealed the fate of the Petrograd strike movement and of the rural insurrections throughout the country. Everywhere the New Economic Policy was blunting the edge of discontent, and Kronstadt would have been no exception.

This is not to suggest that Kronstadt was in any way responsible for the NEP, apart, perhaps, from hastening its implementation. By March 1921 Lenin needed no further convincing to abandon the program of War Communism. He

---

[1] Berkman, *The Kronstadt Rebellion*, pp. 39-40. The same observation was made by a Menshevik writer in *Sotsialisticheskii Vestnik*, April 5, 1921, p. 5. As Engels once wrote: "The defensive is the death of every armed rising."

[2] Lenin, *Polnoe sobranie sochinenii*, XVI, 452-53.

and his associates had been reassessing their economic policies since the end of the Civil War, and had formulated the basic outlines of the NEP some weeks before the rebellion erupted. As early as December 1920, when SR and Menshevik delegates to the Eighth Congress of Soviets called for a halt to food requisitions and for the introduction of a tax in kind, Lenin had already been considering such a move. Several weeks passed, however, before any action was taken. At length, the swelling tide of unrest persuaded him that the survival of Bolshevik rule was at stake, and, at a meeting of the Politburo on February 8, during which the whole question of agrarian policy was carefully reviewed, he outlined a plan to replace forced requisitions by a tax in kind, with the right of the peasant to dispose of his surplus after meeting his obligations to the state. During the succeeding weeks the project was discussed in the Soviet press. On February 24, five days before the outbreak at Kronstadt, a detailed draft based on Lenin's notes was presented to the Central Committee for inclusion on the agenda of the impending Tenth Party Congress.[3]

But the meaning of the rebellion was not lost on the congress when it assembled in Moscow on March 8. By highlighting the intensity of popular opposition, the revolt imparted a sense of urgency to the proceedings and dispelled any doubts about the need for immediate reform. The party saw the writing on the wall. There were those, indeed, who speculated that the rising might never have happened if the NEP had been introduced but a month before.[4] Be that as it may, there was general agreement that the reforms brooked no further delay lest the Bolsheviks be swept from power by a tidal wave of popular anger. Kronstadt, as Lenin put it, "lit up reality better than anything else." Lenin saw that the mutiny was no isolated incident but part of a broad pattern of unrest em-

---

[3] *Ibid.*, XLII, 333. Cf. Carr, *The Bolshevik Revolution*, II, 280-82.
[4] Slepkov, *Kronshtadtskii miatezh*, p. 15.

bracing the risings in the countryside, the disturbances in the factories, and the growing ferment within the armed forces. The economic crisis of War Communism, he noted, had been transformed into "a political one: Kronstadt," and the future of Bolshevism hung in the balance.[5]

The Tenth Party Congress, one of the most dramatic in Bolshevik history, marked a fundamental change in Soviet policy. Years before, Lenin had laid down two conditions for the victory of socialism in Russia: the support of a proletarian revolution in the West and an alliance between the Russian workers and peasants.[6] By 1921 neither of these conditions had been fulfilled. As a result, Lenin was forced to abandon his belief that without the support of a European revolution the transition to socialism was impossible. Here, in essence, lay the seeds of "socialism in one country," a doctrine evolved by Stalin a few years later and entailing a slowing down of the revolutionary process, an accommodation with the capitalist powers abroad and with the peasantry at home. The immediate and overriding need, on which everything else depended, was to placate the rebellious rural population. As Lenin explained to the Tenth Congress, "only an agreement with the peasantry can save the socialist revolution in Russia until the revolution has occurred in other countries."[7] Three years earlier, in March 1918, Lenin had made a similar retreat on the international front when he rejected a "revolutionary war" against Germany and signed the treaty of Brest-Litovsk. Now, in order to secure the "breathing spell" which the Bolsheviks had been denied in 1918, Lenin scrapped War Communism for a more cautious and conciliatory domestic program. "We must satisfy the economic desires of the middle peasantry and introduce free trade," he declared, "or else the preservation of the power of the

---

[5] Lenin, *Polnoe sobranie sochinenii*, XLIII, 138, 387.

[6] See Carr, *The Bolshevik Revolution*, II, 277-79.

[7] *Desiatyi s"ezd RKP(b)*, p. 404.

proletariat in Russia, given the delay in the worldwide revolution, will be impossible."[8]

Thus, on March 15, the Tenth Party Congress adopted what one delegate (the Marxist scholar D. B. Riazanov) called a "peasant Brest."[9] The measure, which formed the cornerstone of the New Economic Policy, replaced compulsory food collections with a tax in kind and conceded the right of the peasant to dispose of his surpluses in the free market. This was but the first of a series of steps in the transition from War Communism to a mixed economy. Valerian Osinsky's proposal for a centrally directed sowing campaign, put forward at the Eighth Congress of Soviets, was abandoned. Armed roadblocks were everywhere withdrawn from the highways and railroads, and trade between city and village was revived. Moreover, Trotsky's labor armies were disbanded and the trade unions granted a measure of autonomy, including the right to elect their own officials and to subject to free debate all issues affecting the interests of the workers. Subsequent decrees restored private retail shops and consumer production, while the state retained the "commanding heights" of the economy—heavy industry, foreign trade, transportation, and communications—in its own hands. Each of these steps drove another nail into the coffin of mass opposition, while stirring new life in the Russian town and village. For several months peasant unrest continued to smolder in Tambov, Siberia, and the Volga basin, but heavy formations of *kursanty* and Cheka troops—the same sort of units used against Kronstadt—were called to the scene, and by the autumn of 1921 effective resistance had been stamped out.

For Lenin the NEP was not intended as a mere stop-gap measure until order had been restored and Bolshevik author-

[8] *Ibid.*, p. 413.

[9] *Ibid.*, p. 468. For the decision abolishing forced requisitions, see *ibid.*, pp. 608-609.

ity consolidated on a more secure footing. "Until we have remolded the peasant," he told the Tenth Congress, "until large-scale machinery has recast him, we must assure him of the possibility of running his economy without restrictions. We must find forms of coexistence with the small farmer." Lenin acknowledged that collectivization had been pushed too far and had alienated the individual peasant proprietor. We shall have to deal with him for many years to come, he said, "since the remaking of the small farmer, the reshaping of his whole psychology and all his habits, is a task requiring generations."[10] By this admission, Lenin tacitly conceded an argument of his Menshevik critics, who in 1917 had warned against any premature attempt to plunge their backward agrarian country into socialism. True Marxists, they had insisted, knew that the moment was not yet ripe, that Russia, with its small proletariat and overwhelming peasant population, lacked the essential conditions for a socialist revolution. Engels too had written that nothing was worse than a premature revolution, that is, one in which a socialist party would come to power before industrialism and democracy had had a proper chance to develop. The Bolsheviks, however, proceeded to attempt what the doctrine of historical materialism declared to be impossible: to make a socialist revolution before the necessary preliminaries had been achieved. The New Economic Policy was an effort to make up these deficiencies. As Lenin envisioned it, the NEP was to be a long period of economic recovery, a period of reconciliation between town and country, during which the groundwork for a socialist society was to be laid.

THE NEP succeeded in relieving a good deal of the tensions in Russian society. Yet it failed to satisfy the demands of Kronstadt and its sympathizers. To be sure, the confiscation

[10] *Ibid.*, pp. 37-38, 406. Cf. Schapiro, *The Origin of the Communist Autocracy*, p. 311.

of grain had been ended and the roadblocks removed, the labor battalions dissolved and the trade unions assured a degree of independence from the state. But the state farms remained intact, and capitalism had been partially restored in the industrial sector. Contrary to the principles of proletarian democracy, moreover, the old directors and technical specialists continued to run the large factories; the workers remained the victims of "wage slavery," excluded as before from a role in management.

Nor, of course, was there any revival of democracy in military life. The right to elect ship committees and political commissars remained a dead issue. After Kronstadt there was no longer any question of decentralizing authority or of relaxing military discipline within the fleet. On the contrary, Lenin proposed to Trotsky that the Baltic Fleet be scrapped since the sailors were unreliable and the ships of questionable military value. But Trotsky managed to persuade his colleague that such a drastic step was unnecessary. Instead, the Soviet Navy was purged of all dissident elements and completely reorganized, with Young Communists filling the naval cadet schools to insure trustworthy leadership in the years ahead. At the same time, discipline was tightened within the Red Army, while plans for a popular militia, to be drawn from peasant and worker volunteers, were forever abandoned.[11]

More important still, not a single political demand of the rebels was fulfilled. What took place, rather, was a hardening of dictatorial rule. The concessions of the NEP, indeed, were made expressly to consolidate the Bolshevik monopoly of power. In his outline for a speech to the Tenth Congress, Lenin noted: "The lesson of Kronstadt: in politics—the closing of the ranks (and discipline) within the party, greater struggle against the Mensheviks and Socialist Revolution-

---

[11] Pukhov, *Kronshtadtskii miatezh*, pp. 185-205; White, *The Growth of the Red Army*, pp. 191-93, 246-49.

aries; in economics—to satisfy as far as possible the middle peasantry."[12] Accordingly, popular initiative remained paralyzed, free soviets a frustrated dream. The state refused to restore freedom of speech, press, and assembly, as called for in the *Petropavlovsk* charter, or to release the socialists and anarchists accused of political crimes. Far from being drawn into a coalition government of revitalized soviets, the left-wing parties were methodically suppressed. On the night of March 17, by a melancholy coincidence, as the Kronstadt Revolutionary Committee was fleeing across the ice to Finland, the deposed Menshevik government of Georgia, the last of its kind in Soviet Russia, left the Black Sea port of Batum for West European exile.[13] During the Civil War, the Bolsheviks, menaced by Whites on every side, had allowed the pro-Soviet parties of the Left a precarious existence under continuous harassment and surveillance. After Kronstadt even this was no longer tolerated. All pretense of a legal opposition was abandoned in May 1921, when Lenin declared that the place for rival socialists was behind bars or in exile, side by side with the White Guards.[14] A new wave of repressions descended on the Mensheviks, SR's, and anarchists, whom the authorities had charged with complicity in the revolt. The more fortunate were permitted to emigrate, but thousands were swept up in the Cheka dragnet and banished to the far north, Siberia, and Central Asia. By the end of the year the active remnants of political opposition had been silenced or driven underground, and the consolidation of one-party rule was all but complete. Thus Kronstadt, like all unsuccessful revolts against authoritarian regimes, achieved the opposite of its intended goal: instead of a new era of

[12] *Desiatyi s"ezd RKP(b)*, p. 625.

[13] Boldin, "Men'sheviki v Kronshtadtskom miatezhe," *Krasnaia Letopis'*, 1931, No. 3, p. 28; Katkov, "The Kronstadt Rising, *St. Antony's Papers*, No. 6, p. 13.

[14] Lenin, *Polnoe sobranie sochinenii*, XLIII, 241.

popular self-government, the Communist dictatorship was fastened upon the country more firmly than ever.

The tightening of Bolshevik rule was accompanied by a drive to end the divisions within the party itself. Far from granting "party democracy," Lenin announced that factional quarrels must cease at once if the regime was to survive the present crisis. "The time has come," he told the Tenth Congress, "to put an end to opposition, to put the lid on it; we have had enough opposition."[15] Lenin used Kronstadt as a cudgel to beat the oppositionists into submission, hinting that their criticisms of party policies had encouraged the rebels to take up arms against the government.[16] His views found strong support among his listeners, who shared his fears that a mass revolt might sweep them from power. "At the present time," one speaker declared, "there are three factions in the party, and this congress must say whether we shall tolerate such a condition in the party any longer. In my opinion, we cannot go against General Kozlovsky with three factions, and the party congress must say so."[17] The delegates readily complied. In a sharply worded resolution they voted to condemn the program of the Workers' Opposition as a "syndicalist and anarchist deviation" from the Marxist tradition. A second resolution, "On Party Unity," cited Kronstadt as an example of how internal disputes might be exploited by the forces of counterrevolution, and it called for the dissolution of all factions and groupings within the party. Its final clause, kept secret for nearly three years, gave the Central Committee extraordinary powers to expel dissident members from the party's ranks.[18] Soon after, Lenin ordered a purge of the party "from top to bottom" to eliminate unreliable elements. By the end of the summer nearly a quarter of the total membership had been excluded.

[15] *Desiatyi s''ezd RKP(b)*, p. 118; Schapiro, *The Origin of the Communist Autocracy*, p. 316.
[16] *Desiatyi s''ezd RKP(b)*, pp. 34-35.
[17] *Ibid.*, p. 276. [18] *Ibid.*, pp. 571-76.

For a sensitive libertarian like Alexander Berkman, Kronstadt was a sobering experience, leading him to a critical reexamination of Bolshevik theory and practice. Yet the rising, for all its tragic drama, did not impress many others at the time as being a decisive event. It played no major role in determining the policies of Lenin's regime; the shift towards a relaxation in foreign and domestic affairs had been under way since the end of the Civil War. Its importance, rather, was primarily as symbol of a broader social crisis—the transition from War Communism to the NEP—which Lenin, in a speech to the Fourth Comintern Congress, called the gravest in Soviet history.[19] But when the passage of time brought a new era of Stalinist totalitarianism, the revolt acquired new significance. "In point of truth," wrote Emma Goldman in 1938, at the height of the Great Purge, "the voices strangled in Kronstadt have grown in volume these seventeen years." "What a pity," she added, that "the silence of the dead sometimes speaks louder than the living voice."[20] From the perspective of the Moscow trials and the Stalinist reign of terror, many saw the rebellion as a fatal crossroads in the history of the Russian Revolution, marking the triumph of bureaucratic repression and the final defeat of the decentralized and libertarian form of socialism.

This is not to say that Soviet totalitarianism began with the suppression of Kronstadt, or even that it was already inevitable at that time. "It is often said," remarked Victor Serge, "that 'the germ of Stalinism was in Bolshevism at its beginning.' Well, I have no objection. Only, Bolsheviks also contained many other germs—a mass of other germs—and those who lived through the enthusiasm of the first years of the first victorious revolution ought not to forget it. To judge the living man by the death germs which the autopsy reveals in a corpse—and which he may have carried with him since

---

[19] Degras, ed., *The Communist International*, I, 213.
[20] Goldman, *Trotsky Protests Too Much*, p. 7.

his birth—is this very sensible?"[21] During the early twenties, in other words, a number of different paths remained open to Soviet society. Yet, as Serge himself emphasized, a pronounced authoritarian streak had always been present in Bolshevik theory and practice. Lenin's ingrained elitism, his insistence on centralized leadership and tight party discipline, his suppression of civil liberties and sanction of terror—all this left a deep imprint on the future development of the Communist party and Soviet state. During the Civil War Lenin had sought to justify these policies as short-term expedients required by an emergency situation. But the emergency was never to end, and meanwhile the apparatus for a future totalitarian regime was being built. With the defeat of Kronstadt and the smothering of the left-wing opposition, the last effective demand for a toilers' democracy passed into history. Thereafter totalitarianism, if not inevitable, was a likely eventuality.

In 1924 Lenin died, and the Bolshevik leadership was plunged into a fierce struggle for power. Three years later a climax was reached when the Central Committee, invoking the secret clause of the Tenth Congress resolution on party unity, expelled Trotsky from the party and soon after drove him into exile. Ironically, when Trotsky formed his own opposition against Stalin's tyranny and bureaucratism, the ghost of Kronstadt was raised against him by libertarian socialists who recalled his role in the crushing of the rebellion. In reply to his critics, Trotsky tried to show that he had not been directly involved. "The fact of the matter," he wrote in 1938, "is that I personally took not the slightest part either in the pacification of the Kronstadt rising or in the repressions which followed."[22] Throughout the affair, he in-

---

[21] Serge, *Memoirs of a Revolutionary*, pp. xv-xvi.

[22] L. Trotskii, "Eshche ob usmirenii Kronshtadta," *Biulleten' Oppozitsii*, October 1938, p. 10; *The New International*, August 1938, pp. 249-50.

sisted, he remained in Moscow; Zinoviev handled matters in Petrograd, and the repressions were the work of the Cheka, headed by Dzerzhinsky, who would brook no interference from any quarter.

In any event, he said, the rebellion had to be crushed. Idealists have always charged the revolution with "excesses," but these in fact "flow from the very nature of revolutions, which are themselves 'excesses' of history." Kronstadt was nothing but "an armed reaction of the petty bourgeoisie against the hardships of social revolution and the severity of the proletarian dictatorship." If the Bolsheviks had not acted swiftly, the revolt might have toppled them and opened the floodgates of counterrevolution. Were his critics denying the government the right to defend itself or to discipline its own armed forces? Could any government tolerate a military mutiny in its midst? Should we have cast our power to the winds without a struggle? What the Bolsheviks did at Kronstadt, Trotsky concluded, was "a tragic necessity."[23]

But his critics were not convinced. For all his assertions to the contrary, Trotsky, as War Commissar and chairman of the Revolutionary War Council, did exercise general responsibility for the suppression of Kronstadt. He did indeed go to Petrograd, where he issued the ultimatum of March 5; he also visited Oranienbaum and Krasnaya Gorka, and played no small part in overseeing Communist military preparations, if not so crucial a role as that of Zinoviev and Tukhachevsky. Moreover, as Dwight Macdonald pointed out, Trotsky never answered the charge that the Bolsheviks handled the revolt with unnecessary intransigence and brutality. How seriously did they attempt to reach a peaceful settlement? If it was true that the Whites would have profited from divisions with-

[23] Trotsky, "Hue and Cry Over Kronstadt," *The New International*, April 1938, pp. 103-105; Trotsky, *Stalin*, New York, 1946, p. 337. Trotsky's remark that excesses "flow from the very nature of revolutions" recalls Engels' dictum that a revolution is "the most authoritarian thing imaginable."

in the party, were not the dangers of an air-tight dictatorship, insulated against mass pressure, even greater? Would a Stalinist clique have been able so easily to usurp control of a party which had allowed greater participation to the masses and greater freedom to the left-wing opposition?[24] In a similar vein, Anton Ciliga challenged the Bolshevik claim that Kronstadt, had it not been subdued, would have let loose the forces of reaction. This is possible, conceded Ciliga, but what is certain is that the revolution perished in 1921.[25]

In the end, the victors at Kronstadt fell victim to the system they had helped to create. Trotsky and Zinoviev were damned as "enemies of the people" who had wittingly abetted the counterrevolution. "Judas Trotsky," declared a Soviet pamphlet of 1939, had packed Kronstadt with his own henchmen, including bandits and White Guards, while deliberately creating a smokescreen with the trade union issue. Another Stalinist work blamed the revolt on Trotsky's "protégé, the commander of the Seventh Army Tukhachevsky," and on "the old Trotskyite Raskolnikov," the head of the Baltic Fleet. To deal with the traitors, it said, the party sent the "true Leninist" and comrade-in-arms of Stalin, Kliment Voroshilov (who actually played a minor role as a commissar at the Kronstadt front).[26] One by one the revolution devoured its makers. Zinoviev, Tukhachevsky, and Dybenko were shot in the Great Purge; Trotsky was murdered in Mexico by an agent of the Soviet secret police; Raskolnikov and Lashevich committed suicide. Many of the party delegates who went to Kronstadt, including Piatakov, Zatonsky,

[24] *The New International*, July 1938, pp. 212-13.

[25] Anton Ciliga, *The Kronstadt Revolt*, London, 1942, p. 13.

[26] *Bol'shaia sovetskaia entsiklopediia*, 1st edn., XXXV, 222; 2nd edn., XXIII, 484; O. Leonidov, *Likvidatsiia Kronshtadtskogo miatezha (mart 1921 g.)*, Moscow, 1939, pp. 8-9, 139; K. Zhakovshchikov, *Razgrom Kronshtadtskogo kontrrevoliutsionnogo miatezha v 1921 godu*, Leningrad, 1941, p. 62. Cf. Abramovitch, *The Soviet Revolution*, p. 209.

and Bubnov, disappeared in Stalin's prisons. Kalinin almost alone died a natural death in 1946. But the martyrs of Kronstadt survived, enshrined in the memory of the people as the revolution's guiltless children.[27]

[27] Cf. Mett, *La Commune de Cronstadt*, p. 6; and I. N. Steinberg, *In the Workshop of the Revolution*, New York, 1953, p. 300.

APPENDIXES
ANNOTATED BIBLIOGRAPHY
INDEX

Appendix A

*Memorandum on the Question of Organizing an Uprising in Kronstadt**

Top Secret   1921

Information emanating from Kronstadt compels one to believe that during the coming spring an uprising will erupt in Kronstadt. If its preparation receives some outside support, one may count entirely on the success of the rising, towards which the following circumstances will be favorable.

At the present time, concentrated in Kronstadt harbor are all the vessels of the Baltic Fleet, which still maintain their military importance. In this connection, the predominant force in Kronstadt rests with the sailors of the active fleet, as well as the sailors on shore duty in the Kronstadt Fortress. All power is concentrated in the hands of a small group of Communist sailors (the local Soviet, the Cheka, the Revolutionary Tribunal, the commissars and party collectives of the ships, and so on). The rest of the garrison and the workers of Kronstadt do not play a significant role. Meanwhile, one can observe among the sailors numerous and unmistakable signs of mass discontent with the existing order. The sailors unanimously will join the ranks of the insurgents, once a small group of individuals by quick and decisive action seizes power in Kronstadt. Among the sailors such a group has already been formed, ready and able to take the most energetic actions.

The Soviet government is well informed about the hostile attitude of the sailors. In this connection, the Soviet government has seen to it that not more than a week's supply of food is available in Kronstadt at any one time, whereas in

* "Dokladnaia zapiska po voprosu ob organizatsii vosstaniia v Kronshtadte," manuscript, Columbia Russian Archive. (Translated by the author.)

235

the past food was shipped to the Kronstadt warehouses for a whole month. So great is the distrust of the sailors by the Soviet authorities that a Red Army infantry regiment has been assigned to guard the routes to Kronstadt across the ice which covers the Finnish Gulf at the present time. But, in the event of an uprising, this regiment will not be able to offer the sailors any serious opposition, for if the rising is properly prepared, the regiment will be taken unawares by the sailors.

The seizure of authority over the fleet and over the fortifications of Kronstadt itself will insure the rebellion's ascendancy over all other forts not situated in the immediate vicinity of Kotlin Island. The artillery of these forts have an angle of fire which will not enable them to shoot at Kronstadt, whereas the batteries of Kronstadt are able to direct their fire at the forts (Fort "Obruchev," which rose in rebellion in May 1919, surrendered half an hour after the Kronstadt batteries opened fire on it).

The only conceivable military resistance to the uprising immediately after it has begun would be for the Bolsheviks to open fire on Kronstadt from the batteries of Krasnaya Gorka (the fort situated on the mainland on the southern coast of the Finnish Gulf). But the artillery of Krasnaya Gorka is completely powerless before the artillery of the ships and batteries of Kronstadt. On the ships in Kronstadt there are at least 32 twelve-inch and 8 ten-inch guns (not counting the guns of smaller caliber, about whose condition there is no reliable information). On Krasnaya Gorka there are only 8 twelve-inch and 4 eight-inch guns; the rest of the guns of Krasnaya Gorka are of insufficient caliber to be of harm to Kronstadt. In addition, the entire supply of shells for the artillery of Kronstadt, Krasnaya Gorka, and the Baltic Fleet are kept in the powder magazines of Kronstadt and will thus be in rebel hands. Therefore, the Bolsheviks will not be able to suppress the uprising in Kronstadt by artillery fire from the batteries of Krasnaya Gorka. On the contrary, one must assume that, in case of an artillery duel between Krasnaya Gorka and Kronstadt, the latter will win (the rising at Krasnaya Gorka in May [June] 1919 was suppressed by Kronstadt after a four-hour bombardment which leveled all the buildings in the Krasnaya Gorka area—the Bolsheviks themselves forbade firing directly at the Krasnaya Gorka batteries in order to preserve them for later use).

From the above it is clear that exceptionally favorable circumstances exist for the success of a Kronstadt uprising: (1) the presence of a closely knit group of energetic organizers for the rising; (2) a corresponding inclination towards rebellion among the sailors; (3) the small area of operations delimited by Kronstadt's narrow contours, which will insure the total success of the uprising; and (4) the possibility of preparing the rising in full secrecy, which is afforded by Kronstadt's isolation from Russia and by the homogeneity and solidarity among the sailors.

If the rebellion is successful, the Bolsheviks, having neither combat-ready ships outside of Kronstadt nor the possibility of concentrating land-based artillery of sufficient power to silence the Kronstadt batteries (particularly in view of Krasnaya Gorka's uselessness against them), will not be in a position to take Kronstadt by shore bombardment or by a coordinated troop landing.[1] It is noteworthy, moreover, that the Kronstadt Fortress and the operational fleet is equipped with anti-invasion artillery so numerous as to create an impenetrable blanket of fire. In order to carry out a landing, it would first be necessary to silence this artillery, a task which the Bolsheviks will be powerless to carry out in view of the support that the heavy guns of Kronstadt and of its fleet will give to the anti-invasion artillery.

In view of the above, the military situation in Kronstadt following the uprising may be regarded as completely secure,

[1] The author of the memorandum assumes that the rising will occur after the ice has melted.

and the base will be able to hold out as long as it has to.

However, the internal living conditions after the rebellion may prove fatal for Kronstadt. There is enough food to last only for a few days after the uprising. If Kronstadt is not supplied immediately after the overturn, and if the future supply of Kronstadt is not properly assured, then the inevitable hunger will force Kronstadt to fall again under the authority of the Bolsheviks. Russian anti-Bolshevik organizations are not strong enough to solve this food problem and are compelled to turn for aid to the French government.

In order to avoid any delay in supplying Kronstadt with food immediately after the uprising, it is necessary that before the appointed time appropriate stores of food be placed on transport vessels which will wait in ports of the Baltic Sea for orders to proceed to Kronstadt.

Apart from the surrender of Kronstadt to the Bolsheviks if food is not provided, there arises the danger of a breakdown of the morale among the rebels themselves, as a result of which Bolshevik authority may be restored in Krondstadt. Such a breakdown in morale would be inevitable if the insurgent sailors were not to receive assurances of sympathy and support from the outside, in particular from the Russian Army commanded by General Wrangel, and also if the sailors were to feel isolated from the rest of Russia by sensing the impossibility of a further development of the rebellion towards the overthrow of Soviet power in Russia itself.

In this regard, it would be extremely desirable that in the shortest possible time after the rising is carried out some French vessels should arrive in Kronstadt, symbolizing the presence of French assistance. Even more desirable would be the arrival in Kronstadt of some units of the Russian Army. For the selection of such units, preference ought to be given to the Russian Black Sea Fleet, now located in Bizerte, for the arrival of Black Sea sailors to help the sailors of the Baltic Fleet would arouse incomparable enthusiasm among the latter.

It must also be kept in mind that one cannot count on the orderly organization of authority in Kronstadt, especially in the first days after the overturn, and that in this connection the arrival of units of the Russian Army or fleet under General Wrangel's command would have extremely beneficial effects, inasmuch as all authority in Kronstadt would automatically devolve upon the ranking officer of these units.

Furthermore, if one assumes that military operations will be launched from Kronstadt to overthrow Soviet authority in Russia, then for this purpose also the dispatch to Kronstadt of General Wrangel's Russian armed forces would be needed. In connection with this, it is appropriate to mention that for such operations—or merely for the threat of such operations—Kronstadt can serve as an invulnerable base. The nearest object of action from Kronstadt would be defenseless Petrograd, whose conquest would mean that half the battle against the Bolsheviks shall have been won.

If, however, a further campaign from Kronstadt against Soviet Russia were for some reason deemed undesirable in the near future, then the fact that Kronstadt had been fortified with anti-Bolshevik Russian troops, acting in concert with the French Command, would still have considerable significance in the development of the overall military and political situation in Europe during the course of the coming spring.

It is necessary, however, to bear in mind that if the initial success of the rising in Kronstadt is cut short because of the inadequate supply of Kronstadt with food, or because of the demoralization of the Baltic sailors and the Kronstadt garrison for lack of moral and military support, then a situation will obtain in which Soviet authority is not weakened but strengthened and its enemies discredited.

In view of the above, Russian anti-Bolshevik organizations should hold the position that they must refrain from contributing to the success of the Kronstadt rebellion if they do not have the full assurance that the French government has decided to take the appropriate steps in this regard, in particular: (1) has taken upon itself to provide financial support for the preparation of the uprising, which for a favorable outcome would require an exceedingly small sum, perhaps in the neighborhood of 200 thousand francs; (2) has taken upon itself the further financing of Kronstadt after the overturn has been carried out; (3) has taken steps to supply Kronstadt with food and has assured the arrival of the first food deliveries immediately after the overturn in Kronstadt has been accomplished; and (4) has declared its agreement to the arrival in Kronstadt after the revolt of French military vessels and also of army and navy units from the armed forces of General Wrangel.

In connection with the above, one must not forget that even if the French Command and the Russian anti-Bolshevik organizations do not take part in the preparation and direction of the uprising, a revolt in Kronstadt will take place all the same during the coming spring, but after a brief period of success it will be doomed to failure. The latter would greatly strengthen the prestige of Soviet authority and deprive its enemies of a very rare opportunity—an opportunity that probably will not be repeated—to seize Kronstadt and inflict upon Bolshevism the heaviest of blows, from which it may not recover.

If the French government should agree in principle to the considerations presented above, then it would be desirable for it to designate an individual with whom representatives of the rebellion's organizers can enter into more detailed agreements on this subject and to whom they may communicate the details of the plan of the uprising and further actions, as well as more exact information concerning the funds required for the organization and further financing of the uprising.

Appendix B

What We Are Fighting For*

After carrying out the October Revolution, the working class had hoped to achieve its emancipation. But the result was an even greater enslavement of the human personality. The power of the police and gendarme monarchy passed into the hands of the Communist usurpers, who, instead of giving the people freedom, instilled in them the constant fear of falling into the torture chambers of the Cheka, which in their horrors far exceed the gendarme administration of the tsarist regime. The bayonets, bullets, and gruff commands of the Cheka *oprichniki*—these are what the workingman of Soviet Russia has won after so much struggle and suffering. The glorious emblem of the workers' state—the sickle and hammer—has in fact been replaced by the Communist authorities with the bayonet and barred window, for the sake of maintaining the calm and carefree life of the new bureaucracy of Communist commissars and functionaries.

But most infamous and criminal of all is the moral servitude which the Communists have inaugurated: they have laid their hands also on the inner world of the toilers, forcing them to think in the Communist way. With the help of the bureaucratized trade unions, they have fastened the workers to their benches, so that labor has become not a joy but a new form of slavery. To the protests of the peasants, expressed in spontaneous uprisings, and those of the workers, whose living conditions have driven them out on strike, they answer with mass executions and bloodletting, in which they have not been surpassed even by the tsarist generals. Russia of the toilers, the first to raise the red banner of labor's emancipation, is drenched in the blood of those martyred for the

* "Za chto my boremsia," *Izvestiia Vremennogo Revoliutsionnogo Komiteta*, March 8, 1921, in *Pravda o Kronshtadte*, pp. 82–84. (Translated by the author.)

glory of Communist domination. In this sea of blood, the Communists are drowning all the great and glowing pledges and watchwords of the workers' revolution. The picture has been drawn more and more sharply, and now it is clear that the Russian Communist party is not the defender of the toilers that it pretends to be. The interests of the working people are alien to it. Having gained power, it is afraid only of losing it, and therefore deems every means permissible: slander, violence, deceit, murder, vengeance upon the families of the rebels.

The long-suffering patience of the toilers is at an end. Here and there the land is lit up by the fires of insurrection in a struggle against oppression and violence. Strikes by the workers have flared up, but the Bolshevik *okhrana* agents have not been asleep and have taken every measure to forestall and suppress the inevitable third revolution. But it has come nevertheless, and it is being made by the hands of the toilers themselves. The generals of Communism see clearly that it is the people who have risen, convinced that the ideas of socialism have been betrayed. Yet, trembling for their skins and aware that there is no escape from the wrath of the workers, they still try, with the help of their *oprichniki*, to terrorize the rebels with prison, firing-squads, and other atrocities. But life under the yoke of the Communist dictatorship has become more terrible than death.

The rebellious working people understand that there is no middle ground in the struggle against the Communists and the new serfdom that they have erected. One must go on to the end. They give the appearance of making concessions: in Petrograd province roadblock detachments have been removed and 10 million gold rubles have been allotted for the purchase of foodstuffs from abroad. But one must not be deceived, for behind this bait is concealed the iron hand of the master, the dictator, who aims to be repaid a hundredfold for his concessions once calm is restored.

No, there can be no middle ground. Victory or death! The example is being set by Red Kronstadt, menace of counterrevolutionaries of the right and of the left. Here the new revolutionary step forward has been taken. Here is raised the banner of rebellion against the three-year-old violence and oppression of Communist rule, which has put in the shade the three-hundred-year yoke of monarchism. Here in Kronstadt has been laid the first stone of the third revolution, striking the last fetters from the laboring masses and opening a broad new road for socialist creativity.

This new revolution will also rouse the laboring masses of the East and of the West, by serving as an example of the new socialist construction as opposed to the bureaucratic Communist "creativity." The laboring masses abroad will see with their own eyes that everything created here until now by the will of the workers and peasants was not socialism. Without a single shot, without a drop of blood, the first step has been taken. The toilers do not need blood. They will shed it only at a moment of self-defense. In spite of all the outrageous acts of the Communists, we have enough restraint to confine ourselves only to isolating them from public life so that their malicious and false agitation will not hinder our revolutionary work.

The workers and peasants steadfastly march forward, leaving behind them the Constituent Assembly, with its bourgeois regime, and the dictatorship of the Communist party, with its Cheka and its state capitalism, whose hangman's noose encircles the necks of the laboring masses and threatens to strangle them to death. The present overturn at last gives the toilers the opportunity to have their freely elected soviets, operating without the slightest force of party pressure, and to remake the bureaucratized trade unions into free associations of workers, peasants, and the laboring intelligentsia. At last the policeman's club of the Communist autocracy has been broken.

Appendix C

Socialism in Quotation Marks[*]

In making the October Revolution, the sailors and Red soldiers, the workers and peasants spilled their blood for the power of the soviets, for the creation of a toilers' Republic. The Communist party paid close attention to the attitudes of the masses. Having inscribed on its banner alluring slogans which stirred up the workers, it drew them into its camp and promised to lead them into the shining Kingdom of Socialism, which only the Bolsheviks knew how to erect.

Naturally, a boundless joy seized hold of the workers and peasants. "At last the slavery we endured under the yoke of the landlords and capitalists is passing into legend," they thought. It seemed as if the time of free labor in the fields, factories, and workshops had come. It seemed as if all power had passed into the hands of the toilers.

By skillful propaganda, the children of the working people were drawn into the ranks of the party, where they were shackled with severe discipline. Then, feeling themselves strong enough, the Communists first removed from power the socialists of other tendencies; then they pushed the workers and peasants themselves from the helm of the ship of state, all the while continuing to rule the country in their name. For the power which they stole, the Communists substituted the arbitrary rule of the commissars over the body and soul of the citizens of Soviet Russia. Against all reason and contrary to the will of the toilers, they began persistently to build state socialism, with slaves instead of free labor.

Having disorganized production under "workers' control," the Bolsheviks proceeded to nationalize the factories and

* "Sotsializm v kavychkakh," *Izvestiia Vremennogo Revoliutsionnogo Komiteta*, March 16, 1921, in *Pravda o Kronshtadte*, pp. 172-74. (Translated by the author.)

shops. From a slave of the capitalist the worker was transformed into a slave of state enterprises. Soon this no longer sufficed, so they planned to introduce the speedup system of labor—the Taylor system. The whole laboring peasantry was declared the enemy of the people and identified with the kulaks. With great energy the Communists set about ruining the peasants, busying themselves with the creation of state farms—the estates of the new landlord, the state. This is what the peasants have received from the socialism of the Bolsheviks instead of the free use of their newly won lands. In exchange for requisitioned grain and confiscated cows and horses, they got Cheka raids and firing squads. A fine system of exchange in a workers' state—lead and bayonets for bread!

The life of the citizen became hopelessly monotonous and routine. One lived according to the timetables established by the powers that be. Instead of the free development of the individual personality and a free laboring life, there emerged an extraordinary and unprecedented slavery. All independent thought, all just criticism of the acts of the criminal rulers became crimes punished by imprisonment and sometimes even by execution. In a "socialist society" capital punishment, that desecration of human dignity, began to flourish.

Such is the shining kingdom of socialism to which the dictatorship of the Communist party has brought us. We have obtained state socialism with soviets of functionaries who vote obediently according to the dictates of the party committee and its infallible commissars. The slogan "He who does not work shall not eat" has been twisted by the new "soviet" order into "Everything for the commissars." For the workers, peasants, and laboring intelligentsia there remains only cheerless and unremitting toil in a prison environment.

The situation has become intolerable, and Revolutionary

Kronstadt has been the first to break the chains and the iron bars of this prison. It is fighting for a different kind of socialism, for a Soviet Republic of the toilers, in which the producer himself will be the sole master and can dispose of his products as he sees fit.

Annotated Bibliography

ARCHIVES

Archive of Russian and East European History and Culture, Columbia University. The archives of the Russian National Committee contain the Secret Memorandum on organizing an uprising in Kronstadt ("Dokladnaia zapiska po voprosu ob organizatsii vosstaniia v Kronshtadte") and other materials reflecting émigré activities around the time of the rebellion. In addition, the Columbia Archive houses a number of valuable memoirs and documents relating to Kronstadt by contemporaries inside Russia. Of these the most important are: G. A. Cheremshansky, "Kronshtadtskoe, vosstanie, 28 fevralia-18 marta 1921"; D. Daragan and N. Zhigulev, "Kronshtadtskoe vosstanie 1921 g."; "K vospominaniiam matrosa sluzhby 1914 goda"; "Khod sobytii v Petrograde vo vremia Kronshtadtskogo vosstaniia," March 1921; and "O raskrytom v Petrograde zagovorov protiv Sovetskoi vlasti," Presidium of Vecheka, August 29, 1921.

The Hoover Institution on War, Revolution, and Peace, Stanford University. Much relevant material is to be found in the archives of M. N. Giers, V. A. Maklakov, General E. K. Miller, and Baron P. N. Wrangel. The following items are particularly significant: (1) In the Giers Archives, letters from Professor D. D. Grimm to M. N. Giers, March 15 and 31, 1921; letter from Professor G. F. Tseidler to President of Russian Red Cross, March 20, 1921; and letters from S. M. Petrichenko and others to Professor Grimm and General Wrangel, May 31, 1921. (2) In the Miller Archives, "Kak nachalos' vosstanie v Kronshtadte," March 12, 1921. (3) In the general collection of the Hoover Library, "Interv'iu s chlenami Vremennogo Revoliutsionnogo Komiteta (s matrosami 'Petropavlovska' Iakovenko, Karpenko i Arkhipovym)"; "Prichiny, povody, techenie i otsenka Kronshtadtskikh sobytii"; and "Svedeniia iz Petrograda ot 12 aprelia: Kronshtadt i otgoloski ego vosstaniia," April 12, 1921.

The National Archives of the United States, Washington, D.C. There are pertinent diplomatic papers in State Department, Records Relating to Internal Affairs of Russia and the Soviet Union, 1910-1929, File Number 861.00, especially the well-informed dispatches of Harold B. Quarton, the American consul in Viborg. The most noteworthy of these are: (1) two reports of April 23, 1921 to the Secretary of State: "Analysis of Foreign Assistance Rendered to the Cronstadt Revolution" and "Cause, Progress and Results of Cronstadt Events" (861.00/8619); and (2) an interview with Petrichenko by Edmond Stratton, an American journalist in Finland, March 19, 1921, in Quarton to Secretary of State, April 9, 1921 (861.00/8470).

The Trotsky Archives, Harvard University. These, unfortunately, contain only one item bearing directly on the rebellion, a message from Trotsky to Lenin, dated March 15, 1921 (T 647), regarding the need to dispel the "wild rumors about Kronstadt." There are, however, a number of firsthand reports on the peasant risings of the period.

In addition to the above, the archives of Professor D. D. Grimm, privately held in Paris, are also of considerable value, particularly with regard to the activities of the émigrés during and after the rebellion.

BOOKS, PAMPHLETS, AND ARTICLES

Abramovitch, Raphael R. *The Soviet Revolution, 1917-1939.* New York, 1962. A useful study by a leading Menshevik.

Alexander, Hunter. "The Kronstadt Revolt of 1921 and Stefan Petrichenko." *Ukrainian Quarterly*, XXIII, Autumn 1967, 255-63.

Antonovshchina. Tambov, 1923. A valuable collection of articles and materials on the Antonov movement.

Anweiler, Oskar. *Die Rätebewegung in Russland, 1905-1921.* Leiden, 1958. A pioneering study of the soviets.

Avrich, Paul. "The Bolshevik Revolution and Workers' Control in Russian Industry." *Slavic Review*, xxii, March 1963, 47-63.

———. *The Russian Anarchists*. Princeton, 1967.

Balabanoff, Angelica. *Impressions of Lenin*. Ann Arbor, 1964.

———. *My Life as a Rebel*. New York, 1938. Reminiscences by the first secretary of the Communist International.

Baltiiskie moriaki v podgotovke i provedenii Velikoi Oktiabr'-skoi sotsialisticheskoi revoliutsii. Ed. R. N. Mordvinov. Moscow, 1957.

Baltiiskii flot v Oktiabr'skoi revoliutsii i grazhdanskoi voine. Ed. A. K. Drezen. Leningrad, 1932.

Barmine, Alexander. *One Who Survived*. New York, 1945.

Berkman, Alexander. *The "Anti-Climax."* Berlin, 1925. Concluding Chapter of Berkman's diary, *The Bolshevik Myth*.

———. *The Bolshevik Myth (Dairy 1920-1922)*. New York, 1925. Absorbing reminiscences by a well-known anarchist who was in Petrograd at the time of the Kronstadt rising.

———. *The Kronstadt Rebellion*. Berlin, 1922. A brief but significant account of the rising from the anarchist point of view.

Bogdanov, A. V. *Moriaki-baltiitsy v 1917 g.* Moscow, 1955.

Bogdanov, M. A. *Razgrom zapadnosibirskogo kulatsko-eserovskogo miatezha 1921 g.* Tiumen', 1961

Boldin, P. I. "Men'sheviki v Kronshtadtskom miatezhe," *Krasnaia Letopis'*, 1931, No. 3, pp. 5-31.

Browder, R. P. and A. F. Kerensky, eds. *The Russian Provisional Government, 1917*. 3 vols., Stanford, 1961.

Bunyan, James. *The Origin of Forced Labor in the Soviet State, 1917-1921: Documents and Materials.* Baltimore, 1967.

Carr, Edward Hallett. *The Bolshevik Revolution, 1917-1923.* 3 vols., New York, 1951-1953. Says little about Kronstadt, but is a monumental study of Bolshevik theory and practice during the revolutionary period.

Carroll, E. Malcolm. *Soviet Communism and Western Opinion, 1919-1921.* Chapel Hill, 1965.

Chamberlin, William Henry. *The Russian Revolution, 1917-1921.* 2 vols., New York, 1935. An outstanding history of the revolution, which retains its value more than thirty years after its original publication.

Ciliga, Anton. *The Kronstadt Revolt.* London, 1942. A brief but penetrating analysis.

Cohn, Norman. *Warrant for Genocide.* London, 1967.

Crossman, Richard, ed. *The God That Failed.* New York, 1950.

Dallin, David and Boris Nicolaevsky. *Forced Labor in Soviet Russia.* New Haven, 1947.

Dan, F. I. *Dva goda skitanii (1919-1921).* Berlin, 1922. An important memoir by a leading Menshevik imprisoned in Petrograd during the rising.

Daniels, Robert V. *The Conscience of the Revolution: Communist Opposition in Soviet Russia.* Cambridge, Mass., 1960. A major study of the opposition movements within the Communist party.

————. "The Kronstadt Revolt of 1921: A Study in the Dynamics of Revolution." *American Slavic and East European Review,* x, December 1951, 241-54. A useful article.

Degras, Jane, ed. *The Communist International, 1919-1943.* 3 vols., London, 1956-1965.

Desiatyi s"ezd RKP(b), mart 1921 goda. Moscow, 1963. Minutes of the dramatic Tenth Party Congress, which met in Moscow at the time of the rebellion.

Deutscher, Isaac. *The Prophet Armed: Trotsky 1879-1921.* New York, 1954. The first volume of a classic three-volume biography.

————. *Soviet Trade Unions.* London, 1950. Has a good brief discussion of the trade-union controversy of 1920-1921.

Dewar, Margaret. *Labour Policy in the USSR, 1917-1928.* London, 1956.

Dukes, Paul. *Red Dusk and the Morrow.* New York, 1922.

————. *The Story of "ST 25."* London, 1938.

Dybenko, P. E. *Iz nedr tsarskogo flota k velikomu Oktiabriu.* Moscow, 1928.

Erickson, John. *The Soviet High Command.* London, 1962. An outstanding history of the emergence of the Soviet armed forces.

Fainsod, Merle. *Smolensk under Soviet Rule.* Cambridge, Mass., 1958.

Fedeli, Ugo. *Dalla insurrezione dei contadini in Ucraina alla rivolta di Cronstadt.* Milan, 1950.

Fischer, Louis. *The Soviets in World Affairs.* 2 vols., Princeton, 1951.

Fisher, Harold H. *The Famine in Soviet Russia, 1919-1923.* New York, 1927.

Flerovskii, I. P. *Bol'shevistskii Kronshtadt v 1917 godu* (*po lichnym vospominaniiam*). Leningrad, 1957.

————. "Iiul'skii politicheskii urok," *Proletarskaia Revoliutsiia*, 1926, No. 7, pp. 57-89.

————. "Miatezh mobilizovannykh matrosov v Peterburge 14 oktiabria 1918 g.," *Proletarskaia Revoliutsiia*, 1926, No. 8, pp. 218-37. A revealing study of a precursor of the 1921 mutiny.

Genkina, E. B. *Perekhod Sovetskogo gosudarstva k novoi ekonomicheskoi politike* (*1921-1922*). Moscow, 1954.

————. "V. I. Lenin i perekhod k novoi ekonomicheskoi politike," *Voprosy Istorii*, 1964, No. 5, pp. 3-27.

Goldman, Emma. *Living My Life*. New York, 1931. A memorable autobiography by the famous anarchist, with vivid impressions of the Kronstadt rising.

―――. *Trotsky Protests Too Much*. Glasgow, 1938. A reply to Trotsky on Kronstadt.

Golinkov, D. L. "Razgrom ochagov vnutrennei kontrrevoliutsii v Sovetskoi Rossii," *Voprosy Istorii*, 1968, No. 1, pp. 133-49.

Goneniia na anarkhizm v Sovetskoi Rossii. Berlin, 1922.

Grazhdanskaia voina, 1918-1921. 3 vols., Moscow, 1928-1930. Volume I has an article on the assault against Kronstadt by S. Uritsky, a Bolshevik military leader, which includes a useful military map.

Great Britain, *Documents on British Foreign Policy, 1919-1939*. First Series, XII, London, 1962.

Iarchuk, E. *Kronshtadt v russkoi revoliutsii*. New York, 1923. An anarchist account of Kronstadt in 1917.

Iz istorii Vserossiiskoi chrezvychainoi komissii, 1917-1921 gg. Sbornik dokumentov. Moscow, 1958.

Kak tambovskie krest'iane boriatsia za svobodu. n.p., 1921. An SR pamphlet from the jacquerie in Tambov.

Katkov, George. "The Kronstadt Rising," *St. Antony's Papers*, No. 6, London, 1959, pp. 9-74. A pioneering study.

Kogan, F. *Kronshtadt v 1905-1906 gg*. Moscow, 1926.

Kolbin, I. N. "Kronshtadt ot fevralia do kornilovskikh dnei," *Krasnaia Letopis'*, 1927, No. 2, pp. 134-61.

―――. *Kronshtadt v 1917 godu*. Moscow, 1932.

Kollontai, Alexandra. *The Workers' Opposition in Russia*. Chicago, 1921.

Korablev, Iu. *Revoliutsionnye vosstaniia na Baltike v 1905-1906 gg*. Leningrad, 1956.

Kornatovskii, N. A., ed. *Kronshtadtskii miatezh: sbornik statei, vospominanii i dokumentov*. Leningrad, 1931. A basic collection of reminiscences and documents on the rising.

Kritsman, L. N. *Geroicheskii period velikoi russkoi revoliutsii*. 2nd edn., Moscow, 1926. A probing study of War Communism.

Kronshtadt: kratkii putevoditel'. Ed. I. P. Vinokurov et al. Leningrad, 1963.

"Kronshtadtskoe vosstanie 1906 g.," *Krasnyi Arkhiv*, 1936, No. 4, pp. 91-116.

Kronshtadtskoe vosstanie, 1921-1956. Berlin, 1956. Of little scholarly value.

Kuz'min, M. *Kronshtadtskii miatezh*. Leningrad, 1931. A popular history of limited use to the specialist.

Kuznetsov, V. *Iz vospominanii politrabotnika*. Moscow, 1930.

Lazarevich [no first name]. "Kronshtadtskoe vosstanie," *Bor'ba*, 1921, Nos. 1-2, pp. 3-8. A useful analysis from the SR viewpoint.

Leites, K. *Recent Economic Developments in Russia*. London, 1922.

Lenin, V. I. *Polnoe sobranie sochinenii*. 5th edn., 55 vols., Moscow, 1958-1965.

Lentsner, L. A. *Kronshtadt v 1905-1906 gg.: vospominaniia*. Moscow, 1956.

Leonidov, O. *Likvidatsiia Kronshtadtskogo miatezha (mart 1921 g.)*. Moscow, 1939. A Stalinist tract.

Liddell Hart, B. H., ed. *The Red Army*. New York, 1956.

Lukomskii, A. S. *Vospominaniia*. 2 vols., Berlin, 1922.

Lur'e, M. L., ed. "Kronshtadtskie moriaki v iiul'skom vystuplenii 1917 goda," *Krasnaia Letopis'*, 1932, No. 3, pp. 76-105.

————. "Kronshtadtskii miatezh 1921 goda v Sovetskoi i beloi literature i pechati," *Krasnaia Letopis'*, 1931, No. 2, pp. 225-40. A useful bibliographical survey.

————. "Otsenka Kronshtadtskogo miatezha v proizvedeniiakh V. I. Lenina," *Krasnaia Letopis'*, 1931, No. 3, pp. 166-75. Lenin's statements about the revolt.

Macdonald, Dwight. "Kronstadt Again," *The New International*, October 1939, pp. 315-16.

————. "Once More: Kronstadt," *The New International*, July 1938, pp. 212-14. An incisive reply to Trotsky.

Makhno, N. I. "Pamiati Kronshtadtskogo vosstaniia," *Delo Truda*, 1926, No. 10, pp. 3-4.

Maximoff, G. P. *The Guillotine at Work*. Chicago, 1940.

Medvedev, V. K. "Kronshtadt v iiul'skie dni 1917 goda," *Istoricheskie Zapiski*, XLII, 1953, 262-75.

Mett, Ida. *La Commune de Cronstadt: Crépuscule sanglant des Soviets*. Paris, 1949. A brief but well-informed and sensitive history from the anarchist perspective. There is a slightly abridged English translation: *The Kronstadt Commune*, London, 1967, published by the Solidarity Press.

Miliukov, P. N. *Russia Today and Tomorrow*. New York, 1922.

Morizet, André. *Chez Lénine et Trotski, Moscou 1921*. Paris, 1922.

Nestroev, G. *Maksimalizm i bol'shevizm*. Moscow, 1919.

Nikulin, L. V. *Tukhachevskii*. Moscow, 1964.

"Obrazovanie severo-zapadnogo Pravitel'stva," *Arkhiv russkoi revoliutsii*, I, 1922, 295-308.

Oktiabr'skii shkval (*Moriaki Baltiiskogo flota v 1917 godu*). Eds. P. F. Kudelli and I. V. Egorov. Leningrad, 1927.

Osinskii, N. [V. V. Obolenskii]. *Gosudarstvennoe regulirovanie krest'ianskogo khoziaistva*. Moscow, 1920.

Parvilahti, Unto. *Beria's Gardens: A Slave Laborer's Experiences in the Soviet Utopia*. New York, 1960.

Pearce, Brian. "1921 and All That." *Labour Review*, V, October-November 1960, 84-92.

Petrash, V. V. *Moriaki Baltiiskogo flota v bor'be za pobedu Oktiabria*. Leningrad, 1966.

Petrichenko, S. M. "O prichinakh Kronshtadtskogo vosstaniia," *Znamia Bor'by*, Nos. 14-15, December 1925-January 1926, pp. 4-8.

————. *Pravda o Kronshtadtskikh sobytiiakh*. n.p., 1921. This and preceding entry are important accounts of the rising by its principal leader.

Petrov-Skitaletz, E. *The Kronstadt Thesis for a Free Russian Government*. New York, 1964.

Poliakov, Iu. A. *Perekhod k nepu i Sovetskoe krest'ianstvo*. Moscow, 1967. An informative work on the Russian peasantry at the time of the rising.

Pollack, Emanuel. *The Kronstadt Rebellion*. New York, 1959. Leans heavily on Berkman and one or two other works.

Pravda o Kronshtadte. Prague, 1921. The most important source, containing all issues of the rebel daily newspaper.

Prokopovitch, S. N. *The Economic Condition of Soviet Russia*. London, 1924.

Pukhov, A. S. *Baltiiskii flot na zashchite Petrograda (1919 g.)*. Moscow, 1958.

————. *Kronshtadtskii miatezh v 1921 g.* Leningrad, 1931. The best Soviet account. A serialized version appeared, in somewhat different form, in *Krasnaia Letopis'* in 1930-1931.

Pukhov, G. S. *Kak vooruzhalsia Petrograd*. Moscow, 1933.

Rabinovich, S. E. "Delegaty 10-go s"ezda RKP(b) pod Kronshtadtom v 1921 godu," *Krasnaia Letopis'*, 1931, No. 2, pp. 22-55.

Rabinowitch, Alexander. *Prelude to Revolution: The Petrograd Bolsheviks and the July 1917 Uprising*. Bloomington, 1968.

Rabota eserov zagranitsei. Moscow, 1922. Contains letters by SR expatriates who raised funds to aid the insurgents.

Rafail, M. A. *Kronshtadtskii miatezh (Iz dnevnika polit-rabotnika)*. n.p. [Kharkov], 1921. Memoirs of a delegate from the Tenth Party Congress who volunteered for the Kronstadt front.

Raskol'nikov, F. F. [Il'in]. *Kronshtadt i Piter v 1917 godu.* Moscow, 1925.

Rotin, I. P. *Stranitsa istorii partii.* Moscow, 1958.

Schapiro, Leonard. *The Communist Party of the Soviet Union.* New York, 1960. The best general history of the party.

————. *The Origin of the Communist Autocracy.* Cambridge, Mass., 1956. An outstanding work, with a good brief analysis of the rebellion.

Scheuer, Georg. *Von Lenin bis . . . ? Die Geschichte einer Konterrevolution.* Vienna, 1954.

Serge, Victor. *Memoirs of a Revolutionary, 1901-1941.* Trans. and ed. Peter Sedgwick. London, 1963. Absorbing memoirs by a sympathetic critic of the rebellion.

————. "Once More: Kronstadt," *The New International,* July 1938, pp. 211-12.

————. "Reply to Trotsky," *The New International,* February 1939, pp. 53-54.

Shelov, A. V. *Istoricheskii ocherk kreposti Kronshtadt.* Kronstadt, 1904. A detailed account of Kronstadt's early history.

Singleton, Seth. "The Tambov Revolt (1920-1921)." *Slavic Review,* xxv, September 1966, 497-512.

Slepkov, A. *Kronshtadtskii miatezh.* Moscow, 1928.

Smith, C. Jay. *Finland and the Russian Revolution, 1917-1922.* Athens, Ga., 1958.

Sofinov, P. G. *Istoricheskii povorot (perekhod k novoi ekonomicheskoi politike).* Moscow, 1964.

Soiuz S-R Maksimalistov. *O rabochem kontrole.* Moscow, 1918.

————. *Trudovaia sovetskaia respublika.* Moscow, 1918.

Steinberg, I. N. *Als ich Volkskommissar war.* Munich, 1929.

————. *In the Workshop of the Revolution.* New York, 1953.

Sukhanov, N. N. *The Russian Revolution, 1917*. Trans. and ed. Joel Carmichael. New York, 1955.

Todorskii, A. I. *Marshal Tukhachevskii*. Moscow, 1963.

Trifonov, I. Ia. *Klassy i klassovaia bor'ba v SSSR v nachale nepa (1921-1923 gg.)*. Vol. I: *Bor'ba s vooruzhennoi kulatskoi kontrrevoliutsiei*. Leningrad, 1964. Has a full bibliographical essay on the peasant revolts of 1920-1922.

Trotskii, L. D. "Eshche ob usmirenii Kronshtadta," *Biulleten' Oppozitsii*, October 1938, p. 10. Translated into English as "More on the Suppression of Kronstadt," *The New International*, August 1938, pp. 249-50.

————. *Kak vooruzhalas' revoliutsiia*. 3 vols. in 5, Moscow, 1923-1925.

————. *The Revolution Betrayed*. New York, 1937.

————. "Shumikha vokrug Kronshtadta," *Biulleten' Oppozitsii*, May-June, 1938, pp. 22-26. Translated into English as "Hue and Cry Over Kronstadt," *The New International*, April 1938, pp. 103-106. This and first entry present Trotsky's defense of his role in the Kronstadt affair.

————. *Stalin: An Appraisal of the Man and His Influence*. New York, 1946.

Tseidler, G. *O snabzhenii Peterburga*. Viborg, 1921.

Tukhachevskii, M. N. "Bor'ba s kontrrevoliutsionnymi vosstaniiami," *Voina i Revoliutsiia*, 1926, No. 8, pp. 3-15. On the suppression of Antonov.

Vardin, I. *Revoliutsiia i men'shevizm*. Moscow, 1925.

V ogne revoliutsii. Ed. L. Gurvich. Moscow, 1933.

Voennye moriaki v period pervoi russkoi revoliutsii, 1905-1907 gg. Ed. S. F. Naida. Moscow, 1955.

Voennye vosstaniia v Baltike v 1905-06 gg. Ed. A. K. Drezen. Moscow, 1933.

Voline [V. M. Eikhenbaum]. *La Révolution inconnue (1917-1921)*. Paris, 1947. Has an interesting section on the rebellion from the anarchist standpoint.

Voronevskii, V. and N. Khenrikson. *Kronshtadtskaia krepost'* —*kliuch k Leningradu.* Leningrad, 1926.

Voroshilov, K. E. "Iz istorii podavleniia Kronshtadtskogo miatezha," *Voenno-Istoricheskii Zhurnal,* 1961, No. 3, pp. 15-35.

Vos'moi vserossiiskii s"ezd sovetov rabochikh, krest'ianskikh, krasnoarmeiskikh i kazach'ikh deputatov. Stenograficheskii otchet (22-29 dekabria 1920 goda). Moscow, 1921.

White, D. Fedotoff. *The Growth of the Red Army.* Princeton, 1944. A valuable work by a well-informed ex-officer in the Russian Imperial Navy. Has a good account of the military side of the revolt.

Wollenberg, Erich. *The Red Army.* London, 1938.

Wrangel, P. N. *The Memoirs of General Wrangel.* London, 1930.

Wright, John G. *The Truth About Kronstadt.* New York, 1938. A defense of the Bolsheviks by a disciple of Trotsky.

Za 5 let, 1917-1922: sbornik Ts.K.R.K.P. Moscow, 1922.

Zhakovshchikov, K. *Razgrom Kronshtadtskogo kontrrevoliutsionnogo miatezha v 1921 godu.* Leningrad, 1941. A Stalinist history.

Zubelevich, Iu. *Kronshtadt: Vospominaniia revoliutsionerki, 1906 god.* Kronstadt, n.d.

CONTEMPORARY NEWSPAPERS AND JOURNALS

Daily Herald. London.

L'Echo de Paris.

Golos Rossii. Berlin.

Izvestiia Vremennogo Revoliutsionnogo Komiteta Matrosov, Krasnoarmeitsev i Rabochikh gor. Kronshtadta. Kronstadt.

Izvestiia Petrogradskogo Soveta Rabochikh i Krasnoarmeiskikh Deputatov. Petrograd.

Izvestiia VTsIK. Moscow.

Krasnaia Gazeta. Petrograd.

Maksimalist. Moscow.

Le Matin. Paris.

Narodnoe Delo. Reval.

New York Times.

New York Tribune.

Novaia Russkaia Zhizn'. Helsingfors.

Novyi Mir. Berlin.

Obshchee Delo. Paris.

Petrogradskaia Pravda. Petrograd.

Poslednie Novosti. Paris.

Pravda. Moscow.

Revoliutsionnaia Rossiia. Prague.

Rul'. Berlin.

Sotsialisticheskii Vestnik. Berlin.

The Times. London.

Voennoe Znanie. Moscow.

Volia Rossii. Prague.

Index